History of
Religions in
The Caribbean

ABOUT THE AUTHOR

Dale A. Bisnauth, a Guyanese, is a graduate of the United Theological College of the West Indies and holds a Ph.D. in History from the University of the West Indies. He has lectured in Comparative Religion and Church History at the United Theological College. He is now a Minister of Religion of the Guyana Presbyterian Church.

All the major religions of the world are found in the Caribbean as well as some indigenous outgrowths of these faiths. In A History of Religions in the Caribbean, Dr. Bisnauth ranges from the vanished beliefs of the Caribs and Arawaks to the Rastafarianism of today. He shows how each religion arrived and developed in the Caribbean area, culminating in the remarkable degree of mutual tolerance which now exists there.

This is an essential book for all who are interested in the history of religion and for students of the region.

ISBN - 976-625-003-0

History of Religions in the Caribbean

DALE BISNAUTH

LMH Publishing Limited

Cover Design by: Linda Donald
Edited by: Leeta Hearne and Mike Henry
Typesetting by: E. McDonald

Published by:
LMH Publishing Limited
7 Norman Road,
LOJ Industrial Complex
Building 10
Kingston C.S.O., Jamaica
Tel: 876-938-0005; 938-0712 Fax: 876-759-8752
Email: lmhbookpublishing@cwjamaica.com

Printed in the U.S.A.   ISBN   976-8202-15-7

For Amy and the children
Alec and Ruth MacDonald

CONTENTS

Pages

PREFACE

PREFACE

The Caribbean is a multi-religious community. Though this work attempts to put together an account of the evolution and establishment of such a community, more emphasis is placed on the actual beliefs and practices of the peoples of the Caribbean.

The book takes us from the time of the Arawak settlement (about 200 A.D.) to about 1950. The *termini a quo* and *ad quem* are not set with strict precision. Our discussion of Rastafarian beliefs sometimes lapses into the present tense, for obvious reasons.

To really understand and appreciate the discussion of religious developments in the Caribbean, one has to bring into perspective historical developments in these parts, as well as on the international scene — which historical developments have in large measure influenced the makeup of the multi-religious mosaic of the Caribbean.

Quotations from books, periodicals and other sources are acknowledged, except in those cases where the information is public knowledge and where the quotes are from the scriptures and other religious writings. The author wishes to acknowledge his gratitude to the authors and editors of those periodicals, journals, monographs and other written material which have contributed to his understanding. A select bibliography is provided.

Finally, thanks are due to Chandra Persaud, Lorraine Lewis and Amy Bisnauth who helped to type the manuscript.

Dale A. Bisnauth

CHAPTER I

THE RELIGIOUS BELIEFS OF THE INDIGENOUS PEOPLES

Introduction

At about the time that the Christian era was being born, a people subsequently described as Arawaks left their homes in the Orinoco basin in South America and migrated northwards. Some of them settled along the way; many others pushed towards the northern waters of the Caribbean Sea and the Atlantic Ocean. The descendants of those who reached the northern waters settled on the islands of the Lesser Antilles; succeeding generations reached as far north as the Bahamas (around 1000 A.D.) and the larger islands of Cuba (around 800 A.D.), Jamaica (around 750 A.D.), Hispaniola, and Puerto Rico (around 250 A.D.)

Almost in the wake of the Arawaks came another migrant people, the Caribs. Indications are that they originated in Brazil, somewhere in the region of the Amazon river. The Caribs occupied Trinidad for a while; then their war canoes pushed northwards following in the path of the Arawaks and actually forcing the latter to seek refuge in more northern waters. The Caribs settled in the islands of the Lesser Antilles as these were vacated by the Arawaks. October 1492 saw the intrusion of the first Europeans into the world of the Arawaks and Caribs. The indigenous peoples were called Indians by the Genoese sailor and discoverer, Christopher Columbus, who thought that they were inhabitants of islands which lay just off the coast of India. The Genoese made another mistake. In writing of the peoples whom he saw in the Caribbean, he asserted: "It seemed to me that they belonged to no religion."[1] To be sure, the Arawaks and the Caribs had no priestly hierarchy, no ecclesiastical organi-

1

sation, no creed or dogma such as the Catholic Columbus was accustomed to; but, nevertheless, they were not lacking in beliefs which were of a religious nature, nor were they lacking in a pattern of worship which both sustained and expressed those beliefs.

Arawak beliefs

The Arawak Indians acknowledged the existence of one, supreme, invisible, immortal and omnipotent creator, whom they called Jocahuna. Jocahuna, however, was not without beginning. He was the son of the goddess Atabei and of a father whose name has not survived. The father and mother of Jocahuna were associated (and, sometimes, identified) with the sun and the moon respectively; but neither Jocahuna nor his parents were represented by images. Jocahuna, like Nohochacyum of the Locandons of Yucatan, was regarded as gentle, benevolent and kind — somewhat like the Arawaks themselves. He was the creator in the sense that it was he who, like Hurakan and Gucumatz of Guatemalan mythology, in the beginning when everything was under water, said "Earth!" and earth appeared. Mountains rose out of the water and the earth became covered with vegetation. Animals appeared on the earth and, at a later time, so did man. These were created by Jocahuna. The Arawaks of Guyana called the creator-god Wamurreti-Kwonci (Our Maker) to indicate that he was the creator of human beings.

Once the work of creation was complete, Jocahuna committed the government of the world to a number of subordinate beings. Most of these had a penchant for mischief with their special delight being that of converting good to evil. Some of these deities were even malignant. Guabancex, who was identified with storms, wind and water, could be beneficent; but she could also be destructive. The storm in its most destructive form was Hurakan. He was as widely known in the Caribbean as was the natural phenomenon to which he gave his name.[2] In Guatemala, he was believed to preside over the whirlwinds and the rumblings which accompanied such winds. In this respect, Hurakan was not unlike Indra of the Indo-Aryans who settled in Northern India, or Shango of the Yorubas in West Africa. The Quiche Mayas of Central America believed that it was Hurakan who gave them fire. As far west as Mexico, he was known as Quetzalcoatl who was forced out of that part of the world by the intrigues of another Azetc deity, Tezcatlipoca. Pushed out

2

of Mexico, as it were, this white-haired, long-bearded old man, set sail on the Eastern Sea (that is the Caribbean Sea) from which he would return one day. Interestingly enough, when the Azetc sentries saw the ships of the Spanish *conquistadores* approaching from the East, they believed that it was Quetzalcoatl returning from his self-imposed exile. Montezuma, the Azetc king, welcomed Cortes, the Spanish conqueror, as Quetzalcoatl and presented to him the snake mask and the feather cloak which were the emblems of the god.

Associated with Quabancex were Coatrischie and Guantuva. Coatrischie was the deity who collected water among the mountains and then let it rush down with destructive force on to the lowlands. Guantauva, the messenger of Guabancex, heralded the approach of the storm goddess. In Guyana, the mysterious and capricious goddess, Orehu, was believed to inhabit the rivers.

No temple or shrine was raised in honour of Jocahuna. In this respect, he was like Brahma of Hindu belief and Oludumare of Yoruba belief. Nor was the god represented by images. It was doubtless felt that Jocahuna did not need to be placated by worship, since he was, by his nature, well-disposed to the Arawaks.[3] Further, Jocahuna had committed the government of these forces to deities who were, in fact, the forces themselves, apotheosised. Worship and intercession were best directed to Hurakan, Guabancex and the gods and goddesses of water, fertility, disease and death — those deities whose actions impinged on the day-to-day life of the Arawaks.

The gods and goddesses were represented in images as toads, reptiles, and distorted human faces. These *zemis* (images) were as horribly conceived as the deities were believed to be malignant. Each village had its house which was consecrated as the residence of the zemis. At Cape Catoche these houses were known as *cues*. The 'godhouses' were inaccessible to all except the *bohitos* (priests) who conveyed the prayers of the Arawaks to the deities. Invariably, the thrust of the prayers was that some danger might be averted or that some catastrophic act of the deities might be stayed. From the cues, the bohitos interpreted the action of the deities in storm or in flood; they brought messages or commands from the gods, and prophecies as to the future visitations of these spirits.

The zemis did not reside only in the cues. The Arawaks carried zemis about their person or kept them in their dwellings.

3

In a world of hostile spirits, it was as prudent as it was comforting to have one's personal or familiar welfare safe-guarded by these tutelary deities. In most cases, the tutelary zemis were those of departed ancestors. The Arawaks did not make any clear distinction between the spirit and its effigy, the zemi. As far as they were concerned, it was the zemi whom they identified as Guabancex, for example, that wrought destruction by wind and water. Nevertheless, Guabancex was free to leave her effigy at her good pleasure and exist independently of it. What was true of Guabancex was true of the other spirits as well.

Sometimes, the power of the tutelary zemi was ineffective against that of the spirits of sickness and death. We do not know the names of these spirits, but among the Arawaks of Guyana, they were known collectively as *Yauhahu.* Pain caused by them was known as *yahauhu simaira* – the evil spirits' arrow. It was the priest or bohito who functioned as the healer in the Arawak village. This is understandable when we bear in mind that as far as the Indians were concerned, sickness was due to the machinations of mischievous and malignant spirits who had to be exorcised if cure was to be effected. Exorcism was properly the function of the bohito.

In his role as exorcist/healer, the bohito of the Arawak village was not unlike the *piai* (priest or medicineman) of the Warrau village in Guyana; neither was the method of exorcising used by the one different from that used by the other. The ritual of exorcism began at nightfall since it was the general belief that the bohito's powers were severely limited during the daytime. In any case, the spirits themselves tended to be somewhat dormant during the hours of daylight and were not accessible then. At nightfall, armed with the sacred rattle (which was made from a gourd), the bohito or piai sought by incantations to exorcise the spirit from the sick man and to expel it from his dwelling-house. The incantations uttered by the priest were punctuated by the blowing of puffs of tobacco smoke from a consecrated cigar into the face of the possessed person. Naturally, if exorcism failed to bring about the desired result, the person died.

Sometimes, untimely death was believed to be brought about by an evil spirit sent specially by the victim's enemy for that purpose. The Macusi Indians of Guyana, among whom the belief was better developed, called that spirit *kanaima.* When death was caused by kanaima, it was generally the responsibility of some close relative of the deceased to avenge his death. In order to effect vengeance, such a relative, in turn, became kanaima who sought out and destroyed the enemy of his deceased kinsman.

The Arawaks believed that at death the spirits of good men went to reside in a pleasant place called *Coyaba*. This Elysium was sometimes described as a valley, and, at other times, as an island. Whether valley or island, it was a place of ease and tranquillity. Here, the *opita* (spirits) of departed ancestors enjoyed cool shade, delicious fruit, and safety from droughts and hurricane. But the rewards of Coyaba were available only to those who had lived upright lives in the Arawak villages.

The Beliefs of the Caribs

The Caribs seem to have had a notion that behind creation there was one great universal cause which might well be a superior, wise and invisible Being of great and irresistible power. But they had no name for this Being. Of much more importance to the Caribs was the earth. To them, the earth was a bountiful parent who provided them with all the good things of life; but it is to be doubted that the earth assumed the status of a deity among the Caribs in the way it did among other peoples. Hindus, for example, have worshipped the earth in the form of Dharti Mata (Mother Earth); the Igbos of West Africa have regarded it as the goddess Ala; the ancient Romans worshipped earth as Tellus Mater. It might well be that the Caribs' high regard for earth did not shade over into worship because they were not altogether dependent on agriculture for their livelihood. Again, it was not the practice of the Caribs (nor of the Arawaks, for that matter) to lavish worshipful attention on forces that were believed to be well disposed to them; in the estimation of the Caribs, the earth was, perhaps, the most beneficent factor in their day-to-day lives.

It was the malignant spirits of wind and water, of disease and death, that had to be kept suitably placated if the Caribs were to live reasonably well in an environment that was shared by these spirits. The names of these spirits have not survived; but it is quite possible that they were known individually and generically as *manitou*.[4] If that was the case, then this particular aspect of Carib belief would not have been different from a belief widely held by the Algonquins and Iroquois of the North American forests. These forest Indians believed that everything

5

in nature – human beings, animals, stones, plants, etc. – was inhabited and animated by a mysterious force or power that could affect and influence other beings. The Algonquins called that power *manitou*. The Iroquois labelled the mysterious force *orenda*.

It was crucial for the Algonquins to control the lesser manitou and to obtain the favourable disposition of the greater ones if they were to survive in their environment. The Caribs of the West Indies felt the same way. The favour of the manitou was sought by worship. The effigies of lesser spirits and of tutelary manitou were offered sacrifices at household altars made of banana leaves and rushes; the propitiatory offering normally consisted of fruit. The more powerful manitou were worshipped at public ceremonies conducted by the *boyez* or priest. The images of these manitou were usually large in size; they were often placed on raised pedestals. At a public ceremony, a kind of blood sacrifice was often offered to the spirits. In this, the Caribs wounded themselves with the teeth of the agouti. They cut their cheeks, their lower lips and other parts of the body, and allowed the blood to drip either in front of, or on, the image of the manitou which was being propitiated. This sacrifice was felt to be most efficacious in securing the favour of the manitou. A similar kind of sacrifice was practised by the Maya Indians of Central America.

The Caribs believed that a man survived death. It is not clear however, whether it was the man himself or his manitou that survived. This pervasive belief did not prevent the Caribs from mourning their dead by cutting their hair and wounding themselves. While there was a general belief that the departed were silent and secret spectators of the conduct of their living relations in whose welfare they were concerned, it was strongly felt that the virtuous and the brave went to some Elysium where they enjoyed great felicity with their wives and with some of the captives whom they had taken in battle. These captives were slain at the funeral of the Carib braves. The wicked and the cowardly, however, were doomed to everlasting punishment. Somewhere, beyond the mountains, the wicked were made to toil unremittingly at labour which disgraced their manhood. The greatest of all afflictions also awaited these unfortunates "beyond the mountains": captivity and a life of servitude among the Arawaks.

Conclusions

Any attempt at an analysis of the beliefs of the indigenous peoples of the Caribbean is a hazardous task. For one thing, the data on which such analysis must be based are rather skimpy; for another thing, such analysis must perforce schematise the beliefs of the Indians in a way that the Indians themselves might not have done. Nevertheless, even at the risk of distortion, such an analysis must be attempted.

It would seem that the Arawaks held to a pattern of beliefs which has been described by ethnologists and anthropologists as animism. Their animism was, however, combined with a form of polydaemonism. Derived from the Latin *anima* (soul/ spirit), animism is used to designate the belief in a large number of spirits, any or all of whom may interfere with human life. These spirits are usually thought of as 'personal' beings who are identified or associated with natural phenomena which they control. They may inhabit, be represented by, or in some way be connected with, physical objects which men worship. They are not, however, to be strictly identified with their effigies in the sense that they are held to be unable to exist independently of those effigies. Much of what we have said above in respect to Arawak beliefs (for example, the association of Guabancex with storms, and the character of the zemi), would suggest that the Arawaks were animists.

A feature of animistic belief is the strongly held conviction that evil spirits must be propitiated or exorcised. This aspect of animism is often categorised as shamanism. Shamanism finds its best expression among the Ural-Altaic peoples of the area around the Behring Strait and the borders of Scandinavia. Among these peoples, the priest or medicine-man is called the *shaman* – hence shamanism. The Arawak bohito was not unlike the shaman. He was credited with the same abnormal qualities which made it possible for shaman and bohito to be mediums through whom men and spirits could communicate. Both used the same method to exorcise evil spirits; both foretold the future and declared the will of the 'gods' while in a trance-like state. [5]

Other features of animistic belief were also found among the Arawaks. These included notions of *tabu* and fetishism. Tabu cannot be understood apart from *mana*. [6] Coming from the world of Melanesian folklore and beliefs, mana is the technical term used to describe that supernormal, diffused, impersonal force which is supposed to pervade all life. Its residence in a special way in objects or persons makes those objects or persons tabu — that is, 'marked off' or forbidden to ordinary usage or relationship. A *fetich* is an object in which a spirit has been induced to dwell. Such an object is then tabu to common handling. The bohito himself was regarded as tabu to common concourse with his fellow villagers. Notions of *mana-tabu* made the 'god-house' inaccessible to anyone but the bohito. Notions of fetichism and mana-tabu forbade the touching of the bohito's rattle as it did the careless handling of zemis.

But the Arawaks were more than animists. Spirits such as Hurakan and Guabancex were much more than local spirits associated only with natural phenomena in a particular village or island. As far as the Arawaks were concerned, their influence was 'universal'. Given time, they might well have developed, together with Jocahuna, into a pantheon of important gods. Meanwhile, in their growing status we see at least the beginnings of an Arawak polydaemonism. As in polydaemonism generally, the spirits (Hurakan, Guabancex, Coatrischie and Guantuval) were recognisably homogeneous. At the same time, the individuality of each of these spirits was fairly well established.

Could Arawak beliefs have evolved in the direction of polytheism and, possibly, even in the direction of monotheism? Probably. For a time, the notion prevailed that Jocahuna was a supreme being. Among almost all people there has been the pervasive notion of a supreme being. It has not been difficult for some of these peoples to hold to a belief in such a being and, at the same time, to be animists, or ancestor or nature cultists. When that being is worshipped as a god and other gods (and/or goddesses) are worshipped as his subordinates or equals, polytheism results. When that god alone is worshipped, polytheism gives way to monotheism. The Arawaks, however, did not reach the stage where Jocahuna was worshipped. Even with Hurakan and the others, Arawak 'worship' was at a rudimentary stage. Its aim was primarily to keep the spirits appeased. No attempt was made to enter into a relationship with them.

The animism of the Caribs was not as advanced as that of the Arawaks. While the spirits which they recognised were no doubt personal, they had little or no individuality. The name manitou embraced all of the powers. There is a strong possibility that the powers of disease, wind, and water were but specialised expressions of the one malignant and pervasive manitou. If this

8

was the case, then the animism of the Caribs was perhaps just emerging from that other kind of primitive belief — animatism, in which a rather diffused kind of force or power is held to pervade all things.[7] The emergence of earth as a distinct object of veneration (if not of worship) among the Caribs, and the fact that manitou was worshipped in distinct and 'individual' forms prevent us from regarding the Caribs' belief as constituting a thoroughgoing animatism.

The prevalent tone of animism is fear; both the Arawaks and the Caribs feared their 'gods'. Their worship was mainly apotropaic in nature in that it was intended to ward off the spirits who were believed to be malignant. In this connection, the blood sacrifice of the Caribs was supposed to possess great apotropaic value. The rattling sound made by the bohito, together with the smoke blown into the face of a sick person, was meant to frighten away the evil spirit which was believed to possess such a person. But there was also an element of propitiation about the worship of Caribs and Arawaks. This was no doubt motivated by the fear that if the spirits were not sufficiently appeased, they would harm their worshippers.

It is to be doubted that the Arawaks or Caribs worshipped ancestral spirits. The Arawaks kept zemis of such spirits mainly for their apotropaic value; but, generally speaking, the 'dead' were believed to reside away from the village, depending on their moral status at death.

The ethical element in animism is generally negligible. Although animists may make a clear distinction between right and wrong, the right in terms of personal behaviour and inter-personal relationships is not based on obedience to the wishes or commands of the spirits, nor is the wrong a violation of such commands. Notions of mana-tabu, however, may impose limits on bloodshed and restraints on indiscriminate sexual activity.

Qualification for bliss in Coyaba (the Arawak Elysium) and in the Carib paradise, was based on aspects of behaviour which the Indians held in high esteem with little if any reference to the 'gods'. Thus, the good Carib was one who was manly in bearing and courageous and resourceful in battle — qualities much prized by a warlike and proud people. The good Arawak, on the other hand, was expected to be gentle, to be able to control his temper, and to restrain his feelings of jealousy. No doubt such qualities were highly prized among the Arawaks because they went a long way towards maintaining stability in the Arawak village.

The beliefs of the indigenous peoples of the Caribbean were undoubtedly shaped by the nature of the environment in which they lived. A hostile environment bred hostile spirits. Whether or not those beliefs would have changed if and when those peoples tamed their environment, we can never know. The intrusion of the Spaniards into the Caribbean halted any further evolution of Arawak and Carib beliefs.

Notes and References

1. Augier and Gordon, *Sources of West Indian History*, p. 1.

2. It is from Hurakan that the word "hurricane" is derived.

3. By calling the supreme god *Wacinaci* (Our Father), the Arawaks of Guyana acknowledged that the deity was benign.

4. Patrick Fermor, who visited the Caribs of Dominica in 1950, tells us that the Caribs worshipped Manitou, apparently agreeing with Père Labat who was an early missionary to the Caribs. See P.L. Fermor, *The Traveller's Tree*, p. 110.

5. For a description of the shaman, see Nathanier Micklem, *Religion*, pp. 22-23.

6. Strictly speaking, notions of *mana-tabu* are related more to animatism — the belief that a diffused life-force inheres all things. Nevertheless, insofar as notions of tabu surround the bohito and his equipment, we will include mana-tabu in our discussion, with the understanding that the state of tabu is brought about by the presence of spirits rather than by impersonal forces.

7. Animism is the name given to the worship of individual spirits which are believed to indwell trees, stones, springs and other natural objects. Animatism is the belief that such natural objects are possessed by a diffused life-force rather than by individual, personal spirits.

CHAPTER II

CATHOLICISM IN THE CARIBBEAN

The year that saw the advent of the first Europeans into the Caribbean, saw also the ascension to the papal throne of Roderigo Borgia who took the name of Alexander VI. It has been said of Pope Alexander VI that his "private and public life made the title 'Vicar of Christ' the most appalling mockery that has ever been perpetrated in the name of religion."[1]

Alexander's eleven-year reign marked the nadir of corruption and immorality at the papal court. The period saw also a weakening of the notion among European peoples that they belonged to a *respublica christiana*. It was only a matter of time before the notion would be destroyed altogether by the Reformation. It is true, however, that it was the Pope, the institutional symbol of whatever sense of community still existed in Europe, who issued the Bulls that granted half the world to the Spanish crown and proposed the dividing line between the Spanish and Portuguese dominions. But the terms of the Bulls might well have emanated from the chancery of Ferdinand and Isabella, the Spanish sovereigns. If that was the case, then the papacy acted not so much as a recognised arbiter between the two rival nations of Portugal and Spain, but simply as an instrument of Spanish diplomacy. To be sure, by 1492, the religious unity of Europe was still formally intact, although papal authority, which was buttressed by canon law, was growing increasingly ineffective throughout the continent. The English monarch was already controlling the appointments to bishoprics. France had forced the papacy to accept the Pragmatic Sanction of Bourges; this gave the French church the appearance of a national church under the control of the king.

In Spain, the Inquisition, an ecclesiastical institution, was being used by Ferdinand and Isabella to unite Spain; papal attempts to restrain its savagery were ineffective. But if the notion that Europe constituted a *respublica christiana* was succumbing to serious erosion because of the rise of powerful nation states in that continent and because of the strong sense of nationalism which characterised those states, its place was to be taken by the conviction that Western Europe shared a unity which had its basis in a common civilisation. That civilisation, in turn, was believed to be rooted in the Christian religion.

The discovery of the New World by Europeans led to what was, for all practical purposes, the extension of the boundaries of Western Europe to these parts. As explorers, discoverers, *conquistadores* and traders sought to open up the region for economic exploitation, missionaries and priests sought to introduce what they considered to be the blessings of European civilisation to the indigenous peoples and to incorporate them into the fold of Catholicism − the religion of the *respublica christiana*. The driving force behind Spain's exploitative thrust in the Caribbean, Central and South America is summed up thus:

> Spain was impelled to two kinds of militant action at that momentous period of her history: the one militarist the other spiritual, both combative and eager to conquer; in the former the purposes to conquer power, territory, and riches prevailed; in the latter the prime aim was to win adherence to Christianity.[2]

The conquistadores made short shrift of much of the civilisation which they found on the far side of the Atlantic: it was upon the gentle Arawaks that the blow of the Spaniards was first to fall. It is not that the Arawaks capitulated without striking a blow; but the reprisals that met such temerity were usually of a savage and brutal nature. In Hispaniola, for example, even when resistance had been quashed, the conquistadores vowed to massacre twelve Indians daily in honour of the twelve apostles. A thirteenth was to be immolated in honour of Jesus Christ! Such was the ruthlessness with which the Spaniards treated the Arawaks that by 1520 their subjugation was complete.

The Caribs of the Lesser Antilles offered stouter resistance to the Spaniards. In the final analysis they were spared not because of their resistance but because the interest of the Europeans had swung away from the Caribbean to the mainland of Central and South America. Gold and silver were found in Central and South America. Hernando Cortes completed the conquest of the Aztecs of Mexico between 1519 and 1521, and Francisco Pizarro completed that of the Incas of Peru in the five years from 1531 to 1536. By 1550, the Caribbean Sea had been converted into a Spanish lake — a *mare clausum* — as Spain was fond of reminding her European rivals.

The task of conquering the Indians was accompanied by that of christianising and civilising them. The latter was sometimes advanced as the reason for the former. In about 1513, the theory was advanced by Martin Fernandez de Enciso, that God had apportioned the Indies to the Spaniards in much the same way that He had given the Promised Land to the Jews. In their conquest of Canaan by force of arms, the Israelites slew many Canaanites and enslaved others. Enciso argued that all this was done by the will of God because the Canaanites were idolaters. Enciso concluded:

> The King of Spain might very justly send men to require those idolatrous Indians to hand over their land to him for it was given him by the Pope. If the Indians would not do this, he might justly wage war against them, kill them and enslave those captured in war, precisely as Joshua treated the inhabitants of the land of Canaan.[3]

Enciso's theory was accepted by the Spanish sovereign. The sovereign caused a manifesto or Requirement to be announced to the Indians before hostilities could be formally launched against them. The document required that the Indians acknowledge the Catholic Church as the Ruler and Superior of the whole world. The high priest was called the Pope, and in his name, the King and Queen of Spain were to be acknowledged as superiors, lords and kings of the Caribbean islands and of the mainland. The document further required that the Indians allow the Christian faith to be preached to them. If the Indians failed to meet the obligations of the Requirement, they were to be subjugated by force to the Church and the Crown.

Whether or not the Indians accepted the Requirement, the outcome was the same: they were to be christianised. Very often, Spaniards razed Indian villages on the excuse that the natives failed to accept the *Requerimiento*. More often than not, the Indians disappeared into the bush before the manifesto was read. Those who heard it read could not understand it.

The task of christianising the indigenous peoples was entrusted to the church. In this regard, the church functioned as an agency of the Crown. King Ferdinand and Queen Isabella of Spain wrung extensive concessions from the Pope by declaring to His Holiness that their ardent aim in promoting expeditions to the Indies was to extend the dominion of the Roman Catholic faith to these parts. The Catholic sovereigns argued that since the task of christianising the natives constituted a valid apostleship, it was natural and necessary that it should be done under the authority and patronage of the successor to the Prince of the Apostles — the Pope. In a series of five Papal Bulls, the Roman pontiff not only gave the Spanish Crown the exclusive privilege of christianizing the natives, but he also gave the crown such extensive control over the church in the Indies, that, for all practical purposes, the king functioned as the Pope's vicar in the New World.

It is a matter of some conjecture as to the effect which this development had on the relationship between the papacy and the crown in Spain itself. Concessions won by the sovereigns from the Pope could have only helped to strengthen the position of the crown *vis-a-vis* that of the papacy. In any case, Alexander VI and his immediate successors to the papal throne were too preoccupied with European politics, the rising threat of Protestantism and the pervasive presence of the Turks in the Mediterranean to supervise the evangelisation of territories discovered by Iberian explorers and adventurers. That responsibility was conveniently delegated by the *Padroado Real* to the Portuguese king.

Meanwhile, the licensing of ecclesiastics for the Indies became the responsibility of the Council of the Indies and the *Casa de Contratacion* — the two metropolitan institutions which were created to govern Spanish America and were answerable to the King alone. In the New World, the movement of priests and friars was subject to the direction of the viceroy or the governor. It was the crown that determined the boundaries of parishes and dioceses; invariably, these coincided with the political territorial divisions.

On the eve of Columbus' arrival in the Caribbean, the Spanish crown, inspired as much by Isabella's passion for religious uniformity as by political considerations, expelled from Spain some two hundred thousand Jews who refused to accept Christian baptism. On November 25, 1491, the Muslim capital of Granada formally capitulated to their Catholic Sovereigns with the understanding that the Muslims would be granted full liberty to exercise their religion as long as they submitted peacefully to Christian rule. In the end, in 1498, the Moors were asked to choose between conversion and exile. Many chose exile. The desire for religious uniformity in the Iberian peninsula, which motivated the crown's action against the Jews and the Muslims, was extended to embrace Spain overseas – the Spanish Indies. It followed, therefore, that the Indians could not be allowed to practise their own religion unmolested; they had to be christianised. The Spanish crown would not have had it otherwise.

The first missionaries to undertake the task of evangelising the indigenous peoples were Franciscan and Dominican friars. The members of these mendicant orders had a tradition of combatting heresy and promoting Christianity by preaching as well as by exemplary living. Both orders arose in the early thirteenth century. The one was founded by St. Francis of Assissi, born Giovanni Bernardone in about 1210, and the other by the erstwhile Augustinian canon, St. Dominic, in about 1215. It was in the towns and universities that were now important factors in the social life of western Europe that the Grey (Franciscan) and Black (Dominican) friars were to recruit their members in the main, as they were to make their most significant contribution to the life and work of the church. Vowed to a life of simplicity and renunciation, the friars gave themselves to the task of preaching and studying in the effort to combat heresy and irreligion with a great single-mindedness of purpose. The ardent desire of the Dominicans had long been to convert heretics, confute Muslim Turks, win over the Greeks to Catholicism, and reach those people in Western Europe who had been left out of the calculations of earlier religious enthusiasts. The discovery of the Amerindians provided the Dominicans with another field for missionary enterprise. Their enthusiasm for the enterprise was matched by that of the Franciscans. More devoted agents than these friars could not have been found to undertake the task of preparing the natives of the Caribbean for inclusion in the *respublica christiana*. The Dominicans and the Franciscans were later joined by the Jesuits and the Mercedarians.

The Mercedarians belonged to an order that was founded in about 1220 by St. Peter Nolasco with the object of tending the sick and of rescuing Christians who had been taken prisoner by the Moors. The order came to be so named because of the monks' dedication to Our Lady of Mercy *(Nuestra Senora de la Merced)*.

By 1502, a Franciscan monastery had been established in Hispaniola; in 1510, the first Dominican monastic centre was established on that island when twelve of the 'Preaching

15

Brothers' led by Pedro de Cardoba arrived. It is of interest to note that the Dominican friars were sent to the New World by Thomas Vio of Cajetanus. Better known as Cajetan, Vio was a scholar of repute in Europe and an acknowledged authority on the Dominican saint and renowned theologian, Thomas Aquinas. Later, in 1518, as a cardinal and papal legate at the Reichstag in Augsburg, Germany, he was to be entrusted with the responsibility of making Martin Luther, then an Augustinian monk, retract his statements which, Cajetan felt, questioned the Pope's authority. At the time the Dominican was despatching friars to the Caribbean, however, Luther was teaching theology at the University of Wittenberg. The Protestant Reformation had not yet begun.

Another point of interest is that it was the Provincial Vicar of the Dominicans, Tomas de Berlanga, who brought the first banana plants to the New World. The plants were brought to Hispaniola, probably from the Canary Islands, around 1516. By 1530, when the Dominicans established their first province, Holy Cross, in the New World, with Santo Domingo as its headquarters, Dominican friars were to be found in Hispaniola, Jamaica, Cuba, Puerto Rico and the mainland of New Spain. No doubt the banana plant was to be found in these places as well.

Special Papal Bulls permitted the friars to administer the sacraments and to perform other clerical duties when and where secular clergymen were unavailable for these duties. Meanwhile, the monasteries served as sources of missionaries and of missionary endeavour to new settlements when these were established by *conquistadores* or *encomenderos*. The Dominican interest in education found expression in the Caribbean in the establishment of the St. Thomas Aquinas University of Santo Domingo in 1538.

By 1499, the *repartimiento-encomienda* system had been established in the Caribbean along much the same lines as in the Canary Islands earlier in the decade. By this system, the Spanish Crown gave or 'commended' Indians to Spanish conquistadores and gentlemen with the understanding that these encomenderos would have the right to exact labour or tribute from the Indians. In return for this favour, the encomenderos were to provide religious instruction for their Indians and to offer them protection, presumably from their fellow Indians. The justification for the *encomienda* ran thus:

> Because of the excessive liberty the Indians have been permitted,
> they flee from Christians and do not work. Therefore they are to

16

be compelled to work, so that the kingdom and the Spaniards may be enriched, and the Indians Christianised.[4]

The avarice of the conquistadores triumphed over the desire of the friars and the crown to have the natives christianised. Pushed to unaccustomed, harsh, and unrelenting labour in mines and fields, the Indians died at an alarming rate. Those of Hispaniola were so decimated that the Tainos or Lucayans of the Bahamas were recruited to take their places and to die in thousands in those places. The transportation of the Lucayans to Hispaniola was authorised by King Ferdinand to provide the Spaniards with labour and to facilitate the conversion of the Indians.

The exploitation of the Indians did not go unnoticed. In Spain, churchmen questioned the justice of the *encomienda*. The result was that, in 1509, the crown decided that Indians were to serve encomenderos for no more than one to two years. But in the New World, the royal decree was observed mainly in the breach. Meanwhile, the plight of the Indians attracted the attention of one of the most brilliant of European theologians – the Dominican, Francisco de Vittoria of the University of Salamanca. Vittoria argued from the principles of natural law and claimed that the Indians of the New World constituted nations in their own rights. Consequently, they were entitled to their liberty, their right to self-government and to the peaceful possession of their property. In the Caribbean in 1511, a protest was voiced over the treatment of the Indians. On the Sunday before Christmas that year, a Dominican friar, Antonio de Montesinos, preaching on the text, "I am the voice of one crying in the wilderness," asked his congregation in Hispaniola:

> Why do you keep [the Indians] so oppressed and weary, not giving them enough to eat nor taking care of them in their illness? For with the excessive work you demand of them they fall ill and die, or rather you kill them with your desire to extract and acquire gold every day. And what care do you take that they should be instructed in religion?[5]

Montesinos' hearers were flabbergasted; they demanded an apology from the friar. He responded by preaching another sermon in which he condemned the cruelty of the Spanish settlers and questioned the right of the Spaniards to rule the Indians, who, in the estimation of the Dominican, were quite capable of governing themselves. In the end, the Dominican Provincial in Hispaniola was ordered by the King through the

Dominican Superior in Spain, Alonso de Loaysa, to prevail upon the friar to desist from preaching such scandalous doctrines. It was felt by Ferdinand that the ideas preached by Montesinos were harmful. But as a result of the debate which the Montesinos incident engendered, the Spanish crown promulgated the *Ley de Burgos* in 1512. This law stipulated that the Indians were not to be treated as slaves; those entrusted to an encomendero were not to be sold or transferred. Further, Indians were to be paid just wages for their labour.

In 1514, another Dominican, Bartholome de Las Casas, raised his voice against the *encomienda*. He was to do so tirelessly, as he condemned the robbery, evil and injustice committed against the indigenous peoples. At Valladolid in 1550-1551, Las Casas engaged Juan Gines de Sepulveda in a debate over the legitimacy of Spain's waging war against the Indians as a necessary step to christianising them. Las Casas' position was: the Indians should be converted by peaceful means. This would make them faithful Spanish subjects afterwards. The Dominican was convinced that the indigenous peoples could be won over to Christianity by the demonstration of peace, love, and good example on the part of the Spaniards. Sepulveda, for his part, advanced four reasons in support of his position that war against the Indians was as just as it was necessary if the barbarians of the Indies were to be conquered, converted to the Christian religion, and made to submit to the jurisdiction of the Spanish Crown.

According to Sepulveda, the gravity of the sins of the Indians, particularly their idolatries and their sins against nature, merited war. So, too, did the rudeness of their natures which placed them under the obligation of serving persons of a more refined nature, such as the Spaniards. Further, the propagation of the Christian faith among the natives demanded their subjugation. Then, there was the need to protect the weaker natives from their more hostile fellows. Sepulveda quoted St. Luke, chapter 14, verse 23: "Go out into the highways and hedges, and compel them to come in, that my house may be filled," as justification for war against the Indians in order to bring them into the Christian fold.

It is of interest to note that at an earlier period, St. Augustine (354-430) had quoted Luke 14:23 in justifying the use of force against Donatist schismatics in North Africa. If Padre Alexandre Valignano is to be believed, Francis Xavier used that verse to justify his missionary methods of recruiting converts on the Fishery Coast of India in the late sixteenth century. Xavier's strategy involved a mixture of threats and blandishments. One threat used by the famous Jesuit missionary was that Portugal might deprive the Indians of fishing privileges and of sea-borne trade if they did not become Christians. The 'forcible' conversion of the natives of India during the Age of Latin Arrogance (late sixteenth century) is, perhaps, understandable. The growth of Protestanism and the revival within Roman Catholicism in Europe led to a hardening of religious differences within Europe itself; in Asia, Christian zeal (if not fanaticism) bred by the developments in Europe expressed itself in a strong intolerance of native religions. These were dismissed as being Satanic in origin. To convert people from them − forcibly or otherwise − was to bestow a great privilege on the converted. Although he lived before the Age of Latin Arrogance, Sepulveda anticipated the mood of that era in his attitude to the Indians of the New World. His strong national pride combined with a distorted understanding of Aristotle's theories concerning slavery and the relationship of superior to inferior men in the city-state, led the Spaniard to believe that it was the responsibility of Catholic Spaniards to enslave the pagan Indians in order to bring about the conversion of the latter.

The important thing about Valladolid is not so much what Las Casas said in refutation of Sepulveda, but the fact that the latter was widely acclaimed and even rewarded by influential Spaniards for his stance in relation to the Indians. He articulated what the mainstream of Iberian Christendom felt about the Indians: that it was right and lawful that the barbarians of the New World should be brought under the dominion of the Christians, simply because − in Sepulveda's estimation − they were "so uncivilised, so barbaric, contaminated with so many impieties and obscenities,"[6] above monkeys to be sure, but at best only "little men (hombrecillos) in whom you will scarcely find even vestiges of humanity."[7] They were certainly not worthy of any consideration that they were in the same class as Spanish Catholics.

Meanwhile, those natives that had not succumbed to the rapacity of Spanish exploitation were herded into pueblos called reducciones. It was felt that this would obviate one of the major difficulties which the missionaries faced in christianizing the Indians: the scattered nature of their settlement. In the reduccion or mision, which was built around the church, the friars could better instruct the Indians in the Christian faith and supervise their growth along lines which their instructors believed to be Christian. In this way, Ferdinand's hope that the Indians might be Christians in fact as well as in name would be realised. In addition to the faith, the aborigines were taught new methods of agriculture and handicrafts at the *mision*. It was hoped that in time the mission might be converted into an Indian parish, or *doctrina*, served by a priest under the administration of a *corregidor*. At the *reduccion*, the Indians were instructed in what the Spanish called the *doctrina christiana*. The general notion was that the natives had but a limited capacity for understanding the intricacies of Catholic theology. Nevertheless, they could be instructed in the elements of Catholicism. Thus, they were taught to make the sign of the cross and to repeat the Lord's Prayer, the Hail Mary and the Apostles' Creed. In addition, they learned by rote: The Ten Commandments, the dogmas of the Church, the Spiritual and Corporal Works of Mercy, the Seven Capital Sins, the Theological Virtues, the Cardinal Virtues and the Sacraments. This training was in preparation for baptism. Sometimes, it took as many as six or seven years for some Indians to be trained for that sacrament. Even so, it is to be doubted that the natives understood with any appreciable degree of clarity the nature of the faith into which they were initiated. Not a few of them managed to combine some elements of Catholicism with the older beliefs in spirits such as Guabancex and Hurakan. This happened much to the disgust of the clergy who sometimes imposed severe physical punishment on the Indians in order to deter them from indulging in 'heathen' practices. Bryan Edwards, no lover of either Spain or Catholicism, tells us, obviously with a great deal of exaggeration, that some Spaniards "more zealous than the rest" forced Indians into the water, and after administering the rite of baptism, slit their throats in order to prevent them from apostatising.[8]

Thousands of Indians were baptised; few were admitted to the sacrament of the Holy Eucharist. The Provincial Synod of the Caribbean which was held in Santo Domingo in September, 1622, was of the opinion that the indigenous peoples lacked the knowledge which would have qualified them to receive the Eucharist. In addition, it was felt that their proneness to their old idolatry certainly disqualified them from receiving the sacrament. While negligent pastors were blamed for the condition of their charges, the resistance of the aborigines to the process of christianisation undoubtedly added to the pastors' already difficult task. Time and again, Indians decamped from the *reducciones.* Many of them repudiated their baptism, with some of them actually applying water to themselves and declaring themselves to be non-Catholics. Some of them, like the Caribs of Dominica, availed themselves of baptism several times in order to receive the gifts which were offered Indians on the occasion of their baptism. Their conversion was obviously superficial.

At best, the programme of christianising and civilising the indigenous peoples of the Caribbean achieved the most minimal results. By 1644, there were about two hundred and fifty Christian Caribs in Trinidad out of a total population of about four thousand. By 1798, there was a small Arawak colony at Iwanee near St. Jago de Cuba in Cuba, where the natives had adopted "the manners and the language of the Spaniards." Elsewhere, the Arawaks had all but disappeared. Some succumbed to diseases brought to the Caribbean by the Europeans; other committed suicide; most were destroyed by the Spaniards. Many of their women were assimilated into the Spanish population by marriage or by concubinage; sometimes, forcibly so. The Caribs too were destroyed, not only by the Spaniards, but also by the English and French when these latecomers to the Caribbean tried to establish a foothold in these parts. For example, Du Parquet, who became one of the early French governors of Martinique, was responsible for the extermination of the Caribs of Grenada. Only in Dominica did a significant number of Caribs survive.

In spite of the outstanding work of such missionaries as the Hieronymite, Roman Pane, and the Mercedarian, Juan Infante, the hope held by both the crown and the friars that the mission to the Indians might result in the establishment of the doctrina or Indian parish, was not realised. Nevertheless, an ecclesiastical hierarchy was established in the Caribbean. In August 1511, three sees were established: Santo Domingo and Concepcion de la Vega in Hispaniola, and San Juan in Puerto Rico. The sees were placed under the jurisdiction of the archdiocese of Seville. In 1517, the first Cuban diocese was established in Baracia; this was transferred to Santiago de Cuba seven years later.

In 1545, Santo Domingo was elevated to the dignity of archdiocese with jurisdiction over the other sees in the Caribbean. This marked the independence of the Caribbean church from the ecclesiastical jurisdiction of Spain; although, theoretically, all ecclesiastical matters in the New World were still supposed to be under the general superintendence of the Patriarch of the Indies. The Patriarchate was created by the Pope around 1513, at the request of the Spanish crown. As vicar-general of the Indies, the Patriarch resided at the king's court in order that he might be in immediate contact with the Council of the Indies. In spite of his title, the Patriarch's office was mainly honorary; he had little (if any) part in the government of the church in the Indies.

The Church received admirable leadership from such men as Don Alonso de Fuenmayor, who was bishop of Santo Domingo from 1539 to 1554, Domingo Fernandez, archbishop of Santo Domingo from 1657 to 1685, and Don Alonso Manso, the first bishop of San Juan, whose office lasted from 1512 to 1534. On the other hand, the church was not without those clerics who used their office to enrich themselves at the expense of their parishioners. Such a clergyman was the second bishop of Cuba, Miguel Ramirez. The bishop and the governor, Gonzalo de Guzman, parcelled out most of the land and the Indians among themselves and their supporters. Protest against that line of action was harshly dealt with. For example, a local judge who opposed Ramirez was subjected to an inquisitorial trial and excommunicated. But generally speaking, clergymen who came to the Caribbean were not as venal as were some Portuguese priests who told the Vicar of Malacca in 1514 that they had gone to the East primarily to amass a fortune in *cruzados.*

Two bishops of Cuba, Juan de Ubite and Diego Sarmiento, left their sees because they considered their efforts futile. Sarmiento, who succeed Ramirez around 1533, was disheartened by the shortage of priests in Cuba; those priests that did serve the diocese were of a poor quality. An additional cause for discouragement was the low level of the spiritual life at the monastery at Santiago.

By the time Sarmiento became bishop of Cuba, Spanish interest in the Indies had swung away from the Caribbean to the mainland of Central and South America. This swing in interest was marked by an exodus of many Spanish settlers from the islands to the mainland. Parishes become depleted in their church membership, and many abler members of the clergy also followed their parishioners to the mainland. Hispaniola suffered less from such losses than did Cuba, Jamaica and Puerto Rico.

By the middle of the sixteenth century, Puerto Rico had only about ten or twelve priests to serve that diocese. Cuba was served mainly by priests who had left Spain to escape the ecclesiastical reforms which were taking place in that country. Those reforms, initially inspired by Gonzalex Ximenes de Cisneros and carried forward by the Spanish Inquisition, were aimed at, among other things, the upgrading of the morals and the education of the clergy. Hispaniola, too, was to attract some clergymen who had fled the Spanish Inquisition, while abler missionary-priests who had hitherto served that island left for Mexico and Peru. If anything, conditions were worse in the abbacy of Jamaica where the church was sometimes without prelate or pastor for long intervals.

In September, 1622, the Provincial Synod of the Caribbean convened at Santo Domingo. In attendance were representatives from Venezuela, Hispaniola, Puerto Rico, Cuba and Jamaica. The deliberations and promulgations of the Synod afford us an insight into the ecclesiastical life of that period. The Synod showed concern over the fact that many clerics were coming to the Caribbean claiming to be holders of certificates and academic degrees which they did not possess. Clerics falsely claiming to be the recipients of patrimony and the holders of benefices elsewhere supplicated on those grounds to be ordained to the priesthood. Clearly, these candidates for the priesthood were not the most honest of men. The Synod forbade priests from absenting themselves from their parishes without permission from their bishops, and ecclesiastics were forbidden to engage in trade or business with the Indians. Apparently, both absentee-ism from their parishes on the part of priests and the practice of clerics engaging in trade with their Indian charges were not unknown. Not unknown too was the practice by both religious and secular clergy of accepting payment from parishioners for the administration of sacraments.

The hub of the church's activities was the church building. Because of this, great emphasis was placed on the construction of churches. The actual task of construction was invariably done by Indians, who, in the course of this kind of work, acquired an expertise in quarrying stones as well as in lime and brick making. As in Europe, the church was not only a centre for the holding of religious services, it was also a refuge for wrong-doers who, having sought the sanctuary of the church, were safe from the harassment of even civil officials. The Synod of 1622 made attendance at religious services on Sunday all but compulsory, particularly for those people who lived within a one-mile radius of the church. At Sunday services, the sacraments were dispensed and the Word of God preached.

Great emphasis was placed on the seven sacraments which were officially sanctioned by the Council of Florence in 1439. Baptism was in the name of the Father, the Son and the Holy Ghost. It was conferred on infants who were brought to the church for the sacrament. In those cases in which infants were baptised at home (a practice that was discouraged after 1622), the ceremonies associated with the rite were performed at the church at the earliest possible time. African slaves and adult Spaniards who were ignorant of Christian doctrine were instructed in the Catholic faith before they were baptised. The sacrament was believed to impart an indelible character on the recipient; it was therefore not to be repeated. But as we have seen above, some Indians availed themselves of baptism two or more times. The belief of the Church was that baptism had a double effect: it brought about the birth of a new nature and it effected the removal of original and actual pre-baptismal sin with the guilt attached to it. It is to be doubted that the Indians understood these things. Normally, the sacrament of confirmation was administered by the bishop. As late as 1574, the sacrament was not administered in the abbacy of Jamaica, since that island did not have a bishop. To correct this the abbot, Mateo Santiago, invited the Bishop of Cuba to visit Jamaica to administer the sacrament. Meanwhile, the abbot sought papal dispensation to enable him to officiate at confirmation. It must be remembered that in comparison with the number baptised, relatively few Indians were confirmed. The children of Spaniards were the principal candidates for the sacrament.

The most important sacrament was the Eucharist. It was believed to provide spiritual nourishment for those who partook of it; it was regarded as a sacrifice for sin which could be offered for those present at its celebration and even for those absent. It could also be beneficial for the dead. Thus, on a visit to Jamaica in March, 1608, the Bishop of Cuba, Don Fray Juan de las Cabesas Altamirando, celebrated a solemn Mass (as the Eucharist was often called) for the dead. Quite in keeping with the theology of the Eucharist or Mass as it developed in medieval Europe and was re-emphasised by the Council of Trent, Caribbean Catholics believed that in the divine sacrifice celebrated

24

in the mass, the same Christ was contained and immolated without blood who on the altar of the cross once offered himself in blood. Christ's body and blood were believed to be contained in the sacrament under the form of bread and wine, the bread being changed into body and the wine into blood by divine power when the words of institution were repeated by the priest. Like their counterparts in Europe, Catholics in the Caribbean partook only of the host. This practice was based on the doctrine of concomitance as it was developed by Hilary of Arles and by Anselm and ratified by the Council of Constance in 1415. The doctrine of concomitance (so called by Thomas Aquinas) taught that the whole Christ was in every particle of bread and wine. If the whole Christ was present in both the bread and the wine, it followed that whoever partook only of the bread received Christ as fully as if he had received the communion in both kinds.

In connection with the Eucharist, the Synod of 1622 ruled that many Indians ought not to receive the sacrament because they lacked an adequate knowledge of the Eucharist. The custom by which the viaticum (that is, communion for the dying) was administered to the sick and to children who, at the point of death, had attained the age of reason but had not made their first holy communion was commended by the Synod. To ensure that Catholics received the Eucharist during the Easter season, priests were required by decree of the 1622 Synod to call on their parishioners on a door to door basis and to insist that they should attend mass.

Catholicism provided a remedy for Christians who lapsed into sin in spite of the new nature bestowed on them at baptism, the grace given to them at confirmation, and the spiritual nourishment which they received in the Eucharist. This remedy was the sacrament of penance. For penance to be effective, the sinner had to be truly penitent for all the conscious, wilful and grave offences which he had committed. Confession of these mortal sins was to be made to an ordained priest who alone had the power to pronounce absolution, which was believed to convey grace, remove guilt and remit eternal punishment. Absolution had to be followed by satisfaction. By rendering some act of satisfaction which involved humiliation, labour or sacrifice, the penitent was believed to have atoned for his wrong-doing. The granting of indulgences (the practice by which one form of satisfaction was substituted for a less onerous form) was not known in the Caribbean where satisfaction more

25

often than not took the forms of prayer, fasting and almsgiving. One reason why the practice of indulgence did not appear in the Caribbean might well have been the fact that by the time Catholicism became established in the area, the 'sale' of indulgences had become greatly discredited in Europe. It was the controversy over indulgences that developed into the movement that came to be described as the Reformation.

Apparently, many Christians in the islands failed to make the minimum of at least one confession annually. To correct this failure, the Synod of 1622 prescribed that everybody should have a written testimony from his pastor indicating that he had been to confession before he would be admitted to holy communion.

The Council of Trent declared: "If anyone says that the married state is to be placed before the state of virginity or celibacy, and that it is not better and more blessed to remain in virginity or celibacy than to be joined in marriage let him be anathema." In spite of that position, however, matrimony was one of the seven sacraments of the Church. Its primary justification was that marriage was a necessary means of raising up members for the Church. Consequently, the grace bestowed on people who entered marriage was believed to enable them to train their children in Christian faith and virtue. It was also believed that the grace conferred in the sacrament purified conjugal relationships and kept them free from sin. In the Caribbean, the sacrament posed for the church special problems related to the validity of pagan marriages. The Synod of 1622 declared that where two pagans (that is, Indians) had been married according to their own rites and one became a Christian, if the pagan partner lived in harmony with the Christian spouse, then they were to be allowed to live as man and wife. A marriage contracted by two pagans at a pagan ceremony was regarded as valid as well. Catholicism, however, strongly discouraged the polygamy practised by Caribbean Indians.

Concerning the sacrament of holy orders, the Synod of 1622 decreed that because Indians were prone to vices and because of their inherent barbarity they were not to be admitted to ordination. In fact, the Synod of 1622 merely formalised what was the practice in the Caribbean and Latin America. By the 1540s, Indians had been barred from ordination in Hispaniola, and the rest of Latin America quickly followed the lead of that island. In 1578, Philip II of Spain decreed that the ordination of Indians, mestizos and mulattoes was forbidden in the Spanish Empire. As a result of the intervention of Pope Gregory XIII, a new decree was issued in September 1588 which permitted the ordination of mestizos, although, around 1590, the king was threatening bishops with deposition should they ordain these 'half-breeds'. It has to be said however, that in spite of the official position, a few Indians and mestizos were ordained into the priesthood. But, this was mainly, of not exclusively, in Mexico and Peru. The Synod of 1622 decreed that while Indians were not to be admitted to orders, mestizos or half-breeds could be ordained. We know of at least one mulatto priest who was attached to the cathedral at Santo Domingo around 1650. He was the only one of the forty priests in Hispaniola at that time who could be described as 'a man of letters'.[10]

It was during the Middle Ages that the practice of praying over the sick and anointing them with oil came to be recognised in Europe as a sacrament. It was called extreme unction and was regarded as marking the end of the Christian's career in much the same way that baptism marked its beginning. According to Thomas Aquinas, the "sacrament removes the remains of sins and makes a man ready for final glory." It was perhaps because the Synod of 1622 felt that the sick, and particularly the dying, should receive this sacrament that it forbade clerical absenteeism from the parish without the permission of the bishop concerned. The Synod noted that the rugged and difficult terrain which priests had to traverse was no excuse for pastors to absent themselves from their parishes lest, in their absence, the Indians should die without the sacraments. Extreme unction was no doubt one of these.

The belief of the Church was that the sacraments conferred grace *ex opere operato* — that is: of or by themselves, by virtue of what they were and not because of the faith of the recipient or the character of the person who administered the sacrament. Nevertheless, it was also held that the good disposition of the recipient who exercised faith and penitence was rewarded by additional grace which was conferred *ex opere operantis*, on the merit of the doer or recipient, so to speak. The majority of the Spain colonists in the Caribbean no doubt believed that the sacraments constituted the very heart of their Christianity. It is to be doubted that those Indians who were christianised held the sacraments in such regard.

Emphasis was also placed on preaching. This emphasis doubtless reflected the Counter-Reformation influence on Caribbean Catholicism. The Synod of 1622 decreed that the Word of God should be preached on feast days such as Christmas, the Incarnation, Epiphany, Pentecost and the Transfiguration so that people might be educated in the Christian religion. Preachers were to be licensed by the bishop and they were to interpret Holy Scripture in accordance with the teachings of the Church and the interpretation of the patristic Fathers. People were to avail themselves of the opportunity to listen to the Word of God. Those who refused to do so, to the point where they attended no more than three or four sermons during their lifetime, were to be anathematised. In order that priests might be better equipped to preach to the Indians, the Synod of 1622 decreed that parish priests were to learn the languages of the aborigines.

The second half of the sixteenth century saw a decline in the Church both in terms of numbers and in the spiritual and moral condition of Caribbean Catholics. This decline was to continue into the next century. Some of the reasons for this decline have been given above. It was in an effort to remedy this state of affairs that the Jesuits came to the Caribbean. They first came to Hispaniola in 1650. Founded by Ignatius Loyola of the Spanish province of Guipuzcoa and formally recognised by the Pope in September, 1540, the Society of Jesus was meant to be a kind of holy militia committed to fight for the papacy against its enemies. It was to be essentially an arm of that movement of Catholic reform in Europe which came to be labelled the Counter-Reformation. Its task was to be the propagation of the faith especially through the education of the young.

No Jesuit of the stature of Francis Xavier, who was a pioneer in missionary activities in India and Japan, came to the Caribbean. Nor could the Catholic Church in the Caribbean of those early times, boast of a man of the courage of the Portuguese Jesuit, Antonio Vieira, who lived and worked in Brazil, and who, in the mid-seventeenth century, castigated the Portuguese planters for their cruelty to the Brazilian Indians. Nevertheless, they did have among their ranks the Italian, Fr. Molinelli (hispanicised to Molina), who was to distinguish himself by his work among Negro slaves. By 1660, because of the activity of the Jesuits, there was a significant change for the better in the spiritual life of Hispaniola.

Later, we shall see how the African slaves understood the

teachings of Catholicism in terms of the beliefs and practices which they had brought with them from Africa. Interesting forms of syncretism developed among Caribbean Blacks because of this process. These included *Vodun* in Haiti; *Santeria* in Cuba and *Shango* in Trinidad. What is little known is that syncretism resulted also from the contact between the beliefs of the indigenous Indians and those of Catholicism. The best efforts of those who desired and those who supervised the christianisation of the Indians were never enough to prevent this process from taking place.

Many Indians resented having been practically forced to become Christians. Many remained animists at heart while they went through the motions demanded by the rituals and ceremonies of Catholicism. Most of them were able to accommodate the beliefs and practices of the new religion by understanding them in terms of their native beliefs.

God the Father, of Catholic belief, they identified with the creator-god, Wamurreti-Kwonci, whom they otherwise knew as the benign Jocahuna. Sometimes they identified Jesus Christ with Jocahuna; at other times they believed him to be the son of Jocahuna or Wamurreti-Kwonci and the Virgin Mary, whom they confused with Atabei, a goddess of Arawak belief.

The practice of Catholics of speaking of Jesus Christ as both God and the Son of God no doubt led to a vagueness in the understanding of the Indians as to the identity of Jesus, which was quite in keeping with the happy vagueness with which they had hitherto regarded the identity of Jocahuna. The Holy Spirit of Catholic teaching was quickly identified as Hurakan, the Mighty Wind, who blew with power whensoever and wheresoever he willed. There were times, however, when the Holy Spirit was identified as Guabancex. The Arawaks saw nothing incongruous in identifying the Holy Spirit with both Hurakan and Guabancex. In their understanding, the Mighty Spirit was free to assume whatever form he wanted. Equally, his worshippers were free to call him by whatever name they wished, since as either Hurakan or Guabancex he was one and the same spirit.

The role of the Catholic priest was perceived as identical with that of the bohito or piai man. The spirit of kanaima was easily identified with Satan, and the heaven of Catholic hopes was identified with Coyaba.

Once these identifications were made to the satisfaction of the Amerindians, they could embrace Catholicism without having much violence done to their former beliefs. At the same time, they could dismiss the new religion as not deserving of any more attention and effort than they had expended on religious exercises before. Little wonder, then, that the ethic of the new faith which priests urged upon them evoked no response from them except surprise that, in its new guise, the old way at the insistence of the new bohitos should be made so demanding.

Notes and References

1. J.C. Wand, *A History of the Modern Church*, p. 3.
2. Fernando de los Rios, "The Action of Spain in America", *Concerning Latin American Culture*, p. 53; cited in C.H. Haring, *The Spanish Empire in America*, p. 166.
3. Cited in Lewis Hanke, *The Spanish Struggle for Justice in the Conquest of America*, p. 32.
4. Cited in Hanke, *op. cit.*, p. 20.
5. Hanke, *op. cit.*, p. 17.
6. *Ibid.*, p. 123.
7. *Ibid.*, p. 122.
8. Bryan Edwards, *The History of the British West Indies*, p. 196.
9. *Ibid.*, p. 170.
10. Justo L. Gonzalez in *The Development of Christianity in the Latin Caribbean*, p. 37.

CHAPTER III

THE CHALLENGE TO SPANISH CATHOLICISM
IN THE CARIBBEAN

Spain's monopoly of the Indies, which was sanctioned by Papal Bulls and recognised by the Treaty of Tordesillas, was challenged by her European rivals from the beginning of the sixteenth century. That challenge took the forms of trade, privateering raids, settlement and conquest. The treaty agreements by which Spain ended armed conflict with France, England and the United Provinces (Netherlands) in 1559, 1604 and 1609 respectively, indicated the increasing degree by which Spain was yielding to the challenges of her rivals.

The first intruders into the Spanish Caribbean were the Portuguese. They conducted a clandestine trade in Negro slaves between Guinea in Africa and Hispaniola in the Caribbean. In addition, the Portuguese supplied the Spanish colonists with manufactured European goods. War between France and Spain between 1512 and 1558, provided the pretext for French privateers such as Jean Fleury, Jean Ango, François le Clerc and Jacques de Sores to plunder Spanish shipping and to hold their towns to ransom. The depredations of the French corsairs were "authorised" by *letters of marque* issued by the French government. The Treaty of Cateau-Cambrésis (1559) ended the Hapsburg-Valois quarrels. But the principle was established that European peace treaties would not be effective west of the Azores. This was expressed in the convention which stated that there would be "no peace beyond the line."

The first Englishman to infringe Spain's monopoly of the Indies was the Elizabethan seaman, John Hawkins, who made his first voyage into the Caribbean in 1562 with the purpose of trading illicitly in Negro slaves. Hawkins was followed by the more belligerent Francis Drake whose exploits had the blessing and support of Queen Elizabeth I. By 1573, what amounted to an English privateering war had developed in the Caribbean. Hostilities were brought to an end by the Treaty of London which was signed in 1604. England's King James I declared on that occasion that, "we are contented to prohibit all repair of our subjects to any places where [the Spaniards or Portuguese] are planted, but only to seek their traffic by their own discoveries in other places whereof there are so infinite dimensions of vast and great territories [in which they] have no interest."[1] As far as England was concerned, the test of possession (or claim to monopoly, by that token) would now be effective occupation. Unoccupied areas would be fair game for English traders.

The truce concluded between Spain and the Netherlands in 1609 ended Dutch privateering activities in the Caribbean. As early as the autumn of 1569, Dutch and Flemish rebels under the Seigneur de Dolhain had begun to plunder Spanish shipping as part of the Dutch resistance to Spanish domination. To force his rebellious Netherlands subjects into submission, Philip II of Spain forbade commerce between Spain and the Netherlands. This in turn precipitated a widespread illicit commerce between Zealand and Holland merchants and Spanish American ports. It was a threat by William Usselincx to organize a West India Company to promote organised Dutch trade in the New World as well as to found colonies there that forced Spain to negotiate for the truce of 1609. The terms of the truce did not mention the Caribbean, but they conceded the right of the Dutch to trade with the Portuguese East Indies. In effect, Spain had been forced to accept, at least tacitly, the principle that any claim on the part of Portugal or of herself, for that matter, to any territory beyond the Azores, had to be based on the effective occupation of that territory.

It was primarily the desire of France, England and the Netherlands to benefit economically at the expense of Spain that motivated those European nations to poach on Spain's preserves in the Indies. The Dutch had an additional motive for fighting Spain related to their struggle for political independence. But religious factors were not without their significance in the challenge to Spain's supremacy in these parts. Up to 1559, this was more the case with the English and the Dutch than it was with the French.

After Cateau-Cambresis, however, the religious motive was strong in the new wave of French privateering activities against Spain. Many of the Frenchmen involved in these activities were Huguenots or French Protestants, often from the Huguenot stronghold of La Rochelle in France. They actually saw their Caribbean exploits as part of the Huguenot struggle against Catholicism. In France itself in the 1560s, the Calvinist Huguenots led by the Prince of Condé were locked in civil war with the Catholics headed by the Duke of Guise. During the struggle, the Guises entered into alliances with Spain whenever the political climate suited such alliances. Naturally, then the Huguenots came to regard Catholic Spain as their enemy. To fight against Spain in the Caribbean, as in Europe, was to promote the Huguenot cause.

The Huguenot war in France forced the French Calvinists to redefine their attitude towards the secular authorities. Down to the early 1560s, the Calvinist policy seems to have been one of non-resistance to the persecution engineered by secular authorities. As Theodore Beza, Calvin's lieutenant, told the King of Navarre in 1562, "Sire, it is truly the lot of the Church of God, for which I speak to endure blows and not to strike them."[2] By mid-1564, however, Beza, now Calvin's successor and Condé's accomplice in revolt, set about the formulation of a theory of armed resistance for Christians. The position of the Calvinists came to be that under certain circumstances (for example), to save the monarch from an illegitimate despotism; when the salvation of the church was at stake) the church should be prepared to associate itself with armed revolt. Protestant pastors judged the circumstances to warrant armed resistance and they exhorted their flock to rally behind the Prince of Condé.

Armed with weapons and the conviction that their cause was just, Huguenot privateers sailed from French Atlantic ports singing the Psalms translated by Calvinist reformers. Inspired as much by Beza's *"Que Dieu se montre seulement"** as by their hatred of Catholicism, these Frenchmen wreaked havoc among Spanish shipping in the Caribbean. So many were the Huguenot privateers in the Caribbean by 1572 that they might well have outnumbered the French corsairs there at the height of the Franco-Spanish wars between 1521 and 1558. Doubtless, the Huguenots' activities had the approval of Gaspard de Coligny, Admiral of France, and, until his assassination on St. Bartholomew's Day, 1572, one of the great leaders of the

Huguenots. Coligny enthusiastically supported his co-religionists in the Netherlands in their fight against Catholic Spain. In all probability, he saw the Huguenot hostility to Spain as calculated to aid the Dutchmen in their cause.

Whatever the motives for the rivalry between Spain on the one hand and England and the Netherlands on the other, that rivalry was made all the more bitter by the fact that Spain was a Catholic country and the other two were Protestant. It is to be remembered that those were days when religious differences coloured and influenced every aspect of European life. As the historian, J.H. Elliot, puts it:

> Individuals and nations found themselves confronted with problems of loyalty which created painful dilemmas and tortured the sensitive conscience. Did an individual's first duty lie with his king or his God? Should a State's foreign policy be guided by considerations of national interest or religious allegiance when as so often happened, the two failed to coincide? . . . for example, should Catherine de Medici of France support the French Protestants in their anti-Spanish policy, or make common cause with France's traditional rival, Spain, against the enemies of the Holy Catholic Church?[3]

This question which was likely to give Catherine de Medici some pause, would not have arisen with Elizabeth I of England or with the States-General of the United Provinces. For these heads of Protestant states, the rivalry between their countries and Spain was less complicated; for them it was a straightforward conflict with a Catholic nation. When the congregation of Plymouth Church flocked out of church on Sunday morning, August 9, 1573, to welcome Francis Drake after a voyage to the Indies, it was as much to congratulate a Protestant on his victories against Catholic Spain as it was to cheer an Englishman home.

In time, the Catholic Pero Menendez's destruction of Ribault's Huguenots, the alleged atrocities committed by the Spanish Inquisition, the Duke of Alva's savage attempt to exterminate the Protestants of the Low Countries, and the Massacre of St. Bartholomew's Day, 1572, when over 8,000 Huguenots were annihilated, would be advanced by the English and the Dutch as overwhelming evidence of Catholic Spain's cruelty. This anti-Spanish propaganda would be buttressed by a Protestant fervour, which, in turn, would give a strong religious flavour to any challenge to Spain's monopoly in the Caribbean by England and the United Provinces.

As we have seen by the treaties of Cateau-Cambrésis (1559) and of London (1604) as well as by the Truce signed between Spain and the Netherlands of April 9, 1609, Spain tacitly accepted the contention that only effective occupation could give her the right to territory beyond the sea. The Lesser Antilles and the Guiana coastlands had not been occupied by Spain; this encouraged Dutch, English and French adventurers to attempt to plant colonies in these parts. In 1616, a Dutch settlement was established by Captain Groenewegen at Kyk-over-al, at the confluence of the Essequibo, Cuyuni and Mazaruni rivers; a second settlement was established on the Berbice river under the direction of Abraham van Peere. In 1622-23, the Englishman, Thomas Warner, founded a colony on St. Christopher. In 1625, the French freebooter, Pierre d'Esnambuc, also landed in St. Christopher; he suggested to Warner that English and French settlers might live together on the island to the mutual benefit of the two European groups. In 1625, John Powell, the commander of a merchantman, landed on Barbados which he claimed in the name of the James I of England. A colony was planted on that island in 1627. From St. Christopher (St. Kitts), English colonists migrated to Nevis (1628), Antigua and Montserrat (1632). By 1642, the Dutch had become established in Curaçao, Bonaire, Aruba, Saba, St. Martin's and St. Eustatius. By this time, too, the French had settled in Martinique and Guadeloupe; Tortuga was in the hands of the French. All in all, some hundred thousand Europeans peopled these settlements and colonies. In 1655, England wrested Jamaica from Spain. From their base in Tortuga, Frenchmen ventured into the western part of Hispaniola which had not been effectively occupied by the Spaniards. Endemic warfare between the French and the Spaniards in Hispaniola might not have been terminated by the Treaty of Ryswick (1697), but that treaty formally acknowledged French sovereignty over the Western section of the island. To the French, their new acquisition was known as St. Domingue. By the time the Treaty of Ryswick was signed, the political map of the Caribbean was vastly different from what it had been a century before — so effectively had Spain's claim to monopoly in the Indies been challenged.

The non-Hispanic peoples who settled in the islands and along the Wild Coast of Guiana belonged to a number of different religious persuasions. The Dutch settlers were mainly Protestants of the Dutch Reformed Church although some of the Dutchmen who came to Guiana were Lutherans. The English colonists were mainly Anglican Protestants. Some English Quakers, however, were to be found in Barbados, in Jamaica and in Nevis where they had been transported in 1660 when the Monarchy was restored in England. The French colonists were mainly Catholics: but some Huguenots under the leadership of Monsieur Le Vasseur, had found refuge in d'Esnambuc's colony in St. Kitts after their stronghold at La Rochelle had fallen. From St. Kitts, some of these Huguenots went to Tortuga where they helped to expel the English in 1639.

Some Jews found their way into the Caribbean. These were mainly the descendants of those who were expelled from Spain in 1492. After their expulsion, some Jews settled in the Netherlands while others migrated to the Balkans and the Levant. From the Netherlands, Jews crossed the Atlantic and settled in Portuguese Brazil in the area around Pernambuco which was captured by the Dutch in the 1630s. With the expulsion of the Dutch from Brazil in 1648, many Jews migrated to various parts of the Caribbean. Some went to the Dutch settlements of St. Eustatius and Curaçao, arriving at the latter place in about 1650. Others went to Barbados at about the same time. Those Jews who originated in Spain have been known as the Sephardim. Ashkenazim Jews who originated in Germany, Russia, Austria and Poland, found their way to Jamaica probably during the reign of Charles II. Like their Sephardic counterparts, the Ashkenazim Jews were sometimes forced to migrate because they were expelled from the countries where they lived. Thus, in December, 1572, Jews were expelled from Vienna when the Emperor of Austria issued a decree that Jews who had been domiciled within his Empire were to depart with kith and kin. They had until Palm Sunday the following year in which to leave. Meanwhile, the privileges which they had hitherto enjoyed were annulled.

The Religious beliefs of the non-Hispanic Europeans

With the exception of the French Catholics and the Jews, the religious beliefs of the non-Hispanic peoples of the Caribbean represented some form of Protestantism.

Protestantism came about as a result of the great schism in Western Christendom which was precipitated in October 31, 1517, when the Church's practice of selling indulgences was challenged by Martin Luther, Professor of Theology at the University of Wittenberg. Indulgences offered the commutation of penance for contributions of money made to causes which were considered worthy by clerics. Thus it was felt that if a contrite sinner confessed his sins, he could be spared the pains of purgatory if he visited at least seven churches on which the papal arms were displayed, reciting in each five Paters and five Aves, and if he made a contribution ranging from twenty-five gold florins to one, depending on his rank, occupation and income. The money might later go towards the erection of a cathedral. Two things in particular angered Luther. The theologian had arrived at the conviction that the assurance of personal salvation consisted in the acceptance of the belief that God was willing to make the sinner just by the power of His love freely bestowed on the true believer. For Luther, this was what St. Paul meant when he said that the "just shall live by faith."[4] In the light of this, Luther felt that the preaching of indulgences encouraged people to hold to a false hope of salvation. Again, the vending of indulgences was a wicked way of exploiting people; it was all the more wicked since it was perpetrated in the name of religion. Luther was at first convinced that the Pope would not sanction the abuse to which the practice of indulgences was put. He declared that Christians ought to be taught that if the Pope knew of the extortions of the mercenary preachers who peddled indulgences, he would rather see the Church of St. Peter in ashes than that it should be built with the skin, flesh and bones of his sheep.

The debate precipitated by Luther, soon shifted from indulgences to the authority of the Pope, the authority of general councils, the function of priests, the rationale behind the sacraments and related subjects. What started as a quarrel over an ecclesiastical practice, developed into a controversy that was to be affected by German nationalism as well as by social and political factors that agitated not only Germany but also Western Europe as a whole. The controversy was not without its violent aspects. Germany was divided into warring religious parties with German princes ranging themselves in opposite camps. The peasants seized the opportunity created by the instability of the times to rise in armed revolt in an attempt to improve their condition.

At the Diet of Augsburg in June 1530, an attempt was made to bring about a reconciliation between the supporters of Luther and their opponents. The princes and other influential supporters of Luther presented a statement of their doctrinal position; they also indicated what changes they had introduced in their liturgy as well as in their approach to church discipline. The statement, which was prepared by Philip Melanchthon, came to be known as the Augsburg Confession. It was to become the broad doctrinal standard of the Lutheran church although the Confession itself speaks of "our Churches" rather than of "the Lutheran Church." The Diet, however, failed to bring about the expected reconciliation between Luther's followers and their opponents, and between the princes in the opposing camps. It was not until 1555 that the religious question which plagued Germany was settled. That year the Peace of Augsburg was signed by the opposing parties.

By the provisions of the Peace of Augsburg, Lutheranism was recognised as a religion with the same status in Germany, as Catholicism. The principle of *cuius regio eius religio* was to be adhered to. By that principle, every secular ruler might hold either to the Augsburg Confession or to Catholicism. Within his territory, no religion other than that professed by the prince was to be tolerated. Free cities had the right to choose their religious persuasion; dissenters were free to migrate to those territories where their religion was practised.

Almost simultaneously with the beginning of the movement in Germany, a reformation was begun in the Swiss canton of Zürich. The man responsible for the reformation in Zürich was Huldreich Zwingli, who, in 1519, was elected the preacher and pastor *(leutpriester)* of the Munster church in Zürich. With the help of the city council, Zwingli was able to reform the Church in Zürich. He abolished the Mass, provided new orders of baptism and communion services, introduced the vernacular into the worship service and emphasised preaching. Zürich, in turn, became an important centre of reformation among the Swiss cantons although all Switzerland was not with Zwingli. Eventually, armed conflict developed between the Catholic cantons and those which opted for Zwingli's reformation. The reformer himself was killed in battle and the leadership of the movement passed to Henry Bullinger. The Peace of Kappel (1531) brought the conflict to an end; but with Zwingli's death, Zürich declined in importance as the centre of the Reformation among the Swiss. Its place was taken by Geneva where the reformer who was to come to fame was the Frenchman, Jean Cauvin, or John Calvin, as he has become known to the English-speaking world.

Calvin came to Geneva in 1536 and was commandeered by William Farel to assist in the task of organising Geneva along reformed lines. By that time, Calvin, who was trained in law and theology and who had been influenced by humanism, had already published his *Institute of the Christian Religion* — a work that has been described as the finest in Reformation literature. The reformer's attempt to impose outward conformity to the beliefs and ethical injunctions of the Gospel, as he understood them, on all the citizens of Geneva met with opposition. As a result, Calvin and Farel were exiled in 1538. Nevertheless, Calvin was recalled to Geneva and by September 1541, he was again in charge of the church there. By the time his work was finished in Geneva, Calvin "gave [the Genevan] Church a trained and tested ministry, its homes an educated people who could give a reason for their faith, and to the whole city an heroic soul which enabled the little town to stand forth as the Citadel and City of Refuge for the oppressed Protestants of Europe."[5] What was more, in the *Institutes of Calvin,* Protestantism had received a strong theological statement which was based on "a breadth of scriptural and patristic learning."[6]

Meanwhile, Lutheranism (which came to be designated Evangelical Protestantism) spread rapidly to the Scandinavian countries of Denmark, Norway and Sweden. In these countries, the Lutheran movement had the blessing of the several governments. In France, Calvinism (which came to be designated Reformed Protestantism) supplanted Lutheranism in influence. The Protestants there came to be known as Huguenots after 1560. After that date, too, they became a persecuted people. Nevertheless, the movement developed in France as it attracted followers from every rank of society, with peasants and artisans outnumbering the other converts. By 1561, when the French government protested to the Republic of Geneva for sending preachers to France who caused sedition in that kingdom, there were about 2,150 Protestant congregations in France. That year, a National Synod adopted a confession of faith, the *Confessio Gallicana,* which was based on a draft prepared by John Calvin.

As we have seen above, Reformed Protestantism in France became inextricably bound up with political rivalries in that land. Between 1562 and 1589, the nation was in a state of intermittent civil war in which the Huguenots were regarded as dissidents and persecuted as such. The Edict of Nantes (1598) granted toleration to the Protestants, regarding them as a body politic with France. That edict was, however, revoked in 1685 and Protestantism was to remain proscribed in France until 1789.

As it did in France, Calvinism was to outstrip Evangelical Protestantism in influence in the Netherlands which it penetrated in the 1550s, also becoming more important than the Anabaptist movement in that land. Again, as in France, Protestantism became identified with dissent from and opposition to the Catholic Philip's purpose of uniting the Netherlands along Catholic lines by suppressing heresy. Armed resistance to Philip II was declared permissible by a Calvinist synod that convened at Antwerp on December 1, 1566. The outcome of the struggle that ensued was that the Netherlands was divided into a Catholic south and a Calvinist north in 1579. A national Protestant church, *De Nederlandsch Hervormde Kerk*, or Dutch Reformed Church, was established; its Confession of Faith, the *Confessio Belgica*, was approved by the Synod held at Antwerp in 1566.

It was in Scotland that Calvin's ideals were to achieve their fullest realisation. Here, again, Calvinism was the faith around which political dissent was to centre. Opposition, this time, was to the foreign domination of Scotland by France, the result of a royal marriage into the powerful Catholic Guise family. The Scottish reform was led by George Wishart and then by his disciple, John Knox. In 1559, the reformation gathered momentum. It resulted in the abolition of papal jurisdiction in Scotland and of the Mass. Both were abolished by the Scottish parliament. In 1560, a Confession of Faith *(the Confessio Scoticana)* was adopted along with the First Book of Discipline. The former was to remain the standard of belief in the Church of Scotland until 1647 when the Westminister Confession was adopted.

England's break with Rome might well be dated from 1534 when Henry VIII declared himself "Supreme Head of the English Church and Clergy." However, it was not until 1560 that that break was complete. It was no lofty theological principle which motivated Henry to break with papal jurisdiction. It was more the refusal of Pope Clement VIII to annul the king's marriage with Catherine of Aragon, in order to make it possible for him to marry Anne Boleyn, that precipitated that momentous move.

Nevertheless, even a Henry VIII would not have been able to effect that break with Rome had it not been for widespread dissatisfaction felt in England over the papacy, papal control and ecclesiastical abuses in that country. Lutheran ideas as well as the much earlier teachings of John Wycliffe were not without their influence in England at that time. But Henry's reformation resulted in little more than the transference of the headship of the Church in England from the Pope to the sovereign of England. Henry's subjects were as devout, obedient, catholic, and humble children of God and Holy Church as any people within any Christian realm. The act which forbade the payment of Peter's Pence to Rome indicated that the Church of England had no intention of departing from Christ's Church in anything concerning the Articles of the Catholic Faith in Christendom, or in any other thing declared by Holy Scripture and the Word of God as necessary for salvation.

Under Edward VI, the Reformation in England proceeded along more radical lines. However, in 1553, the accession of Mary Tudor saw the resurgence of Catholicism in England and the restoration of ecclesiastical relationships with Rome. Mary was succeeded by Elizabeth I in 1558. Her very first parliament repealed Mary's religious Acts, revived those of Henry VIII and Edward VI, and re-established the supremacy of the crown over the English Church. Elizabeth I, however, chose to designate herself the Supreme Governor of the Church on the ground that Christ alone is the Supreme Head of the Church.

Under Elizabeth I, the Church of England embraced both Catholic and Protestant elements. The understanding was that the Church followed the *via media* or middle way between the extremes of Protestantism and Catholicism. It is perhaps because of this that the beliefs and practices of the Church of England represent a fusion of elements derived from Lutheranism, Zwinglianism, Calvinism and Roman Catholicism in the unique synthesis of Anglicanism. Of this Church, Archbishop Bramhall wrote:

> We do not arrogate to ourselves a new Church, or a new religion or new Holy Orders . . . Our religion is the same it was; our Holy Orders the same they were, in substance; differing only from what they were formerly as a garden unweeded from a garden weeded.[7]

The Church of England was the church of the whole nation. As Richard Hooker observed:

> "There is not any man of the Church of England but the same man is also a member of the commonwealth; nor any man a member of the commonwealth, which is not also of the Church of England."[8]

Nevertheless, there were those people who had no desire to

walk the *via media*. They wished to see the Church organised according to the best reformed model. These people were Calvinist in doctrine and Presbyterian in church policy; they were called Puritans. During the Commonwealth period in the following century, Puritanism gained the ascendancy in England. Archbishop Laud, the staunch opponent of Puritanism, was executed; the Westminister Assembly of July 1643 abolished the Prayer Book and produced the Longer and Shorter Catechisms and a Directory for Public Worship. More than a thousand clergymen who refused to accept the Directory were deprived of their cures. In 1660, however, the monarchy was restored and the Church of England was re-established. In 1662, the Book of Common Prayer was revised. That same year, some two thousand Puritan clergymen who refused to accept it were ejected. Among them was the Rev. John Pinney, the vicar of Broadwindsor in Dorset, whose son Azariah was transported to Nevis because he was involved in the Monmouth Rebellion of 1685.

With the exception of the Puritan development which took place in the Church of England in the first half of the seventeenth century, the changes described above had already been established before the non-Hispanic Europeans settled in the Caribbean. The beliefs of those people had, for all practical purposes, become fixed by the time the Dutch settled at Kykover-al and Fort Nassau on the wild coast of Guiana. It was these beliefs that the settlers brought with them.

Dutch Reformed and Lutheran Christians in Guiana

The Dutch were either Lutherans or members of the Dutch Reformed Church. Very little is known of their religious practices in Guiana during the seventeenth century. Perhaps they were too busy establishing their settlements to bother with religion. In about 1668, the Dutch Reformed Church was established in Surinam which had been awarded to the Dutch by the Treaty of Breda (1667). A Dutch Reformed Church was erected in about 1720, at the mouth of the Wieronie river. Services were held irregularly because of the difficulty involved in obtaining *predicants* to serve as pastors to the church at the small salary offered. To meet this difficulty, the Reformed Church was constituted the State Church by an Act of the Berbice Association which was promulgated on February 21, 1735. Taxes were imposed on the Berbice citizenry to provide funds for the church. On January 7, 1736, Johannes Frauendorff was appointed predicant of Berbice. At that time, the church services were well attended, but the religious and

42

moral tone of the colony of Berbice was very low. The Dutch Reformed Church was established in Essequibo also. A church building was erected on Fort Island on the Essequibo River for those Dutch planters and merchants who chose to attend services there.

On October 15, 1743, the Dutch Lutherans in the colony of Berbice met at the home of one Lodewyk Abbensetts to consider the possibility of establishing a Lutheran church in Berbice. They were perhaps encouraged by the fact that their counterparts in Surinam had organised a congregation there on November 15, 1741. The Lutherans first professed adherence to the unaltered Augsburg Confession; then the meeting resolved ". . . that petitions should be forwarded to the Honourable Court of Policy (the colonial legislature), and to the Most Honourable, the Directors of the Colony, and the High Mightinesses, the States General of the Netherlands, praying for the privilege of the free exercise of their religion; and that at the same time applications should be made by letter to the Reverend Consistory of Amsterdam, soliciting their aid and co-operation in this urgent matter, and also their good services in procuring a clergyman for the community."[9] Nine years later, Johan Henrik Faerkenius arrived as the first Lutheran pastor to Berbice. The first preaching service was held at Fort Nassau on October 22, 1752. For administrative purposes, the congregation elected four elders — Spielman, Abbensetts, Schirmeister and George, and two deacons — Wantrel and Kridlowsky.

Unlike the Dutch Reformed Church, the Lutheran Church was financially self-supporting. Doctrinal differences were inevitable between the Lutherans and the Calvinistic members of the Reformed Church. Although the Evangelical Protestants shared many beliefs with their Reformed countrymen, they shared as well, something of the bitterness which years of theological controversy had bred between Evangelical and Reformed churchmen in Europe. However, in Guiana, where the small European community needed to be closely knit for social reasons as well as to maintain ascendancy over the slave population, this bitterness was not allowed to destroy the relationships between Lutherans and Reformed churchmen.

Both sets of Protestants believed that justification was by faith. For the Lutherans, justification was more the subjective assurance of salvation which came to the sinner who confidently appropriated the promises of the gospel, among which was the

43

Biblical affirmation that "the just shall live by faith." Calvinists, on the other hand, held to the more objective doctrinal view that God having received men into his favour regarded them as righteous. Such men's sins were remitted and Christ's righteousness imputed to them. It was the sovereign God who predestined some men to salvation and others to damnation. Calvinists believed that their doctrine of election was derived from St. Paul and St. Augustine.

Calvinists and Lutherans alike held to the belief that the Scripture was normative for doctrine and discipline. If anything, Calvinists had more thoroughgoing doctrine of the Scripture itself. They saw the Scripture as the *aeternae veritatis regula** — the norm on which were to be based not only the organisation and discipline of the church, but the moral standards and the sanctions of the Christian community as well. The Scripture was also to be the basis of the whole system of Christian doctrine.

The Lutheran doctrine of the sacraments (baptism and eucharist) was hammered out by Martin Luther in controversy with the Catholics on the one hand, and with the Zwinglians on the other, In fact, it may well be said that Luther's position on the sacraments represented a *via media* between that of the Roman Catholic Church and that of the more radical Zwinglian element of the Reformation, which Luther branded as 'enthusiasm'. For Luther (and Lutherans), the Word of God was closely bound up with the sacraments. He declared:

> In every promise of God there are two things which one must consider: the word and the sign. As in baptism there are the words of the baptiser and the dipping in water, so in the Mass there are the words and the bread and wine. The words are the divine vow, promise and testament. The signs are the sacraments, that is, sacred signs.[10]

Calvinists would not have found this Lutheran doctrine repugnant since they too believed that the Word was indispensable to the sacrament since it was "the promise which, proclaimed aloud by the minister, leads the people by the hand to that to which the sign tends and direct us."[11] It was on the question of the presence of Christ in the Supper that Lutherans and Calvinists differed. The position of John Calvin has been stated thus:

> The presence of Christ in the Supper we must hold to be such as neither affixes him to the element of bread, nor encloses him in any way (this would obviously detract from his celestial glory);

44

and it must, moreover, be such as neither divests him of his just dimensions, nor dissevers him by differences of place, nor assigns to him a body of boundless dimensions, diffused through heaven and earth. All these things are clearly repugnant to his true human nature.[12]

The Lutheran belief that the glorified body of Christ was ubiquitous (that is, present everywhere at the same time), and therefore in the consecrated elements substantially, was rejected by Calvinists as semi-Catholic. The French reformer felt that it was derogatory to the heavenly glory of Christ for him to be "brought under the corruptible elements of this world."[13]

Calvinists have traditionally been seen as holding sombre and austere personal ethics. It is not without significance that Puritanism is identified with Calvinism. But there was something tragic (or absured) about the ethics of the Dutch of the Reformed tradition in Demerara. Many of them might have been like Hubertus van Groenwegel, who led his family often in prayers and was "in all things, piety unexcepted, a man of rigid resolve."[14] But in the frontier days of the early settlement of the Wild Coast, when few European women had yet arrived, sexual promiscuity was prevalent among the Dutch. Later, when the plantation society developed and Negro slaves were imported to supply labour on the plantation, Dutch planters, overseers and merchants exploited female slaves sexually. Marriage to them was considered improper. The institution of slavery itself was not questioned. Yet shades of Calvin's Geneva legislation are to be seen in the following: In Demerara, in 1756, every person who cursed in a tavern had to put four shillings, by way of fine, into a locked box that was kept for that purpose; in 1757, one Jacques Salignal was fined 25 guilders for permitting card playing and rum-drinking on Thanksgiving Day. On all holy days, no one was allowed to give strong drinks to slaves.

A disastrous year for the Lutheran church in Berbice was 1763 when the slave rebellion in that colony resulted in the death of many of its members. Hitherto, the Lutheran church had served exclusively as a chaplaincy to Lutheran Dutchmen in Berbice, in much the same way that the Dutch Reformed church had functioned in respect to Dutchmen of a Calvinistic turn of mind. It is not surprising, therefore, that the rebellion was seen by the African slaves as much as a revolt against Christians as it was against the European masters. When Mr. George, the manager of the Beerestyn Plantation, and probably a deacon of the Lutheran congregation, asked the rebellious slaves why they were treating the Christians with hostility, Cosala, one of the leaders of the revolt, stated that Christians were too cruel to them and that they had decided that they would not tolerate any more Christians or whites in the country.

Later, in 1778, the Lutheran church was to be the employer (and owner) of slave labour. That year, Lutherans bought the estate Die Kleine Maripaan and renamed it Augsburg Plantation. Slaves who once served as domestics to the Rev. Mr. Glendtkamp were employed to cultivate the estate. Later, their numbers were augmented by other slaves who were purchased to work at Augsburg. Die Kleine Maripaan had originally been bought because it was felt that its cultivation would help to finance the Lutheran church in Berbice. The members of that church had to meet the expenses involved in the operations of their own church; they were also taxed in order to provide funds for the Dutch Reformed church.

Both the Dutch Reformed and the Lutheran congregations passed through periods when they were without pastors. Nevertheless, when the colonies of Essequibo, Demerara and Berbice became British territory in 1803, the Lutheran church was still active in Berbice, and a Dutch Reformed Church was still to be found on Fort Island on the Essequibo River.

The Church of England in the Caribbean

If Richard Hooker was right, then those Englishmen who settled in the Caribbean were mainly members of the Church of England, however well or poorly they practised their religion. The first Englishmen in the Caribbean, we are told, were men "deeply sensible of the obligations which rested upon them as baptised members of the Church of Christ in their native England."[15]

The first settlers went to St. Christopher under the leadership of Thomas Warner. With them went the Rev. John Featly, who was probably the first Church of England cleric in those parts. He was certainly the first preacher to minister in St. Christopher (St. Kitts). The earliest settlers in the Leeward Islands probably saw themselves as seventeenth century "Israelities" about to break the strongholds of heathen unbelievers, or, perhaps, like crusaders about to wrest land from infidels. At least, they were encouraged to see themselves in that light by the Rev. Mr. Featly. In a sermon based on Joshua chapter 1: verse 9, and preached at St. Botolph's, Aldersgate, on September 6, 1629, before Warner and his company who were about to

46

depart to the West Indies, Featly declared:

> God will be with us in peace to preserve us in unity, in
> to give us the victory, in our native soil to bless us with plenty,
> and in foreign parts to enrich us with prosperity; provided always
> that (with Joshua) we receive our command from the God of
> Heaven . . . Our religion must be as well clad in sincerity, as our
> strength in courage; that so, those ignorant infidels, observing our
> religious conversation, may join with us in a happy resolution.[16]

Featly continued:

> ". . . If the company of Indian archers rank themselves against us,
> yea and promise to themselves our utter confusion yet must we
> know that the Lord, which is a Man of War (as he hath styled him-
> self) which breaketh the bow in pieces, and knappeth the arrows
> in sunder, can prevent their fury."[17]

Whether it was the inspiration of their religion, or their need
for safety, or both, that motivated them in 1625, the Englishmen in St. Kitts with the help of the French settlers under
Pierre Belain d'Esnambuc, surprised the Caribs and massacred
them. Even chief Tegremond, without whose goodwill the
settlement could not have been founded, was killed. The
argument has been advanced that the Europeans thought that
it was politic to slaughter the Caribs in order to prevent them
from treacherously attacking the whites in the way that Indians
had attacked English settlers in Virginia in 1622. Those Caribs
that survived were enslaved by the white settlers. The Christians
might well have felt that it was "the Man of War which breaketh
the bow in pieces and knappeth the arrows" that had given them
the victory.

In 1625, Barbados was claimed by John Powell in the name
of James I, king of England. By that token, the island was
claimed for both the State and the Church, as the planting of
the flag and the cross at Hole Town signified. Dispute over the
proprietorship of Barbados created such factiousness among
the settlers that Nicolas Leverton, the first chaplain ever to
Barbados, fled the island in despair. Another clergyman, the
Rev. M. Kentlane, had to act as arbiter between the contending
parties.

The island was divided into parishes in 1629 by the governor,
Sir William Tufton. The parishes established that year were
Christ Church, St. Michael, St. James, St. Thomas, St. Peter and
St. Lucy. Later, in 1650, when Philip Bell was Lieutenant-
Governor of the island, five other parishes − St. George, St.
Philip, St. John, St. Andrew and St. Joseph − were established.

By 1634, the Church of England was to be found in Nevis, Antigua and Montserrat. In that year, Archbishop William Laud, Primate of England, obtained from King Charles I an Order in Council which extended the jurisdiction of the Bishop of London over English congregations and clergy abroad. This meant, in effect, that the Church of England in the Caribbean was considered an extension of the diocese of London.

To emphasize the point: the Church of England was the church of the Englishmen who resided in the colonies. It was not, for example, the church of those Irish people who came to the islands as indentured servants. The Irish were mostly Catholics. It was no doubt their Catholicism that made them sympathetic to the cause of their co-religionists, the Spaniards. Thus, in 1629, when the Spanish fleet attacked Nevis, the Irishmen who served in the island's militia not only deserted, but some of them proved useful collaborators to the Spaniards. When Sir Henry Colt visited St. Kitts in 1631, he discovered that the Irish indentured servants there were hoping that the Spaniards might come to free them from their English masters. In fact, it was Irish Catholics from St. Kitts who, on the expiry of their indentures, went to Montserrat and began the settlement of that island in 1632. They were joined a short while later by some of their country-men (and co-religionists) from Virginia. These 'Virginians' came to Montserrat because of the religious intolerance which they experienced in the North American colony. Not that Catholicism was formally tolerated in Montserrat. The official religion of that island was held to be that of the Church of England. Catholic priests were not allowed legal entry into the island; but, nevertheless, some did visit clandestinely to celebrate mass.

It was the responsibility of the Bishop of London to enquire into the manners and conduct of all rectors, ministers, curates, parish clerks and incumbents and to punish them if he found them at fault by "removal, deprivation, suspension, excommunication, or other ecclesiastical censure."[18] It turned out, however, that the bishop's jurisdiction over the Church of England in the Caribbean, was purely nominal. It was the responsibility of the Governor, acting on behalf of the crown, to appoint clergymen. No doubt, the Governor consulted with the parish vestry before he made appointments. But, in those days, when even in England itself clergymen succeeded to offices mainly because of their known political inclination, it would not have been considered irregular if the governor appointed a protege to

48

office without consulting the vestry concerned. In any case, because priests were hard to come by in the seventeenth century, few vestries would have quibbled over an appointment such as that of Samuel Harman who was appointed to a Leeward Islands cure. Harman's primary qualification for office was that he was once secretary to the Governor of the Leeward Islands. The Governor who appointed clergymen could no doubt remove them from office.

The white planters who comprised the several vestries were generally jealous of their power in ecclesiastical matters in their parishes. Thomas Lane, the first minister of St. Michael's, complained to Laud in 1637, that the Minister was little more than the hired hand of the vestry. Such planters would undoubtedly resent the authority of the Bishop of London. Later on, some of their counterparts who comprised the Jamaican Assembly would express that resentment when they decreed that "no ecclesiastical law, or jurisdiction shall have power to enforce, confirm or establish any penal mulct or punishment in any case whatsoever."[19] Later, too, when the Bishop of London tried to put into effect the authority granted him by the King's Order in Council and appointed a commissary (deputy) in Barbados, in the person of the Rev. Mr. Gordon, the rector of St. Michael's, Governor Lowther strenuously opposed the move. The Governor's opposition was based on the ground that the erection of a spiritual court such as was contemplated by the King's Order in Council would clash with the laws of Barbados, embarrass the government, torment the gentry, improverish the larger free-holders and ruin the common people.

Behind Governor Lowther's opposition was the principle of Erastianism which was influential in determining the relationship between the State and the Church of England at that time. Named after Thomas Erastus (b. 1524), the principle asserts that the church ought to be subordinate to the state. Erastus held the view that to claim 'visible' power for the church was tantamount to robbing Caesar of what rightly belonged to him. Erastians such as Grotius and Althusius taught that since God had entrusted the sum total of visible government to the Christian magistrate in a Christian country (such as England was), the church had no right to exercise a power of repression that was distinct from and independent of that of the state. Far from the church having the right to establish its own court, it was felt that the state should legislate for the church. Strictly speaking, the Erastian principle admitted no division between the church and the state; the former was but the latter at prayer. It was in keeping with this principle that the English Parliament enacted legislation on ecclesiastical matters. In 1619, when an assembly was established in the colony of Virginia in North America, it proceeded to legislate for the church of the English settlers — the Church of England. Governor Yeardley of Virginia would have regarded it as unthinkable, as Lowther later did in the case of Barbados, that a separate body should be established to regulate ecclesiastical matters in the English colony, its Puritan character notwithstanding.

Barbados remained stubbornly royalist during the Civil War in England. Because of this, the island's legislature (and church) had no patience with the Puritanism of Cromwell's Commonwealth. In fact, it may well be said, that during that time, Barbados was more Anglican than England itself. On May 3, 1650, the Barbadian Assembly proclaimed Charles Stuart (i.e. Charles II) King of England, Scotland, France and Ireland. The Book of Common Prayer was declared the only true pattern of worship; it was commanded that it be distinctly and duly read in every parish church every Lord's Day. In England, at that time, not only had the episcopacy been abolished, but the Confession of Faith and the *Directory of Worship* had replaced the Book of Common Prayer. Cavaliers (i.e. royalists) who were exiled by Cromwell to Barbados might have helped to strengthen the resolve of the Barbadian plantocracy to be both royalist and Anglican.

To guard against the erosion of the influence of the Church of England in the island and to secure conformity to the teachings of that Church, the island's Assembly enacted that:

> All persons whatsoever inhabiting or resident, or which shall inhabit or reside in this Island, are, in his Majesty's name hereby strictly charged and commanded that they, from henceforth give due obedience, and conform themselves unto the Government and Discipline of the Church of England, as the same hath been established by several Acts of Parliament.[20]

In addition, regulations were promulgated for regular attendance at the parish church or chapel on the Sabbath, the preaching of the Scripture, and "the Catechizing and questioning [of] all the Youth, and others that shall come before them" by ministers, in "the Fundamentals of the Christian Religion, and all the Articles of the Christian Faith."[21] Those who infringed these regulations could be fined forty pounds of sugar, or ten

50

pounds of cotton or be placed in stocks, depending on the nature of the infringement.

In 1655, English settlers in Barbados were recruited by Admiral Penn and General Venables to form part of an expedition against the Spaniards of Hispaniola. Whether it was because as royalists they had little or no sympathy with Cromwell's Western Design for the mastery of the Indies of which the expedition was a part, or because the religion practised and encouraged in Barbados had little influence on them, they turned out to be a sorry lot. Venables wrote of them that they were "not to be commanded as soldiers, nor to be kept in any civil order, being the most profane, debauched persons that we ever saw, scorners of religion; and indeed, men kept so loose as not to be kept under discipline, and so cowardly as not to be made to fight." It could be, however, that the criticism of the Barbadians by Venables was an attempt to blame the islanders for the failure of the expedition to capture Hispaniola. Further, the criticism of Venables might well have reflected the Puritan prejudice against non-Puritan members of the Church of England.

The expedition of Penn and Venables, however, captured Jamaica in 1655. The expedition included seven ministers of religion who were naval and military chaplains. And it would seem that the religious motive was not lacking in the conquest of Jamaica. Shortly after the conquest of the island, General Fortescue, the president of a Military Council that administered Jamaica for a short while, wrote to Cromwell:

> Forasmuch as we conceive the propagation of the Gospel was the thing principally aimed at and intended in this expedition, I humbly desire that His Highness will please to order that some godly, sober and learned minister may be sent to us, which may be instrumental in planting and propagating of the Gospel.[22]

Further, in 1653-4, when the Lord Protector of England was proposing his Western Design to the United Provinces, he had, in fact, suggested that England and the United Provinces might send out teachers imbued with the knowledge of Jesus Christ to propagate the Gospel and the ways of Christ as part of that Design. The two Protestant nations would not only be the richer for the Design, but they would have the glory of being responsible for the spread of true religion.

Since the Design was aimed primarily against Spain, it was of necessity hostile to Catholicism. That hostility vented itself against the two Spanish Catholic churches at St. Jago de la Vega.

51

The churches were destroyed by the Puritan soldiers of the Commonwealth. Harsh terms of evacuation were imposed on the Spaniards; priests in particular, were expelled from Jamaica. The antagonism shown to the Catholics on this occasion might well have been regarded by the Puritans as just revenge for the plunder of the Puritan colony of Providence by Don Francisco Diaz de Pimienta in May, 1641. The origins of this event went back to 1615 when the Earl of Warwick, a bitter enemy of Spaniards, initiated a series of attempts to settle the Bermudas or Somers Island. The experiment was a disappointment to both Warwick and the settlers. However, in 1629, when English Puritans were looking for a place where their supporters might find refuge from persecution in England, Warwick suggested that a settlement might be established in the Caribbean. In 1630, Warwick, John Pym, John Hampden, Oliver Cromwell and others, incorporated the Providence Island Company for the establishment of such a settlement. The island chosen for the settlement was Santa Catalina (renamed Providence), which was just off the Mosquito Coast and ideally situated for intercepting Spanish shipping. In a short time the character of Providence changed. The attempt to establish a colony along Puritan lines was abandoned as the settlers turned to privateering at the expense of Spain. To Philip IV of Spain and his ministers, the presence and the activities of the heretics on Providence constituted an impudent affront to Catholicism as well as to Spanish power. The colony had to be destroyed. And destroyed it was by Pimienta in 1641 with a force of nine ships and more than two thousand men. Englishmen at the time vowed that, "this unexpected and undeserved act of the Spaniard . . . will ere long be requited."[24] The revenge came in Jamaica in 1655.

The Commonwealth came to an end in 1660. With its termination, Puritanism was eclipsed. The Church of England that became established in Jamaica was the church of the Restoration. In 1661, General Edward D'Oyley, the first governor of the island, was instructed to "discourage vice and debauchery and to encourage ministers that Christianity and the Protestant religion, according to the Church of England, might have due reverence and exercise"[25] in Jamaica. The first Church of England building was erected at St. Jago de la Vega on the site of the Red Cross Catholic church that had been destroyed by the Puritan soldiers. In England, the Restoration was followed by a series of Acts — the Act of Uniformity (1661). The

Corporation Act (1661). The Conventicle Act (1664), the Five Mile Act (1665) and the Test Act (1678) – which severely restricted the liberties of those people (clergy and laity alike) who would not swear unfeigned assent and consent to everything in the Book of Common Prayer. Dissenting clergymen were ejected from their cures; some (e.g. Richard Baxter) were gaoled, while others were exiled. Dissenting laymen were excluded from public office and their prayer meetings were declared illegal. But the scruples which Charles II might have had regarding the religious purity of Jamaica were set aside because of the urgent need to populate the island. The king gave instructions that "persons of different judgement and opinions in matters of religion"[26] might be transported to Jamaica. This was no doubt felt to be one way by which England herself might be rid of dissenters. In any case, once the transportees were in the island they were not to be discriminated against on account of their religious scruples. Those who might succeed to governmental office, except for those who might become members and officers of the Privy Council, were not to be required to take the oaths of supremacy and allegiance. Some other way of securing their allegiance was to be devised.

Charles II's instructions regarding Jamaica anticipated in some measure the Toleration Act of William and Mary (1689) which declared that penal laws were no longer to be enforced against the Protestant (i.e. Dissenting) subjects of the sovereigns providing that they took the oaths of allegiance and supremacy and denounced the Catholic doctrine of transubstantiation. Quakers were excused from taking the oaths because of their abhorrence of swearing. They were asked, however, solemnly to denounce the papacy. Charles' instructions might well have resulted in the advent of a motley group of Dissenters to the island.

In Barbados, dissenting churchmen, who in 1676 were identifiable, later went over to the Church of England when they became members of the sugar planter class. Presbyterians, Baptists, and even Jews, became Anglicans, with only the Quakers as a group maintaining their religious integrity. The Quakers did this in the face of persecution. A similar thing might well have happened in Jamaica with only the Quakers and the Jews resisting the process of change in that island. There the disappearance of Dissenters would have been rapid since Jamaica became a sugar producing island almost from the time it became an English possession. Lack of religious leadership among the Dissenters, the fragmented nature of that group and the status and influence which the Church of England enjoyed in the island, would have encouraged the transference of religious allegiance. This change in church membership was not peculiar to the Caribbean. In England, where the Established Church of England became the church of the squirearchy, and Nonconformity the religion of the poorer classes, it was not unknown for many an erstwhile Dissenter to join the Established Church once he became wealthy enough to be regarded as belonging to a higher social class. He would have had, of course, to acquire the graces of his new class.

Their formal Church of England membership notwithstanding, Jamaicans nurtured a spirit of dissent. Not a few of them developed an attitude of cynicism to matters of religion — an attitude often characteristic of people who became adherents of a religion for motives other than a conviction that their new religion teaches the truth. The result was that members of the Church of England in Jamaica were either indifferent or hostile to the authority of the Church or they were lax in the practice of their religion. These attitudes in turn were to harden into a tradition which was to plague the Church for a long time to come.

Like the Church in Barbados, that in Jamaica came under the espiscopal authority of the Bishop of London. The island's Assembly, however, was quick to circumscribe the power of that bishop by decreeing that "no ecclesiastical law, or jurisdiction, shall have power to enforce, confirm or establish any penal mulct or punishment in any case whatever."[27] It was not only the case that the Assembly probably regarded it as absurd that the Bishop of London should exercise jurisdiction over the Church in Jamaica from a distance of four thousand miles away, it was also the case that the Assembly was not willing to relinquish its control over the Church to anybody.

In its relationship to the established Church of England in the island, the Jamaican Legislature adhered to strict Erastian principles. As late as in April, 1826, about a year after Dr. Christopher Lipscomb, the first Bishop of Jamaica, arrived in the island to assume the episcopacy, the Assembly enacted legislation to the effect that "all such laws, ordinances, and canons ecclesiastical as are now used in England, so far as relates [sic] to the due ordering and ecclesiastical regimen of, and jurisdiction over, the clergy, shall be in force within this land."[28] The legislation carefully excluded the Bishop from any judicial authority, spiritual or temporal, over the lay inhabitants of the island. The Governor, as the crown's representative in the island, was to continue to function as the Ordinary. That is, he was the person responsible for actually appointing clergymen to vacant benefices.

Even some clergymen over whom the bishop's jurisdiction extended resented Lipscomb's authority. The resentment found spiteful utterance in such complaints as that of the Rev. G.W. Bridtes. That reverend gentleman wrote in 1828. that:

> Upon his arrival, the Bishop of Jamaica found the livings and curacies occupied chiefly by creoles, but some of them by British clergymen; and looking forward to the possession of the patronage, his avowed principle was that no good could be expected from his mission until "the old clergy", that is, those who owed their appointments to the Duke of Manchester (Governor of Jamaica, 1808-1827), were exterminated.[29]

The Jamaicans were not noted for their piety. The early (perhaps Puritanical) zeal noted by Sir Thomas Modyford which led people to meet in each other's houses "as the primitive Christians did . . . to pray, read a chapter, sing a psalm"[30] at a time when only five parishes had churches, gave way to indifference. Lady Maria Nugent, who came to the island at the beginning of the nineteenth century, noted that the military had not attended church for nearly three years. She held a conversation with some men on religion and discovered to her chagrin that not one professed to have the least religion while some declared that religion was all a farce. While at Black River, the Governor's wife noted that the clergyman's wife excused herself from attending church on the ground that the service was likely to be too long! An observer in 1807 recorded that the average congregation comprised the curate, the clerk, and sexton, one or two magistrates, a dozen gentlemen, and about twice that number of ladies. For many people, Sunday was a gala day on which overseers met to dine, play cards, drink and dance.

As for morals, many white men, whether married or single, lived in a state of licentiousness with their female slaves. Overseers in particular, were without principle, religion or morality. There were, however, the odd proprietor, attorney and professional man, who were known for high-mindedness and good character. On the whole, the women seemed to have been better behaved than the men. But for their addiction to horse-racing their love of dancing and entertaining, and their tendency to be proud, avaricious, and sometimes cruel, the women, though no paragons of virtue, were no more immoral than their sisters in England.

'Anglican'[31] governments in the Caribbean reflected the intolerance shown by the government to non-Anglicans in Great Britain, particularly to Roman Catholics. In Jamaica, for example, the liberty of conscience granted to Dissenters by William and Mary was extended to all except 'Papists'. In the 1760s, when Roman Catholic inhabitants of Grenada applied to the Secretary of State for the Colonies for permission to exercise the elective franchise and to be regarded as eligible for office in the House of Assembly and on the Board of Council, opposition to the application came from the Governor, General Melville, the Members of the Council, the Speaker, and most of the Members of the House of Assembly. Objections were based on the ground that it was incompatible with the British constitution to grant the desired privileges to Roman Catholics. It was felt that the extension of such privileges to Catholics would constitute an injustice to the members of the 'English Church' who had purchased lands and had settled on the island on the good faith that their rights would be guaranteed by the British constitution.

Further, in 1763, when Grenada was ceded to the British, it became the stated policy of the government of the island that in order that the Church of England might be established both in principle and in practice, the French (Catholic) inhabitants of the island were to be induced to embrace the Protestant religion. Their children were to be brought up in the principles of Anglicanism. For that purpose, Protestant schools were to be established in the island, and provision was to be made for the maintenance of a Protestant ministry. It was not until 1785 that Roman Catholics in Grenada were regarded as being on the same footing as tolerated Dissenters on the island. By way of contrast, when Tobago was ceded to France in 1783, the Protestant inhabitants of that island were allowed the free exercise of their religion and their clergymen were given the assurance that they would not be deprived of their benefices.

Reasons of state, more than anything else, were responsible for the official Anglican attitude of intolerance to the Catholics in Grenada. Only a few generations before, Catholicism had been treasonable in England. And in Grenada, the Catholics were Frenchmen who — it might have been felt — could hardly

56

be transformed into 'English' colonists unless they were Anglicanised. With the French, on the other hand, while Roman Catholicism was very strong in France it was not identical with French nationalism. Nor was Protestantism in the latter half of the eighteenth century there regarded as antithetical to nationalism. It is true that with the Revocation of the Edict of Nantes in 1685, Protestantism was officially proscribed in France, and that it was to remain so until 1789. But by the 1770s, public sentiment in France was much against any kind of religious fanaticism that might have engendered intolerance. The writings of Voltaire and the *philosophes* were having their effect. These men had poured scepticism and mockery on Catholicism. New ideas inspired by men such as Toussaint, Diderot, Montesquieu, Buffon and Condillac, severely tempered the persecuting spirit of the Church; so, too, did the prolonged vendetta between the French *parlementaires* and the Jesuits. That vendetta was to end with the abolition of the Society of Jesus in France, in 1762, when that body was charged with the repudiation of the sovereignty of the throne, and when Jesuit doctrines were described as perverse, destructive of all principles of religion, injurious to Christian morals, and pernicious and seditious to civil society. These developments in France were, no doubt, behind the tolerance which the French officials in Tobago showed to the Protestants on the island.

Not only was the Church of England established by law; its beliefs, and its liturgy were settled by Parliamentary legislation, although these did not, by that token, originate with Parliament. In any case, Parliamentary legislation which related to the Church's faith and order was invariably ratified by Convocation. In 1717, Convocation was prorogued; it was not to meet again until 1855 in the case of Canterbury, and until 1863 in the case of York. But by 1717 the Church's doctrines had become established. These doctrines were adhered to by the Church in the Caribbean.

Church of England orthodoxy was believed to be enshrined in the Thirty-nine Articles of Faith and the Book of Common Prayer. The Articles declare that the Scriptures of the Old and New Testaments contain "all doctrine required of necessity for eternal salvation through faith in Jesus Christ". In addition, the eighth Article declares the Apostles', the Nicene and the Athanasian Creeds to be "thoroughly received and believed; for they may be proved by most certain warrants of Holy Scriptures."

According to the Articles, man is justified by faith alone. Article XI states: "We are accounted righteous before God, only for the merit of our Lord and Saviour Jesus Christ by Faith, and not for our own works or deservings. Wherefore, that we are justified by Faith only is a most wholesome doctrine and very full of comfort." Article XXII repudiates "the Romish doctrine concerning Purgatory, Pardons, Worshipping and Adoration, as well as of Images and of Reliques, and also invocation of saints." On the Eucharist, the Articles (XXVIII and XXIX) are strongly Calvinist in character. The Catholic doctrine of transubstantiation which explains how the Presence of Christ is related to the sacrament, is repudiated, as is the Lutheran theory of the ubiquity or natural omnipresence of the 'glorified' Body of Christ in the sacrament. The position of the Articles is that: "The Body of Christ is given, taken and eaten, in the Supper, only after a heavenly and spiritual manner. And the means whereby the Body of Christ is received and eaten in the Supper is Faith." As for the wicked and those who lack faith, "they are in no wise partakers of Christ."

Article XXI states that "general councils may not be gathered together without the commandment and will of Princes." Another Article, however, while acknowledging that the Sovereign possesses the chief government of the Church, declares that "we give not to our Princes the ministering either of God's Word or of the Sacraments . . . but that only prerogative which we see to have been given always to all godly Princes in Holy Scriptures by God Himself." (Article XXVII). Part of the prerogative of the Sovereign was to nominate clergymen to the bishoprics; it was his prerogative also to appoint priests to benefices. In the Caribbean, the latter privilege was exercised by the representative of the crown — the Governor.

As important as the Thirty-nine Articles as a standard of orthodoxy was the Book of Common Prayer. The use of the Book of Common Prayer in church was prescribed by the Act of Uniformity which was passed by Parliament in 1661; the Prayer Book that came into widespread usage was that which was revised in 1662 following the re-establishment of the Anglican Church. By that Act, ministers of religion were obliged to swear unfeigned assent and consent to everything in the Book of Common Prayer. At ordination, the candidate for the priesthood promised to "use the form in the said book and none other except in so far as may be prescribed by lawful

58

authority." Not only was the Prayer Book regarded as normative for liturgy; it was held to be normative for doctrine also.

Edward Long, the eighteenth century Jamaican historian, observed that "it has always been the rule in our West India Islands to assimilate their religion, as well as laws, to those of the mother country."[32] The islanders doubtless subscribed to the orthodoxy contained in the Articles and the Book of Common Prayer. However, the extent to which they could "assimilate their religion" to that of England was limited. Parishes were demarcated in the several islands, but there were never enough clergymen to supply the churches in the parishes; there were even cases in which parishes were without churches. Sometimes, as in Portland (Jamaica) in Long's time where there was neither church nor rector, the services were performed in some planter's house about once or twice a year. As late as 1812, the seven parishes of Tobago had but one clergyman and no church building. In Barbados in 1680, only five of the eleven parishes were supplied with priests.

The scarcity of Church of England clergymen in the Caribbean forced the Bishop of London to ordain men for the colonies who were less qualified than their counterparts in England. Edward Long, commenting on the clergymen in Jamaica, declared that some were "much better qualified to be retailers of salt-fish, or boatswains to privateers, than ministers of the Gospel." Sometimes priests were recruited from among unsuccessful planters, merchants and ex-military officers. Sometimes clergymen came to the Caribbean as chaplains to expeditions, or to better their position in some way. Some, perhaps, came in order to avoid persecution in England. Many were appointed to cures in the Caribbean not by the Bishop of London, but by the local vestries. Such appointments were then ratified by the Governor, who more often than not was anxious to see that the several parishes were as adequately staffed as the circumstances would permit.

It was not until 1825 that bishops were appointed to the Caribbean. With no bishops in the Caribbean, the sacrament of ordination could not be performed, therefore, no one could be ordained to the diaconate. This, in turn, meant that the Church of England's three-fold order of ministry — bishop, priest and deacon — did not exist in the Caribbean before 1825. The only clergymen in the islands were priests. In addition, the sacrament of confirmation by which baptized persons were admitted to the Eucharist, and which could only be performed by a bishop, could not be observed in the Caribbean. Little wonder that Maria Nugent encountered people in Jamaica who were old enough to be admitted to the Eucharist but who had not yet been confirmed.

The absence of bishops in the Caribbean posed a very serious problem for the Church. This related to the discipline of the clergy — a problem that was undoubtedly exacerbated by the fact that many of the clergymen appointed to the region were deficient in both learning and piety. As Long noted of them:

> There have seldom been wanting some who were equally respectable for their learning, piety, and exemplary good behaviour; others have been detestable for their addition to lewdness, drinking, gambling and iniquity; having no control but their own sense of their function, and the censures of the Governor.[34]

Among those clergymen who were noted for their exemplary zeal and conduct were Galpin, Johnstone and May of Jamaica, Knox and Bryan of Antigua, and Dent of Grenada.

J.B. Ellis said of the eighteenth century Church of Jamaica what might well have been said of the Church of England in the Caribbean as a whole: that it was little more than a respectable and ornamental adjunct of the state, the survival of a harmless home institution which would not have been tolerated (apparently by the white plantocracy whom it served and who largely comprised it) had it shown any signs of energy and activity which were not in keeping with the character and role that its membership had assigned to it. Johnston and Osborne have expressed the opinion that the Caribbean Church was a *blasé*, contented and rather "dull sort of church", because it was modelled after the Church of England.[35]

The truth is that at the time when Anglicanism was becoming established in the Caribbean, the Church in England was far from being *blasé*, contented and dull. It was agitated by one controversy after another. That was a time when religion was at the heart of many a dispute between men of differing shades of beliefs and opinions regarding doctrine and church order. The crown as well as Parliament was involved in these quarrels. And not a few clergymen lost their lives in the changing fortunes of these controversies. Not a few persons, too, were forced to flee England in order to escape religious persecution. Meanwhile, theologians such as the Cambridge Platonists, Benjamin Whichcote (1609-83) and Ralph Cudworth (1617-88), were concerned to defend Christianity from the attacks of philosophers such as Roger Bacon and Thomas Hobbes, and
60

from scientists who were hostile to certain aspects of the Christian religion. Theological speculation developed in the direction of deism — the vague belief in a First Cause or Supreme Being — and in natural morality. The title of John Toland's book, *Christianity not Mysterious* (1696), epitomised the theological spirit of the age which insisted that the essentials of faith had to be made plain and obvious so that any reasonable man might comprehend them. Whatever the style of theological speculation in the Church of England, the point is that a church involved in such speculation was hardly contented and *blasé.*

The church in the Caribbean was little more than an ornamental adjunct to the state not only because that church was a somewhat defective replica of the 'home institution' but mainly because the Caribbean church was so thoroughly dominated by the influence of sugar planters and governmental officials in the colonies. The salaries of clergymen (who were thought of as the 'church') were voted by the planter-Assemblies. Clergymen held office at the pleasure of the Governor. At the level of the parish, the vestry, which was composed of planters and which functioned as a civil as well as an ecclesiastical body, dictated the policy and the programme of the parish church. The fact that the Caribbean church before 1825 lacked any kind of Convocation and the fact that without bishops residing in the area it was bereft of local spiritual leadership did not help to reduce the influence which the plantocracy had on the Church. Further, the fact that many clergymen were deficient in both learning and piety did not help to make the Church a creative force or the clergy an imaginative body.

The Society of Friends in the Caribbean

The Quakers or members of the Society of Friends were among the Dissenters who had been transported from Britain to the Caribbean. They were brought to Barbados, Jamaica and Nevis in 1665. In Barbados, the Friends settled primarily in Carrington's Village in St. Michael. By 1671, the community of Friends in Jamaica had become sufficiently important to warrant a visit from George Fox, the founder of the movement. In Barbados by that time, the Friends were beginning to attract the attention of the island's legislature.

The movement itself was one of several that had their genesis in England between 1640 and 1660. During that time, the country experienced such a ferment of religious ideas that it has been said that that period was perhaps the most profoundly and thoughtfully religious in English experience since the Middle Ages. The religious ideas current in those times were not without their implications for politics. There were the theological ideas held by the 'rational' theologians such as William Chillingworth of Oxford and John Hales of Eton. An important sympathiser of this group was Archbishop Laud. The 'rational' theologians were Royalist in their political sympathies. They had little, if any, liking for dogmatism. As far as they were concerned, the fundamental beliefs that Christians were required to hold were few in number. Provided they adhered to these, they could leave the interpretation of Scripture to their reason as it was guided by divine revelation. The 'rational' theologians, advocating moderation in all things, found little wrong in drama, poetry and sport. The Court's patronage of dramatists such as Shakespeare and Ben Johnson and of poets such as John Donne and George Herbert had their approval.

In contrast (and probably in opposition) to the ideas of the 'rational' school of thought were those held by the Seekers — the forerunners of the Society of Friends. Led by Dr. John Everard, the Seekers maintained that since Antichrist had ruled over the Church for so long, no true Christ, in fact, existed anywhere. Truth, they maintained, could only come from within as an interior experience. In keeping with their beliefs, they left all organised churches and societies and went in search of Truth. In the words of William Penn, they "wandered up and down as sheep without a shepherd and as doves without their mates, seeking their Beloved." George Fox, who was born at Drayton-in-the-Clay in Leicestershire in July, 1624, was one such Seeker. In this quest for the saving experience, he fancied that he heard a voice which informed him that, "There is one, even Christ Jesus, that can speak to thy condition." This was the beginning of a profound mystical experience which was to dominate Fox's life and influence his religion. He wrote:

> The Lord God opened to me by his invisible power, how every man was enlightened by the divine light of Christ. I saw it shine through all, and they that believed in it came out of condemnation to the light of life, and became the children of it; but they that hated it, and did not believe in it, were condemned by it, though they made a profession of Christ. This I saw in the pure openings of the light without the help of any man, neither did I then know where to find it in the Scriptures.[36]

Following Fox, the Friends emphasised the mystical experience by which a man came to know the inward light that came from Christ. Spiritual insight was to be authenticated by conduct that was believed to be becoming to the children of light. Friends refused to take oaths, believing that to do so was to uphold a double standard of morality and to disobey Christ who said, "Swear not at all." They objected to the wearing of gaudy apparel. They would have nothing to do with sport or with the theatre. They refused to doff the hat to any man believing that that sign of respect was due to God alone. They used 'thee' and 'thou' ('thou' was used at that time for addressing inferiors) instead of 'you'.

The Friends had little or no use for the Church of England. They refused to conform to its rites and regarded parish churches as 'steeple houses'. George Fox taught that God who made the world did not dwell in temples made with hands. The Friends disregarded constituted authority to such an extent that they felt that no act was so religious as the resistance of authority. But resistance was not to take the form of violence, since violence for them was anathema.

Fox assembled a congregation at Mansfield around 1647. Members called themselves the Children of Light or the Society of Friends. In 1650, they were dubbed Quakers by a Puritan magistrate, Gervase Bennett. The Quakers rejected all creeds, the sacraments and the institutional ministry. Their authority and source of truth was the inner light from God shining in the heart of the individual. The greater part of their meeting for worship was spent in silence as they waited upon God for illumination. The silence was broken only when someone duly illuminated felt led by the Spirit to speak or to offer prayer.

The adherence of the Friends to the precepts of the Society made them very unpopular in the Caribbean. Holding war to be ungodly, they refused to participate in militia manoeuvres. Participation in such manoeuvres was a requirement that was made of all able-bodied white men in the islands. It was felt that this was necessary to keep the whites in readiness in case there were slave revolts. These island militias would also be useful in the event of war with England's enemies should the fighting shift to the Caribbean. The refusal of the Friends to participate in the manoeuvres was, in the eyes of their fellow whites, tantamount to a betrayal of the Englishmen's cause and of the plantocracy. That betrayal was complete when the Friends began to encourage slaves to attend their meetings. In Barbados, in 1676, the Assembly passed an Act forbidding Quakers to bring Negroes to their meetings.

The repugnance which the Friends felt for the Established Church found expression in their refusal to pay tithes from which the stipends of Church of England clergymen would be met. Unlike other Dissenters, they did not find the Church of England attractive when they accumulated enough wealth to move higher up the social ladder. In contrast to their attitude to the Church of England, the Quakers were accommodating to the missionaries of the Evangelical churches when these came to the Caribbean. In fact, the Moravian church was able to gain a foothold in Barbados primarily because a Quaker, a Mr. Jackman, allowed the missionaries of the Unitas Fratrum to preach on his estate near Bridgetown. Before the evangelicals arrived on the Caribbean scene, the Quakers had themselves attempted to convert slaves, much to the disgust of their fellow colonists. In the light of this, it is understandable that the Friends should be tolerant of the evangelicals since their work was primarily among slaves and ex-slaves; and, particularly, since the Quakers would have recognised in the missionaries fellow dissenters from the established order.

Consistent with the practice of Friends generally, those of the Caribbean refused to swear oaths. They refused, for example, to take the oaths of supremacy and allegiance. It was this fact more than anything else that led Charles II to order that Dissenters in Jamaica should not be compelled to take the oaths. In Barbados and elsewhere in the Caribbean, law court officials found the Friends most disconcerting whenever they had to appear in court; they simply would not swear the required oath before testifying. In short, much of the intransigence which led to their having been transported (or 'Barbadosed') to the Caribbean in the first place was to persist. What was to persist as well, to their credit, was their liberal attitude to Negro slaves. We have noted above, their tendency to invite slaves to their meetings. In 1755, they forbade their members to trade in slaves; and, later, they were among the first people in the Caribbean to agitate for the abolition of the slave trade and the emancipation of slaves.

French Catholicism in the Caribbean

French Catholicism was first brought to the Caribbean when the French colonists under D'Esnambuc settled on St. Christopher in 1626. From St. Kitts, French settlers moved to Martinique and Guadeloupe. The following year, after the Sieur du Parquet bought Grenada and St. Lucia from the *Compagnie des Isles d'Amerique* (1650), French arrived in those islands as well. The pioneers who settled on Guadeloupe, Martinique, St. Lucia and Grenada were Normans, Bretons and Gascons. They were doubtless Catholics as well. These Frenchmen were later joined by Irishmen with names like O'Rourke, O'Kelly, O'Donnell and Dillon. They were in all probability Catholics who might have fled the persecution of Catholicism in Britain. The names O'Donnell and O'Rourke (O'Ruark) appear with some frequency among the names of Irishmen who resisted attempts to introduce Protestantism (i.e. Anglicanism) into Ireland. Later, French planters settled on the neutral island of Dominica and in the process established the Catholic faith there. This meant that the Catholicism that was to become established in the Lesser Antilles was that of the French Church.

The Catholic church in the Lesser Antilles suffered from a shortage of missionaries and priests. Before 1666, for example, there were no regular missionaries in St. Lucia. The Catholic community there was served by monks who went there from time to time. The legendary Père du Tertre began his ministry in St. Lucia around 1666. Very much in keeping with the instructions of the Provincial Synod of 1622 and with the tradition of the Dominican Order, du Tertre learned the language of the Caribs in order to preach to them. In addition, along with Father Breton, he wrote a part of the Church's liturgy in the language of the Caribs. Another legendary religious to serve the French islands of the Lesser Antilles was the Dominican, Père Jean Baptiste Labat of Paris; he came to the Caribbean towards the end of the seventeenth century.

The French Catholic mission to the Caribs was almost barren of results. The efforts of men like du Tertre and Labat were frustrated by the hostility of the Caribs to Europeans generally, and by their reluctance to accept the Catholic religion which they no doubt found difficult to comprehend. In the end, in most of the islands; the Caribs were unfortunately annihilated by the French settlers, but not before these indigenous people had taken some toll of the lives of the Europeans.

The French officials were at first tolerant in their attitude toward non-Catholics. In this respect, they were faithful to Edict of Nantes (1598), which had guaranteed the Huguenots in France liberty of conscience. Perhaps another reason for this tolerance – at least before the Caribs were exterminated – was the anxiety of the officials to maintain a united front against possible attacks from the Caribs. When Monsieur de Poincy, the Governor of the French settlement in St. Kitts, sent the Huguenots under La Vasseur to oust Roger Flood's men from Tortuga around 1640, he did so in order to rid St. Kitts of the Calvinists. This was not because de Poincy was intolerant of Protestantism but because he hoped that by sending these rather militant Protestants away from the island he would bring peace to the French settlement that had been hitherto troubled by the rivalry between the Catholic and Huguenot settlers. This rivalry was exacerbated by the presence of Le Vasseur and his group in St. Kitts. These Huguenots were the remnants of the followers of the Seigneur de Soubise who had opposed Cardinal Richelieu's policy of imposing Catholicism on Bearn and had taken up arms at La Rochelle in their conflict with the cardinal. With the fall of La Rochelle, they had become wanderers until they joined d'Esnambuc's settlement shortly after 1625.

With the Revocation of the Edict of Nantes in 1625, Protestants and Jews in the French colonies of Martinique, Guadeloupe, St. Lucia and Grenada were subjected to persecution and expulsion from the island. By this time, the Carib threat had been removed. This persecution of non-Catholics in an effort to establish a single religion, Catholicism, in the French islands, reflected in miniature what was happening in France. In the Caribbean, however, there was no resistance comparable to the Camisard revolt which erupted in the Cevennes in France.

The non-Catholics in the islands were too few and too powerless to offer any opposition. Not that the non-Catholics lacked important people among their numbers. Among the Jews who were expelled from Martinique, for example, were the descendants of Benjamin d'Costa who was responsible for introducing sugar-cane into the island in 1654. Among the Protestants who suffered expulsion from Martinique were the co-religionists of Mademoiselle d'Aubigné who had once lived on the island with her father, a government official. Later, as Madame de Maintenon, the former Mlle d'Aubigné married King Louis XIV. It has been said that it was the Jesuits who, working through Madame de Maintenon, influenced the king to persecute the non-Catholics in order to demonstrate his orthodoxy to Rome. Madame de Maintenon had by that time converted to Catholicism. Her conversion in faraway France was to have disastrous effects on her former co-religionists in Martinique.

Meanwhile, Frenchmen were settling in the western section of Hispaniola. Many of these settlers had come directly from

66

France; others came from the island of Tortuga where Frenchmen had established a settlement. By 1640, this section of Hispaniola had a widely scattered French population of about six thousand, served by thirteen churches and eight priests. From around 1684, French Dominicans came to minister among their countrymen. The Treaty of Ryswick (1697) granted the western section of Hispaniola to the French who named it St. Dominigue. Seven years later, Jesuits, members of the most powerful and influential religious order in France of the *ancien régime,* arrived in St. Domingue; and, in 1705, the colony was divided into two apostolic prefectures – the *Préfecture du Nord* and the *Préfecture du Sud.* The former was to be the scene of Jesuit activity and the latter that of Dominican activity. The Huguenots, by this time, had been either absorbed by the predominantly Catholic population, or had been forced to leave the colony because of the disadvantages which they suffered when the Edict of Nantes was revoked. The work of the Dominicans in the *Préfecture du Sud* was hampered by many difficulties. Climatic conditions and the hardships involved in travel over dangerous terrain took their toll. In the other prefecture, the Jesuits fared slightly better. The outstanding Jesuits of this early period were Father Le Pers and Father Boutin. The former was responsible for founding new parishes and the latter for starting a school for girls.

At the level of formal legislation, the French government was liberal in its attitude to the christianisation of African slaves in a way that the English government was not. In 1685, the *Code Noir* was promulgated by Louis XIV as part of his attempt to impose uniformity, in the form of Catholicism, on all his subjects. Under the Code, slaves in the French islands were to be baptised and instructed in the Catholic faith. Earlier, Louis XIII had sanctioned the importation of slaves into the French colonies only after he had been led to believe by the French planters that slavery was the only means by which Africans could be brought into the Catholic fold.

There was a vast difference between the intent behind the legislation of the *Code Noir* and what was in fact done as far as the christianisation of slaves was concerned. In St. Domingue, both Father Le Pers and Father Boutin worked hard at converting the slaves. Father Boutin actually learned several African dialects in order to preach more effectively among the blacks; he also introduced the 'Negro Mass' which was celebrated on Sundays after the regular Mass. In spite of the efforts of the

67

Jesuits, however, the results achieved among the slaves of St. Domingue were minimal. Elsewhere in the French Caribbean, the scarcity of missionaries to serve the rapidly growing slave population and the resistance of the Africans themselves to the process of christianisation were factors which were responsible for the lack of any appreciable success in the effort to convert the slaves. Another important factor in this regard was the hostility with which many French planters viewed the education of the blacks, even in matters that were mainly religious in nature. Fenelon, a government official, expressed the sentiment of the French plantocracy when he declared that the safety of the whites who were less numerous than the blacks demanded that the slaves be kept in the most profound ignorance.

We shall discuss the impact of Christianity on the slaves in Haiti at another point. But it can be indicated here that the work of the Catholic Church in St. Domingue suffered a serious setback with the outbreak of the St. Domingue slave revolt in 1789. Many churches were sacked and destroyed and many congregations were dispersed. The fact that the lives of many priests were spared at a time when thousands of whites were killed would seem to indicate that the blacks had come to develop a favourable regard for these servants of French Catholicism.

A discussion of the beliefs of the French Catholics is not necessary since those beliefs were not essentially different from those held by the Spanish Catholics. A characteristic of French Catholicism, however, was its emphasis on preaching. This was perhaps demanded by the situation in which there were Caribs and African slaves to be evangelised. A contributing factor might well have been the emphasis which Catholicism of the post-Tridentine period placed on preaching – an emphasis which was no doubt inspired by the success gained by Protestant preaching in Europe. The preachers of French Catholicism in the Caribbean were the Jesuits and the Dominicans.

It may be of interest to indicate how the French Caribbean was in some measure involved in the eventual abolition of the Society of Jesus in France. Between 1716 and 1756, France experienced considerable economic growth and commercial expansion. This prosperity had its basis in the French colonies of which the islands in the Caribbean were considered to be the jewels of the French crown. Between four and five hundred ships left the French Atlantic ports annually to convey slaves from Africa and manufactured goods from France to the West

68

Indies. From the Caribbean, the ships returned with cargoes of sugar, rum, molasses, cotton and indigo. The fishing fleets of St. Malo conducted a very profitable trade in fish with the French West Indies; the fish was used in the slaves' diet. This trade between France and her colonies was regulated by *l'exclusif* – the French version of mercantilism. When the *Compagnie des Indes* lost the monopoly of the trade to the Caribbean, individual merchants, shipowners and other interests conducted that trade to their profit as well as to France's economic growth. One person to invest in the Caribbean trade was Pere Lavalette, the Jesuit Superior of Mission to the Leeward Isles. As a result of Lavalette's investments, a not inconsiderable commercial enterprise was built up in Martinique. That enterprise collapsed during the Seven Years' War (1756-1763) and Lavalette's creditors obtained judgement against the Society of Jesus. The Society appealed to *Parlement* of Paris against the decision. The society had apparently forgotten that at that time the French *Parlements* were involved in a campaign against the *richerisme* of the lower clergy. In any case, the Paris *Parlement* decided that the Society should pay all the debts of Lavalette. Further, a commission was set up to examine the Jesuit statutes. When the commission reported in 1762, *Parlement* decreed the abolition of the Society on the grounds that while it was ostensibly engaged in combatting heresy, it had actually established an alien authority in France.

The Jewish Diaspora in the Caribbean

Among the first Jews to come to the Caribbean were those who settled in Jamaica when that island was colonised by Don Juan de Esquivel in 1509. Although at that time their co-religionists were being persecuted in Spain, Jews who settled in Jamaica enjoyed the protection of the Spanish discoverers and *conquistadores*. As a special favour to Christopher Columbus, the Spanish crown had forbidden the Inquisition to operate in the island in the way it did in Hispaniola and Cuba. Thus, from its early history as a European colony, Jamaica was to be a refuge for Jews. Later, immigration from the Netherlands and England increased the number of Jews who settled in Jamaica. In about 1622, the Jews in Jamaica were joined by their fellows who had been expelled from Brazil when a Dutch settlement there was temporarily dispersed by the Portuguese. The Catholic nations of Portugal and Spain were at that time hostile to

Jews while the Dutch, on the other hand, were more tolerant of them. The tendency was, therefore, for Jews to settle among the Dutch. This meant that the fortunes of the Jews in the Caribbean fluctuated with those of the Dutch. During the latter half of the seventeenth century, Jews continued to come to Jamaica from Portugal, Brazil, Guiana (now Guyana) and Surinam. In almost every case, the migration of these Jews was prompted by religious intolerance, if not persecution.

The Jamaican Jews at this time were almost exclusively Sephardic. Not only were they related to those who had settled in London, but it was the London-based synagogue at Bevis Marks that supplied the Jamaican congregation with its *kazanim* or leaders. After the English conquest of Jamaica in 1655, the Jewish community in the island (and, indeed, the English settlers as well) benefitted greatly from the advice of Simon de Caceres, an Amsterdam Jew, who had settled in London and who had business connections with the island. Much of this advice might well have been related to the sugar industry. Later, de Caceres, who was Cromwell's secret adviser on Jamaican affairs, settled in the island.

When Spain granted the *asiento* to the English in 1713, a lively trade sprang up between Jamaica and the Spanish islands and mainland in slaves and manufactured goods. Much of this trade was in Jewish hands. Jews were allowed to own landed property, but they were excluded from the political franchise — a factor which caused them much dissatisfaction. It was not until 1831 that, as a result of the first Jewish Emancipation Bill in Britain, all legal disabilities were removed from the Jews of Jamaica. In 1760, however, the Jews had two further causes for complaint: the island's legislature was contemplating the imposition of a special tax on them, and they suffered the inconvenience of the martial law that was imposed on the island following the revolt of the slaves under Tacky in that year. It was here that the connections between the Kingston and London congregations were important. The Jamaican Jews sought the help and advice of the Jewish Board of Deputies that had just been formed in London. The advice of the Board was that as long as martial law was in force in the island, the Jews were to obey without question all the orders that were issued during the state of emergency even if it meant that in so doing they would have to desecrate the Sabbath. On the matter of the taxation, Jacob Nunes Gonzales and Joseph Jessurun Rodrigues, elders of the 'Portuguese Nation' (i.e.

70

the London synagogue) and members of the Board of Deputies, were able to obtain an undertaking from William Henry Lyttleton, the newly appointed Governor to Jamaica who was still in England, that the special taxation of Jews would not be tolerated even if the local legislature were to adopt it. The Governor also assured the deputies that the Jamaican Jews might be relieved from performing militia duties on the Sabbath.

Writing of the Jews in Jamaica in the early 1770s, Edward Long noted that they were numerous in the island and that they had a burial ground at some distance outside Kingston. They assembled in their synagogue with its "several well-adapted ornaments"[37] to read from the Law and Prophets every Sabbath. They observed most of the feasts and fasts of their forefathers, married circumcised, and buried their dead according to inherited Jewish custom. In addition, the Jewish community had its own butcher who slaughtered animals in the prescribed Mosaic manner and thus provided the community with *kosher* (ritually approved) food.

The Jews known to Long were of the Sephardic tradition, since it was not until about 1781 that Ashkenazi Jews were to come to the island. The first Sephardic synagogue is thought to have been that built at Port Royal shortly after the disastrous earthquake of 1692. This was perhaps the first Jewish place of worship to be built in the Caribbean, although this distinction has also been claimed for the synagogue in Curaçao. The Jamaican synagogue was named *Kahal Kadosh Nevnh Zedek* (Holy Congregation, Dwelling Place of Righteousness). People such as Moses Ferro, Esther Baruh Alvares, Sarah Lopez Torres and Sarah Nunes belonged to the Port Royal Jewish community. The family of Sarah Torres had fled Portugal to avoid the dangers of the Inquisition there, while Sarah Nunes' father, Abraham, was among the earliest settlers in Jamaica. Abraham and his brother Jacob had first settled in Barbados and then moved to Jamaica. It is highly probable that Abraham's pilgrimage brought him to Jamaica from Portugal *via* Brazil and Barbados. Tombs discovered at Dickenson's Run in St. Elizabeth with inscriptions in Hebrew and Portuguese indicate that Sephardim had also settled in that area at an early date. Probably, they were among those Jews who left Surinam in 1667 for Barbados and Jamaica, when Surinam was ceded to the Dutch by the British in exchange for New Amsterdam (New York) in North America.

Ashkenazi Jews came to Jamaica from Germany by way of

71

England. Some might have come, however, from the United States of America following the War of Independence. Those who settled in Kingston organized themselves into the *Kahal Kadosh Shaangare Yosher* (Holy Congregation, Gates of Righteousness). Their counterparts in Spanish Town built their synagogue, the *Kahal Kadosh Nikveh Yisroeil* (Holy Congregation, The Hope of Israel), in 1796. The *Kazan* of the *Mikveh Yisroeil* was the Rev. Jehiel Lopes. While the Sephardim buried their dead at Hunt's Bay, the Ashkenazim buried theirs in their Elletson Road cemetery.

When the Sephardic and the Ashkenazi synagogues were destroyed by the great Kingston fire of 1882, the Jewish community in the island decided to attempt to form a united congregation and to worship in one synagogue. It was the London synagogue of Bevis Marks that suggested to the Sephardim that they might unite with the Ashkenazim in this manner. Bevis Marks also provided the book of ritual that the United Congregation of Israelites in Jamaica was to use. Thus, the disaster of 1882 helped to effect in Jamaica a union of Sephardim and Ashkenazim that had not been achieved elsewhere at that date. Although the union was not total at first, it finally resulted in the complete amalgamation of the congregation in 1921.

Meanwhile, Sephardic Jews had settled in the Dutch island of St. Eustatius. In November, 1772, the congregation there wrote to the Jews in Barbados asking for financial assistance towards the rebuilding of their synagogue. The English island had a Sephardic synagogue by 1688. A much more important community of Jews settled in Curaçao after that island was captured by the Dutch in 1634. In 1651-52 the Sephardim, Joao de Ilhao and Joseph Nunes de Fonseca who were of Brazilian birth, were licensed by the Dutch West India Company to establish an agricultural settlement in Curaçao. At around the same time, the Jews were guaranteed freedom of worship in the island. When farming failed, the Jews became traders. So well did they do as traders that they replaced the Protestant merchants there in a fairly short time. The Jews were even sent on trade missions to the Spanish Main by the Dutch West India Company. No doubt their ability to speak Spanish and Portuguese as well as their entrepreneurial skill qualified them for these missions. There was, however, no social intercourse between the Protestant Dutch and the Sephardim. In fact, the two communities lived apart from each other, effectively

72

separated by a bay.

The Sephardic community in Curaçao built their synagogue, the *Mikveh Yisroeil,* in 1732. Before the synagogue was erected, they worshipped in private homes. Worship in the synagogue was conducted in Portuguese until 1870 when Dutch was introduced. The introduction of Dutch into the *Mikveh* indicated that the Jews had decided to regard Curaçao as their home. The time of the innovation coincided with another significant development in the Jewish community – that of the appointment of Jews to offices in the government. Undoubtedly there was a strong connection between these two developments involving the Jewish community in Curaçao. Religious schools or *midrasj* were established in the early eighteenth century. From these, Sephardic youths could graduate to the *Yeshivah* – a Jewish academy.

Another important Sephardic community was established on the island of Barbados almost as soon as the island was settled in 1627. The Barbadian Jews, many of whose fore fathers had originated in Spain and Portugal, were among those planters who pioneered in sugar cultivation in the island. In the heyday of the sugar industry, rich Jews migrated to London to retire among their kinsmen and co-religionists after they had accumulated their wealth in Barbados. Younger members of the London community went out to Barbados to seek their fortune there. Given their connections with Barbados, these young Jews were not likely to fail at that venture. Around the middle of the seventeenth century, Jews from the southern Caribbean joined their co-religionists in Barbados. For some of these migrants, Barbados was but a stop-over on their way to Jamaica.

As in the case of synagogues elsewhere in the Caribbean, Bevis Marks exercised great influence over the *Kaal Kadosh Nidhe Israel* (Holy Congregation of the Remnant of Israel) as the congregation in Barbados was named. The *Kaal Kadosh* depended on the London community for its *Kazanim.* It was through Bevis Marks that the Jews in Barbados sent a relief of £20 in 1791 to distressed Jews in Tetuan. Similarly, in 1815, a remittance was sent to London for the relief of their brethren in the Holy Land. Because of the relationship between Jews Street in Bridgetown and London, names that were commonplace at Bevis Marks were also familiar in Barbados. These included such names as Henriques, Massiah, Barrow, Nabarro and Bueno de Mesquita.

73

The differences between the Sephardim (who originated in Spain and Portugal mainly) and the Askenazim (who originated in Germany, Poland and Russia) were in liturgy, the practice of various customs, the method of studying and the pronunciation and spelling of Hebrew. The Sephardim and the Ashkenazim differed, for example, in the recital of the *piyyutim*. They differed also in the number of benedictions recited while they were putting on the *tephillin;* the Ashkenazim preferred two recitations while the *Sephardim* thought that one was enough. The Sephardim turned their eyes downwards when saying, "Kadosh, Kadosh, Kadosh." ("Holy, Holy, Holy."). The Ashkenazim, on the other hand, looked upwards. In their study of the Bible (i.e. the Old Testament) the Ashkenazim preferred a homiletical and literal approach; the Sephardim tended to be allegorical in their interpretations of the Bible and the Talmud. But as far as the central beliefs of Judaism were concerned, there was little, if any, difference between the Sephardim and the Ashkenazim.

In an attempt to formulate a series of cardinal beliefs in Judaism, the twelfth century Jewish philosopher Moses Maimonides listed thirteen Articles of Faith. These called for belief (1) in the existence of God; (2) in His Unity; (3) in His incorporeality; (4) in the eternity of God; (5) that worship is due to Him alone; (6) in prophecy; (7) that Moses was the greatest of all prophets; (8) that the Torah (the written and oral law) was revealed to Moses on Sinai; (9) that the Torah is immutable; (10) that God is omniscient; (11) in reward and punishment in the after life; (12) in the coming of the Messiah; (13) in the resurrection of the dead. While these articles were included in the Jewish prayer book, they were by no means considered to constitute a creed.

The Jews in the Caribbean would have believed in much the same body of faith as that outlined by Maimonides. In this regard, their beliefs would not have been different from those held by their co-religionists throughout the centuries. From earliest times, the Jews believed themselves to have had both a lofty and unique vision of God and a unique relationship with that God whom they named Yahweh. Their religion evolved slowly over hundreds of years as their prophets and wise men interpreted their historical experiences in the light of that ancient vision of God. The religion of the Jews (or Israelites) was closely related to Palestine, the land of their abode, which they saw as the Promised Land in that it was given by way of promise by God to Abraham, the father of the race. Their understanding of social justice, righteousness and mercy was related to the ownership and usage of land as well as the use of the produce of the land. The invasion of their land by surrounding nations was seen as the judgement of their God upon them for having infringed His holy laws. Deliverance from those enemies was viewed as the intervention of Yahweh in history to bring about their salvation. This interpretation of historical events was given by prophets such as Isaiah, Jeremiah, Ezekiel, Amos and Hosea.

Although the 'children of Israel' felt themselves to be God's chosen people, they believed that eventually God would honour a covenant made with Noah by communicating His saving truth to all nations. In this connection, the Jews were to play a crucial role. The knowledge of the God of love, justice, truth and mercy was to be communicated to the Gentiles (i.e. the nations) by the descendants of Abraham who were required to live in a manner that was in keeping with those attributes of God. The Torah (Law) was given to the Israelites as a guide to holy living. It was given through the medium of Moses, the greatest prophet of all times, not long after the Israelites had been miraculously delivered from bondage in Egypt.

In addition to the Torah, the Jews had the Talmud (Teaching) for their guidance. This consisted of two parts: the Mishna and the Gemara. The Mishna was supposed to be the revelation of Yahweh that was whispered into the ear of Moses. Originally, this revelation was not written down as the Pentateuch was, but was transmitted in an unbroken line through men such as Joshua and the elders, Hillel and Shammai. After the destruction of Judaea by Hadrian, the Mishna was reduced to writing. But even the Mishna (which was meant to elaborate on the Torah) had to be reinterpreted to meet the specific needs of the Jewish people at specific periods in their history. This 'contextualisation' of the Mishna was to occupy the rabbis of Galilee and Babylonia for some two and a half centuries. The result of this rabbinic deliberation was the compilation of the Gemara (Completion). While the Torah consisted of five books, the Mishna and the Gemara (i.e. the Talmud) occupied five hundred and twenty-three. Talmudic study was to become the preoccupation of the Ashkenazim of Cracow and Lublin in Poland before the atrocities of Chmielnicki in 1648 and 1649 forced the Jews to leave that country. Even so, they took their love of Talmudic studies with them wherever they went in

Europe. Because of this, the Talmud was to wield an important influence on European Judaism.

During the seventeenth century, two other movements influenced European Judaism. One was the Kabbala or Jewish mysticism; the other was a philosophical scepticism which arose against both Talmudic sophistry and Kabbalistic excesses. The reaction was led by Uriel de Costa (1590-1647), Rabbi Leo of Modena and Joseph Delmedigo. Baruch Spinoza (1632-1677), represented another kind of reaction against Judaism. Spinoza was a member of the Sephardic congregation of Amsterdam. Trained in Jewish law and philosophy and in Latin and physics, Spinoza found it difficult to live within the framework of Jewish orthodoxy of his times. Reacting against the dualistic philosophy of René Descartes who had, in his teaching, separated God from the world of rational man, Spinoza advanced the theory of the unity of God and man, mind and matter. According to the monism of the Jewish philosopher, things were not really things, but one or another of different 'modes' by which the Thing (i.e. Deity) was expressed. Neither Christians nor Jews found Spinoza's philosophy acceptable. A renaissance within European Judaism in the eighteenth century, led by Moses Mendelssohn and Naphtali Wessely, helped Judaism to survive the scepticism of the previous century.

Ever since the destruction of the Temple of Jerusalem in A.D. 70, Jewish worship had come to be centred in the synagogue which was known variously as the House of Prayer, the House of Study, and the House of Assembly. The destruction of the Temple also meant that the priest, whose function was associated with the Temple, had to give way to the rabbi or teacher and interpreter of Torah and Talmud. No formal administrative, judicial or disciplinary hierarchy developed in Judaism. Every rabbi was free to ordain suitable disciples to succeed him. Such ordinations were recognised by all Jewry; no rabbi was allowed to infringe on the area of jurisdiction of a duly ordained fellow rabbi. At the time of the establishment of Judaism in the Caribbean, however, the Hakhan (Chief Rabbi) of Bevis Marks was regarded as the highest court of appeal for the Sephardim.

The influence of Bevis Marks on Judaism in the Caribbean cannot be underestimated. The Jewish congregations of Jamaica, Barbados, Curaçao, St. Eustatius and St. Thomas maintained close contacts with the London synagogue. Even after Ashkenazim in Jamaica joined with Sephardim to form the United

Congregation of Israel in 1883, the Jamaican synagogue continued its relationship with Bevis Marks. As late as 1924, Bevis Marks accepted the responsibility for the Jewish cemetery in Nevis. Three years later, when the community in Barbados went out of existence, the London congregation was appointed its heir and executor.

The synagogue of Nevis was to go the way of that of Barbados; but that of Jamaica, like that of Curaçao, was to remain a centre of Judaism in the Caribbean. Jews in Jamaica and Curaçao came to positions of prominence and influence in these islands. As early as 1849, eight of the forty-seven members of the Jamaican House of Assembly were Jews. On September 26 that year, the Jewish members of the Assembly managed to have the House adjourn its sitting in order that they might observe *Yom Kippur* (the Day of Atonement) — such was the growing influence of Judaism on that important body in Jamaica.

We have dealt in some detail on the beliefs to which the non-Hispanic Europeans in the Caribbean subscribed and which they brought with them to the area. These Europeans, with the exception of the members of the Society of the French and Catholics, did not attempt in a deliberate way to communicate their beliefs either to the indigenous peoples whom they encountered in the Caribbean or to the African slaves who would be brought to work on the sugar plantations in most of the colonies, or in the salt-pans in Bonaire.

The Dutch Reformed and Lutheran Churches in Guiana served as chaplaincies to the Dutch settlers in that colony; so too, did the Church of England to the English settlers in the British colonies and the synagogue to Jewish communities in the Caribbean. Those were the days when it was widely felt by Europeans that the blessings of Christendom were properly the heritage of Europeans and that to extend the gospel to non-Europeans was to barbarise it. Judaism of the Caribbean Diaspora was not interested in proselytisation among African slaves. The impact therefore of these religions on the Amerindians and the African slaves was, at best, negligible.

The Society of Friends was much too small and too little wide-spread a group to have any significant influence on the African slaves, despite the goodwill of the Friends to the slaves. French Catholicism, as will be seen, was to have a significant impact on the blacks, particularly in St. Domingue.

Notes and References

1. A.P. Newton, *The European Nations in the West Indies*, p. 126.
2. Quoted in Owen Chadwick, *The Reformation*, p. 159.
3. J.H. Elliot, *Europe Divided, 1559-1598*, p. 39.
4. *Romans* 1:17.
5. T.M. Lindsay, *A History of the Reformation*, ii, p. 131.
6. G.R. Elton, *Reformation Europe, 1517-1559*, p. 214.
7. H.G.G. Herklots, *These Denominations*, p. 29
8. *Ibid.*, p. 30
9. Paul Beatty, *A History of the Lutheran Church in Guyana*, pp. 3-4.
10. Martin Luther's Works (55 vols.) *Word and Sacrament I* ed. E.T. Bachman, Muhlenberg Press, Philadelphia, 1960, v. 35, p. 91.
11. John Calvin, *Institutes of the Christian Religion*, translated by Henry Beveridge, ii, p. 494.
12. *Ibid.*, p. 571
13. *Ibid*, p. 571.
14. Edgar Mittelholzer, *Kaywana Stock*, p. 5.
15. James Anderson, *A History of the Church of England in the Colonies and Foreign Dependencies of the British Empire*, ii, p. 194.
16. *Ibid.*, p. 190.
17. *Ibid*, p. 192.
18. Canon J.E. Reece and Canon C.G. Clark Hunt, eds. *Barbados Diocesan History*, p. 11.
19. J.B. Ellis, *The Diocese of Jamaica*, p. 33.
20. James Anderson, *op. cit.*, pp. 204-205.
21. *Ibid.*, p. 206.
22. Quoted in Newton, *op. cit.*, p. 216.
23. Ellis, *op. cit.*, p. 27.
24. Newton, *op. cit.*, p. 192.
25. Ellis, *op. cit.*, p. 30.
26. *Ibid.*, p. 35.
27. *Ibid.*, p. 33.
28. *Ibid.*, p. 62.
29. *Ibid.*, p. 64.
30. *Ibid.*, p. 31.
31. The term 'Anglican' came to be used of the Church of England in the nineteenth century. It has sometimes been used to distinguish the tradition that developed in the

Church from Puritanism.

32. Quoted in A. Caldecott, *The Church in the West Indies,* p. 44.
33. Quoted in L.J. Ragatz, *The Fall of the Planter Class in the British Caribbean,* 1763-1833, p. 19.
34. *Ibid,* p. 19.
35. F.J. Osborne and G. Johnston, *Coastlands and Islands,* p. 26
36. Quoted in H.G.C. Herklots, *P.O. CT.* p. 97
37. Edward Long, *The History of Jamaica,* p. 18.

CHAPTER IV

AFRICANS AND AFRICANISM IN THE CARIBBEAN

In 1517, Las Casas and a number of ecclesiastics presented a memorial to the King of Spain in which it was suggested that the development of Spanish-Indian communities in the New World might be encouraged. It was suggested, at the same time, that Negro slaves might be employed in place of Indian labour since the Negroes could better undertake the heavy work demanded by the Spanish settlers. Later, Las Casas deeply regretted the suggestion to which he had subscribed and declared that it was as unjust to enslave Negroes as it was to enslave Indians. But he has never been forgiven for having made that suggestion.

The enslavement of Africans by Europeans came about as a result of the development of contact between West Africa and Western Europe in the late fifteenth century. Soon after 1470, the Portuguese reached the Niger delta; by 1510 they were shipping more than three thousand five hundred African slaves annually to markets in the Cape Verde Islands, the Iberian peninsula, Madeira and the Canary Islands. It was soon realised that the value of the New World discovered by Columbus in 1492, lay in bullion and possibly in tropical agricultural products. The exploitation of both mine and field (so it was felt) needed an abundant labour force that was inured to tropical conditions. With the rapid depletion of the Indians, the Spaniards found such a labour force in African slaves. Their Iberian neighbours, the Portuguese, were ready suppliers to these slaves. African slaves were brought to the Caribbean as early as 1510 when they were put to work in the mines of Hispaniola. This was some seven years before the ecclesiastics presented their memorial to the Spanish throne. From 1517 onwards, however, slaves were brought in large numbers to the islands of Hispaniola. Cuba, Jamaica and Puerto Rico, and to the mainland. With the development of the sugar plantations in the New World, African slaves were brought in their hundreds of thousands to the Caribbean.

The sugar plantation first developed in Portuguese Brazil on the north-eastern coastal plains of that country. The labour force for the plantation was supplied partly by enslaved Indians and partly by slaves imported from coastal Africa to which the Portuguese had ready access. Such was the prosperity of coastal Brazil that by 1580 it was the most important source of sugar for Europe.

The Dutch, who from the early years of the seventeenth century were to dominate trade with the Spanish Empire in the Caribbean, were not unaware of the economic advantage of sugar. It was an advantage on which they were to capitalize heavily between 1630 and 1654. During that time, the Dutch West India Company gained control of a part of north-east Brazil. The period saw the rise to supremacy of the Dutch in naval warfare and their capture of the Portuguese slave trading forts on the Gold Coast, Arguin and Goree. The Dutch were not interested in developing sugar plantations for themselves in the Caribbean. They were interested in the trading aspects of the industry. They passed on to the English and French who had settled in St. Kitts, Barbados, Antigua, Martinique and Guadeloupe the expertise in sugar technology which they had learnt in Pernambuco. In addition, the Dutch supplied the islands with slaves from Africa and provided shipping for the transportation of sugar to European markets.

With the introduction of sugar into the Caribbean, the islands underwent a dramatic change. Between 1640 and 1655 they were transformed into sugar colonies. Small farms gave way to large plantations; tobacco was superseded by sugar; many small farmers and indentured labourers were ousted to make room for African slaves. When Jamaica was acquired by the English and St. Domingue by the French, they too became sugar colonies. The Dutch were excluded from trading with the English islands from 1651 and with the French islands from 1664. But the English began their own slave trade which lasted from 1651 to 1808 and which introduced an estimated 1,900,000 Africans into the Caribbean. The French trade in slaves lasted from 1664 to 1830, transporting some 1,650,000 Africans. Meanwhile, the Dutch brought another 900,000 to the Guianas, Curaçao, Aruba, Bon Aire and St. Eustatius.

The bulk of the African slaves were brought from Senegambia,

81

Sierra Leone, the Windward Coast, Gold Coast and the Bight of Benin. They belonged to several tribes and to several different language groups. Many of those that came from the Windward Coast and Sierra Leone were Mandingoes, while the Koromantyns came from the Gold Coast and the Papaws from Whydah on the Bight of Benin. In time, the descendants of the African slaves were to become the most numerous of the several ethnic groups that were to people the Caribbean. Every facet of Caribbean life, including that of religion, was affected by the presence of the African in the New World.

Richard Ligon, an early settler in Barbados, declared in 1647 that the Africans did not 'know' any religion.[1] This opinion was repeated by the Jamaican planter, Matthew 'Monk' Lewis, in 1817. Ligon and Lewis represented the general view of English planters that the African slaves did not hold to a system of beliefs that could be described as a religion. At best — so the planters felt — their beliefs amounted to nothing more than heathenish superstition. Not a few of them, perhaps, felt that the Africans were incapable of a religious sentiment since they seemed "void of genius and . . . almost incapable of making any progress in civility or science".[2]

The Africans, however, were religious. In fact, religion pervaded their lives. The religious beliefs held by the slaves were derived mainly from their homeland. But there were some slaves who had had contact with Islam. Some of the Mandingoes, for example, were Muslims. Bryan Edwards knew Mandingoes in Jamaica who practised circumcision, recited morning and evening prayers and fasted on Friday, the Islamic holy day. They were also literate in Arabic. The 'Jamaican' Mandingoes were not unlike those encountered by Mungo Park on the Niger river in the late 1790s. So religious were the Muslim Mandingoes encountered by Park that they felt that Europeans were "a race of Formidable but ignorant heathens".[3] Toby, a Hausa slave who was known to John Wray, a missionary to Guiana in the early nineteenth century, held a similarly low estimation of the religion of the whites in Guiana. Toby was a Muslim. Islam had penetrated West Africa from the north by way of the Sahara desert. The religion did not long survive the rigours of the Middle Passage and of the plantation system. The practice of the planters of separating tribesmen from one another and discouraging the assembling of slaves for any purpose whatsoever was not calculated to allow Islam to survive. Again, the small number of Muslims that came to the Caribbean lacked

82

the leadership of *imams* and the possession of the Qu'ran, the Muslim holy book. Then, too, plantation life did not lend itself for long to prayers at set times, worship on a set day, fasting at prescribed periods, or feasting on holidays that did not coincide with those observed by the plantocracy. The development of Islam in the Caribbean would have demanded mosques around which the religious life could centre, *imams* who could expound the Qu'ran and give guidance to holy living according to Qu'ranic prescriptions and, above all, freedom in which the Islamic community could shape its life according to the teachings of the mosque, the *imam* and the Qu'ran. The plantation which was geared exclusively to sugar production gave no scope for the development of Islam as the African village did.

Indigenous African religious ideas, however, did survive the difficulties of estate life. This testified to the vitality of those beliefs and to the reality of the Weltanschauung, the world picture, which those beliefs provided for the Africans in their homeland. In the Caribbean, however, African religious ideas were to undergo significant changes but they remained recognisably 'African' in structure. Two factors were mainly responsible for these changes. In the first place, African religious ideas were capable of modification in response to the new circumstances of estate life. Secondly, the practice of African religion was frowned upon by the estate authorities. This meant that the religion could only be practised clandestinely and irregularly. The result was that some aspects of African religious practices withered away.

After 1760, it became an offence punishable by death for slaves to practise *obeah* in Jamaica. That year, Koromantyn slaves on an estate in the parish of St. Mary broke out in insurrection. It was alleged that Tacky, the leader of the insurgents, had furnished the slaves with a magical preparation that was supposed to render them invulnerable to the weapons of the authorities. Inspired by the belief that they were immune to injury, the slaves created great havoc in St. Mary. The law passed by the Jamaican legislature was meant to prevent the practice of *obeah* since it was felt that that practice could inspire slaves to further revolts. Since any aspect of African religion was likely to be described as *obeah* by those who administered the law in Jamaica, it meant that the practice of that religion was now under official ban. That ban extended across the British Caribbean, since the other English islands followed Jamaica in legislating against *obeah*. In the French and Spanish colonies where the practice of African religion was not formally legislated against, the hostility of the plantocracy to any such observance was enough to force the slaves to refrain from practising their religion in public.

The policy of the plantocracy of separating African tribesmen from one another (as far as this was practicable) also affected the development of African religion in the Caribbean, since that religion has traditionally had a strong link with the tribe. While the slaves did not lack "religious" leadership, their leaders were not as well trained or as carefully chosen as the priests and priestesses who served the African villages and compounds. The process of creolisation by which the blacks began to adopt (however imperfectly) some of the habits of their European masters and to neglect some of their traditional practices had grave implications for the religion of their forefathers.

Given the massive difficulties which the practice of African religion faced in the Caribbean, it must surely be one of the most remarkable things in the region's history that so many aspects of that religion survived. One such aspect was the African belief in the existence of an almighty god. The people of West Africa from among whom the slaves were recruited knew this deity by several names. The Akan-speaking Ashanti, Fanti and Brong peoples knew him as 'Nyame or Nyankopon; the Yorubas of the lower Niger, central Dahomey and Togoland called him Oludumare or Olurun; the Ewe-speaking Fon of Abomey, Allada of Porto Novo, Ge of Togo and Ga of the Gold Coast called him Mawu. To the Igbos he was Chukwu.

The supreme being was believed to be the author and preserver of creation; he was almighty, omnipresent and omniscient. In addition, he was infinitely good. The fact that he was associated with the sky testified to the widely-held belief that he was transcendent. Many myths told how the supreme god withdrew from the physical company of men to live in or above the sky. In almost every case, women were responsible for the deity's withdrawal. In spite of his withdrawal, however, he continued to care for the welfare of his creation.

Not every tribe had priests, temples or rituals dedicated to the worship of the supreme god. It was felt that an almighty god who had the welfare of his people at heart did not need to be persuaded by sacrifices and prayers to act in the interest of that people. The Akan, however, worshipped 'Nyame or Nyankopon regularly. Nearly every Akan compound had its

84

Nyamedua or 'God tree' which served as an altar. Their sacrifices and offerings were made by priests dedicated to the life-long service of 'Nyame. A prayer which accompanied offerings, ran:

> Nyankopon Kwame, Twereduampon, Creator, who made the rain and made the sunshine, come with thy consort Asase Yaa and receive this offering and let peace come upon this house and all people. Long life to the Ashanti nation. May we never at any time suffer defeat.[4]

The bystanders responded to the prayer by the Ashanti equivalent of 'Amen' — *Mmo ne kasa.*

Bryan Edwards, the eighteenth century Jamaican historian, noted that the Koromantyns (i.e. the Ashantis) who were in Jamaica, believed in Accompong, the creator god of the heavens, although they did not sacrifice to him. They did however, offer libations to Assarci, the 'god' of earth. The historian's references must have been to Nyankopon and Asase Yaa. The latter was regarded among the Akan people as the *yere* (wife) of Nyankopon and the goddess of the earth. If there is any merit in the observations of the historian, we may conclude that the active worship of Nyankopon had begun by Edwards' time to succumb to the rigours of the Atlantic crossing and the baleful conditions of plantation life. The policy employed by the plantocracy by which slaves were recruited for the plantation, and the arrangement by which the Africans were housed on the estate, made it impossible for any identifiable Ashanti compound to emerge which could set up its Nyamedua in Nyankopan's honour. In any case, if by some happy chance such a compound did emerge, the initial hostility of the plantocracy and then the formal legislation against the practice of African religion forbade the performance of those rituals and ceremonies which were vital for the survival of the active worship of 'Nyame. In addition, the plantocracy would have regarded it as unthinkable that some men and women should be released from plantation labour in order that they might be devoted exclusively to the service of the African god. The active worship of Nyankopon ('Accompong') in the traditional Akan manner, therefore, was bound to lapse.

The belief in the existence of a supreme god however, survived. Both Richard Ligon and Matthew Lewis attested to the fact that the slaves recognised the existence of a supreme being who was associated with the sky or heaven. That god was known as 'God A'mity' (i.e. 'God Almighty'). While the slaves

85

did not accord him formal worship, they made frequent mention of his name in salutations such as: 'God bless you!', "God preserve you!". These salutations and ejaculations were strikingly like those employed by West Africans as short spontaneous prayers of invocation addressed to the supreme deity. These prayers included, "God pity me,", "God give (us) rain!", "God go with you!"

Except for the Ashanti Nyankopon that was known to the slaves in eighteenth century Jamaica, the African names for the supreme being did not survive the Atlantic crossing for any great length of time. These names (including Nyankopon eventually) gave way to 'God A'mity' (sometimes, 'Gara-mighty'). It was not so much that the slaves substituted the Almighty God of their 'Christian' masters for the supreme deity of their forefathers, it was more the case that they recognised in Almighty God (or more correctly God Almighty) the Mawu, Olurun and 'Nyame that they had always believed in. As African languages gave way to English and French in the Caribbean, so too did the African names for the supreme being. In English-speaking colonies the name God Almighty was used; in French-speaking colonies the deity was known as *Le Bon Dieu*.

The Yorubas of West Africa, who paid little formal homage to Oludumare, lavished their worship on divinities such as Obatala, Ogun, Shango and Ifa, the *orish-nla* (gods) of the sky, iron or war, thunder and divination, respectively. The Akan worshipped a number of similar *abosom* (lesser gods) whom they regarded as sons of 'Nyame. The Ewe too, had their *vodu* (gods/spirits) whom they worshipped with due ceremony. These included Sakpata, So or Xevioso and Legba. Sakpata was the earth-smallpox divinity, So the thunder-god, and Legba the messenger of Mawu. At Abomey, even Mawu was regarded as one of the vodu. The deity was believed to be female and was worshipped in conjunction with her partner, Lisa. In this case, the supreme being was the 'universal' Mawu or Nana Bulu-ku. But generally, the vodu were regarded by the Ewe as Manu-vi (sons of Mawu).

The orish-nla, vodu and abosom were regarded as functionaries or ministers of the supreme being, who was the absolute controller of the universe. They were all derived from the supreme being. While the supreme being was transcendent, universal and somewhat removed from the human situation, his 'sons' functioned in the local situation and presided, as it were,

86

over the operations of earth, sky, thunder, sun, water, agriculture and so on. In time, it came to be felt that the divinities were the channels through which men should approach the supreme being.

The worship of the divinities was directed by trained and duly accredited priests and priestesses at village or compound shrines and temples. An Ewe priest (vodu-no) normally served a novitiate of about three years. Akan priests (akomfo) also served a long novitiate during which they were expected to live with instructors and to take the vow of chastity. During the period of his novitiate, a neophyte was expected to become increasingly responsive to the influence of the deity (Akan: obosom)[5] whom he was to serve eventually as a priest. Sometimes the village chief or the most senior person in the village functioned in a priestly role. This happened on those occasions when the chief or village elder approached the ancestral spirits on behalf of the village or tribe.

An important part of the worship service devoted to the 'lesser' gods consisted of an elaborate ceremonial dance in which priests, priestesses and devotees of the gods danced until some of the worshippers became 'possessed' by the gods. The dance was done to the rhythm of drums. The gods who made their appearance at the dance were greeted with a litany of praise and with gifts in the form of sacrifices or libations. Sometimes the priests interpreting the mood of the gods spoke words of counsel and warning to the assembly of worshippers.

Despite the attitude of the plantocracy to African religious practices in the Caribbean and the formal legislation against such practices, the worship of the African divinities survived. In Guyana, "komfo' (i.e. akomfo) dancing with its emphasis on spirit possession has had a long tradition. In Trinidad, the worship of Shango, Ogun, Eshu and other recognisably African 'spirits' survived. In St. Domingue, slaves worshipped Damballa, Legba, Shango and other gods of identifiably Dahomean origin. In both Trinidad and St. Domingue (Haiti), the worship of African divinities was to combine with that of Roman Catholic saints. Meanwhile, it was noted by Bryan Edwards that the Koromantyns (i.e. Ashantis) in eighteenth century Jamaica worshipped Assarci (Asase Yaa). The Bush Negroes of Surinam worshipped gods whom they associated with the woods and the rivers in the manner of their African forefathers. The *kele* ceremony as well as the *katumba* dance which survived in St.

Lucia undoubtedly had its origin in the worship of African divinities. In the French islands in the eighteenth century, the belief in the 'water mother' existed, as it did in the Dutch colony of Surinam. In fact, this belief in the spirit of the rivers and streams was known in the British islands as well. It was no doubt derived from the West African belief that rivers and streams were the wives of such divinities as Tano (Ashanti) and Shango (Yoruba). In Spanish Cuba of the second half of the nineteenth century, the Lucumi Negroes (i.e. those from Nigeria and the Gulf of Guinea) worshipped the recognisably Yoruba gods, Obatala, Chango (Shango), Eleggua (Legba) and Oggun (Ogun). Without doubt, the worship of these spirits went back to an earlier period in Cuba's history.

Some features of Lucumi worship resembled those of the Akan worship of the obosom. In Akan worship, a brass pan was usually regarded as the localized dwelling place of the obosom. On solemn occasions, the pan was filled with medicinal herbs and various sacred objects. The god was summoned to take up his residence in the pan by the sounding of bells and by a ceremonial dance in which priests, priestesses and worshippers participated. Offerings and prayers were then made to the god. Esteban Montejo, who was once a slave in Cuba, described the worship service of the Lucumi as it was practised in the nineteenth century in that island, thus:

> A *nganga,* or large pot, was placed in the centre of the patio. The powers were inside the pot . . . People started drumming and singing. They took offerings to the pot and asked for health for themselves and their brothers and peace among themselves.[6]

The actual belief in the African divinities together with their worship underwent significant changes in the Caribbean. In the first place, the more localized gods (i.e. those who were associated with local West African rivers, streams or animals) did not survive the Middle Passage. Such divinities included Togo, the god of the Agbomi lagoon of that name, Elo, the crocodile god of the Dahomeans, and Oya, the goddess of the Niger. This elimination of local gods (in these cases brought about by the transportation of blacks to the Caribbean) was a process that had in fact already begun among some West African peoples. Among the Ewe, for example, the tendency was for people to believe in a god who presided over rivers rather than in several local gods or goddesses each presiding over one local river. A second change that took place in the Caribbean was that the divinities of different tribes became grouped together as slaves of different tribal backgrounds were made to live and work together on the same plantation. This merging of the gods, so to speak, was facilitated by the fact that while many of the tribal divinities differed in names they shared almost identical attributes and functions. Thus, the Ewe Xevioso was, for all practical purposes, identical with Shango of the Yorubas. Generally, the name of the god of the dominant tribal group survived. Thus, in Northern Haiti, the Igbo, Congo and Arada names for many West African divinities gave way to Yoruba names.

In time, many of the names of the African divinities would survive mainly in the syncretistic Afro-Christian cults – the Cuban *santeria,* the Haitian *vodu* and the Trinidadian *shango,* which we shall discuss later. Otherwise, blacks would speak only of African spirits or powers without identifying them by African names. Sometimes they were known by local names. In Surinam, for example, the Bush Negroes called the god of the woods Bambo, and that of waters, Boembe. Sasabonsam, an evil spirit, and Nyankopon Kweku, the cruel and malevolent counterpart of Nyankopon Kwame, came to be identified in the English islands as the Devil, in the Spanish islands as El Diablo and in the French islands as Le Diable. Sasabonsam and Nyankopon Kweku were both Akan spirits.

A significant change came over the role of the priest. This is best illustrated by contrasting the Akan *okomfo* (priest) with the *obayifo* (wizard). In West Africa, the priest mediated between the tribe and its gods. His role was a social one and the worship services at which he officiated were public affairs. One of his functions was to challenge and condemn the operations of the obayifo. The obayifo (from whose name the work obeah is derived) was regarded as a disciple of Sasabonsam. Possessed of supernatural powers, this functionary used his gifts to injure or kill people, usually for a price. The obayifo worked clandestinely at nights. He was regarded as evil, and his functions were regarded as disruptive of the welfare of the tribe or village. People guarded themselves against the machinations of the obayifo by wearing *suman* (amulets or charms) which were often provided by the okomfo. (plural, *akomfo)* Sometimes, the aid of a *bonsam komfo* (witch doctor) was enlisted to unearth the obayifo and to render his work ineffective.

The general disfavour with which the plantocracy in the Caribbean regarded slave religious practices, and the official ban

89

that was put on those practices in some territories, forced the okomfo to perform his office clandestinely in much the same way that the obayifo did in West Africa. That office was now performed on behalf of an amalgam of blacks that cut across tribal groupings. While intercession with the spirits for the prosperity of the slaves was not neglected, many an okomfo found that the welfare of his charges demanded that he sought to injure the whites who were responsible for keeping the slaves in bondage and for punishing them when they were recalcitrant. Many of the attempts to poison planters and over-seers might well have been inspired by the okomfo. Violent resistance to the plantocracy was led by men who were akomfo. These included Cuffy, the slave who led a revolt in Guyana in 1763, Tacky who inspired the 1760 rebellion in Jamaica, and Boukman, who triggered the St. Domingue slave revolt in 1790. While such men were regarded by the whites as obeah-men (i.e. obayifo), in fact, they were not. Like Joe of Dagerad, Guyana, who was known to the missionary, John Wray, they were opposed to the practice of obeah. Their inspiration and power were derived from the 'good' spirits of African belief; they functioned in the interest of the slave community of which they were a part. The Caribbean obayifo, on the other hand, wrought harm to slaves on behalf of clients for fees; or, sometimes, to avenge himself on those who crossed him. The source of the obayifo's power was the recognisably evil Sasabonsam.

The distinction between the priest and the obeah-man was not clear to the whites in the Caribbean; it was not always clear even to the blacks. People sometimes resorted to the same person for cures for illnesses as well as to seek help in avenging themselves on other people, or to discover and punish adulterers or thieves. At other times, they obtained charms and amulets from him with which to ward off evil spirits. It is quite possible that the confusion was compounded by the fact that unscru-pulous priests doubled as obeah-men. Whether functioning as priest or sorcerer, they were invariably African by birth and not creole. That is to say, they were born in Africa and not in the Caribbean.

Both the okomfo and the obayifo wielded considerable influence over the blacks. Sometimes, the influence of the obayifo was strong enough to bring about death. 'Monk' Lewis has told the story of a Negro gaoler who was told by Plata, a condemned rebel who was also an obeah-man, that he would

90

die before long. The gaoler fell ill and neither medicine nor a voyage to America could cure him. Within twelve months he had withered away and died. How was this phenomenon to be explained? To the African slave the answer was simple. It was caused by the power of obeah.

Caribbean obeah derived its rationale from two strands of African belief and practice: that which was related to witchcraft, and that which was connected with magic. Witchcraft, in turn, involved a theory of causation that was concerned with the explanation of misfortune or evil. To the African mind, every evil occurrence demanded two explanations: How did it occur? And why did it occur? The "how" could be answered by commonsense, empirical observation. Thus, it could be shown that a man died because he was bitten by a snake. But that did not explain why that particular man was bitten at a particular place, at a certain time, and with such disastrous results. Could it be the will of 'Nyame, the results of the machinations of Sasabonsam or the action of the ancestral spirits? Since 'Nyame and the ancestral spirits were normally well-disposed to people, a likely explanation was that Sasabonsam was responsible for the tragedy. In that case, it was felt that the immediate cause of death would most likely be the work of Sasabonsam's agent — the obayifo or sorcerer.

The sorcerer's art included the ability to use rites, spells and substances related to his craft to harm people. The confidence which he, his clients, and his victims had in his skill, was derived from their belief in magic. This brings us to the second strand of African belief which gave Caribbean obeah its rationale — magic.

Magic has had a tradition that is perhaps as old as the history of mankind itself. It is related to one of the ways in which people have viewed the universe and, particularly, the agent or author responsible for its creation. When the power-behind-creation has been recognized as a divine, personal being, the approach to him has generally been one of supplication, communion, communication and fellowship. This approach has been regarded as necessary if people were to cope adequately with the creator's world. This was the approach of the akomfo, the voduno, and of those people who waited on the abosom or orish-nla in glad worship. On the other hand, when the power-behind-creation has been conceived or either as an impersonal, elemental force, or as spirits that are susceptible to the control of man, the approach to the force or to the spirits has been one of *awe-ful,* but confident mastery on the part of those equipped with the technique of manipulating and utilising the force or the spirits to serve some desired end. The obayifo was supposed to possess that esoteric knowledge which qualified him to control and utilise the spirits, or, at least, some of the spirits that presided over men's lives. Those who availed themselves of the obayifo's craft believed in his ability to persuade or cajole the spirits to do his bidding by the correct technique and the correct application of some esoteric ritual. Much more important, his victims shared that belief; this, more than anything else, was responsible for their undoing.

The obeah-man in the Caribbean often used poison to hurt those who did not believe in his power. In particular, attempts were made to poison overseers. With those slaves who believed in his ability, the obeah-man used the power of suggestion. His magic was believed to operate on three major principles: similarity, contiguity and unusualness. The principle of similarity was based on the belief that there was a similarity between an act that was performed and the result that was to be achieved. Thus, if the effigy of the victim was sprinkled with "guinea" pepper, the victim himself was expected to burn with a fever that was like the heat of pepper. To put it another way: When a person suffered from an unusually hot fever, he was likely to blame the fever on the obeah that he believed someone had placed on him by sprinkling pepper on his effigy.

The principle of contiguity was based on the belief that things which were in contact with each other at one time would continue to interact although the contact was broken. The continued interaction could be induced by the 'spell' of the obeah-man. Thus, if the victim's foot-print was lacerated with a poisoned knife, it was believed that the foot which had made the print would itself become poisoned. Similarly, if some of the victim's hair could be obtained on the obeah-man's instructions and burned by him, the victim might contract a fever in the head.

Magic which was believed to operate on the principle of unusualness was often employed to prevent something from happening. Thus, if Quashee wanted to prevent Quasheba from leaving him for another man, he might, at the direction of the obeah-man, go through a ritual in which he stood on his head, spat in the palms of his hands and dribbled at the corners of his mouth. Meanwhile, an incantation would be made to the effect that until Quashee's rival did the same thing, Quasheba would not prefer him to her mate.

Both the priest and the obeah-man used herbs and plants which were believed to have medicinal or magical qualities – the one to heal and the other to hurt. The whangra was one such plant. Thus, Pickle, one of Monk Lewis' slaves, made out that the root of the whangra was used to obeah him. West Africans believed that plants with curative or magical qualities came from the gods in much the same way that the special gift to bring about healing came to some people from the gods. This belief was brought to the Caribbean. Esteban Montejo articulated it when he remarked that all medicines came from herbs, that the whole of nature was full of cures for illnesses, and that practically any plant had curative powers. But healing was not brought about simply by the use of herbs or plants. Such use was accompanied by gestures and incantations designed to invoke the favour of the gods.

The belief that healing was the work of the divine order was the corollary of that other belief that human disorder or sickness was brought about by the operations of the spirit world. In addition to the use of herbs and medicinal plants, the healer (who was not always a priest) sometimes used exorcism. At other times, he advised the use of *suman* (amulets) to counteract and nullify the work of malignant spirits that were creating disorder in a person. This put the healers (Ashanti: *suman-kwafo)* into the category of 'spiritual' men. Other such men were the okomfo and the bonsam komfo (witch doctor). There was a tendency in the Caribbean for the suman-kwafo to be confused with the obeah-man – much to the chagrin of the former.

As widespread in the Caribbean as the belief in the efficacy of obeah, was the belief in the continuing existence of people who died. This belief was West African in origin. The departed were supposed to exist in the spirit realm and to have great interest in the welfare of their living relatives. Because they could affect the lives of their relations for good or for ill, it was imperative that those relations keep the ancestral spirits in good humour. That was done by venerating those spirits. It is debatable whether veneration shaded over into worship. In any case, the ancestors could not be neglected. Thus, when the Igbo of Nigeria went through their morning ritual they made their invocation: "Chuku (Deity), come and eat kola-nut; Ala (Earth Goddess), come and eat kola-nut; Ndiche (Ancestors), come and eat kola-nut."[7]

This respect for the ancestral spirits travelled with the slaves to the West Indies. It must have been a deeply traumatic experience for the Africans to be separated from those things with which the ancestral spirits were associated in Africa. However, they survived the religious and psychological crises imposed by that forced separation, and, in a short time, practices associated with the veneration of the dead began to appear in the West Indies. One such practice was that of burying the dead with due ceremony and in fine style. It was not unusual for the body of the deceased to be dressed in the finest clothing for disposal by burial, and for the funeral to be followed by a celebration. On the anniversary of the funeral, the relatives assembled around the grave (which was usually near the slave compound) and were led in prayers by the oldest male. Sacrifices were offered to the divinities and feasting followed at which the ancestral spirits were believed to be present. Libations (often in the form of rum) were offered to the dead whenever the blacks had cause for celebration. Before a grave was dug in a burial ground, libations of rum were poured on the ground which was considered the dwelling-place of the ancestral spirits. In this way, the spirits were persuaded to allow a new grave to be dug in their preserve, and, more important, to allow a new person to be admitted into their company.

Strictly speaking, the spirits venerated in the Caribbean were those of older members of families who had died there. The tribal ancestors who, in Africa, were invoked to send rain and to make the hunt successful, were usually quite closely identified with tribal lands. They were believed to be back home in Africa. Meanwhile, on occasions of birth, sickness or death, the family ancestral spirits were invoked to bless or to help as the occasion warranted. The practice whereby slaves were sold or transferred from estate to estate made it difficult for many slaves to keep track of their relatives or to remember where their parents and other relations were buried. In spite of these difficulties however, the practice of the veneration of the dead — the 'old people' — survived.

Closely related to the belief in the continuing existence of the deceased was the belief that a man was indwelt by a number of spirits or personalities. In Ewe thought, one such personality was the *luwo* (Akan: *kra*) a pre-existent spirit which might well have indwelt a long series of men. The belief was that the luwo entered a new-born human body shortly after leaving the body of a person who died. In fact, it was because the luwo or kra left the body of that person that he was said to have died. While it was without a body, the luwo existed as a *noli* (i.e. house-less spirit) and, for a while, lingered about the grave in which its one-time 'house' was buried. If the person whom it once indwelt was good, and if he died by natural causes and was properly buried, the luwo might be reborn in a new-born child. Otherwise, it might wander about as a homeless noli doing good or evil accord to its disposition. It might possess animals or be used for evil purposes by sorcerers. Meanwhile, the man's other personality or 'soul', the *shraman* (Akan), continued its existence in the world of the ancestral spirits. A burial with due ceremony was calculated to speed him on his way to the place of the ancestors while a ceremonial 'second burial' was helpful to confer on him the status of an ancestor.

Rites and ceremonies which surrounded birth and death on the plantation indicated that notions of the multiple nature of man's personality were actively held by the slaves. For example, the naming of a new-born baby was delayed until it could be ascertained whether or not an ancestral kra was incarnated in the baby. If it was the case that an ancestor was incarnated in the child, then the child was given the name of that ancestor. Once the quickening in the womb took place, care was exercised by the pregnant woman to ensure that the possible reincarnation of the kra was not jeopardised. Sexual intercourse was discouraged. It was at this stage that the male often had recourse to another woman. One of 'Monk' Lewis' slaves, Cubina's wife, objected to being christened while she was pregnant; she did not know what change christening might bring about in the unborn child. Perhaps she feared for the safe reincarnation of some kra or another.

Slaves pooled their meagre resources in order to secure a decent burial for their dead. This was to ensure both the reincarnation of the kra and the proper dismissal of the shraman or the 'shadow' personality to the place of the ancestral spirits. Other funeral ceremonies were sometimes held on the ninth night after death, and, at other times, on the fortieth night when the shraman (literally: guardian of the family) was believed to attain the status of an ancestor.

'African' birth and funeral rites survived in the Caribbean long after many blacks could explain the rationale behind the rites. This happened in spite of the fragmented nature of the black family which was brought about by the conditions of slavery. An indication of the cruelty and oppressiveness of those conditions is the fact that sometimes women aborted their pregnancies or smothered their babies rather than have their children born and grow up to be slaves. Given the general belief in the possible reincarnation of the ancestral kra in the new-born baby, such abortion or smothering could only have been inspired by a horror greater than the fear of offending the ancestors and consigning the kra or luwo to an existence of aimless wandering.

Ancestral spirits were generally believed to be well-disposed to the living. Not well-disposed to the living were those spirits that were associated with trees (particularly, the silk-cotton tree) rivers, streams and rocks. These nameless spirits were the ghost-spirits of those people who had died tragically – during pregnancy, by drowning or by hanging. They were capable of entering birds, animals and snakes in order to harm people. The paraphernalia used by obeah-men: feathers, beaks of birds, dogs' teeth, alligators' teeth, indicated that the obeah-man used these spirits to hurt people. In Jamaica, the spirits were known as duppies; elsewhere in the Caribbean, they were called zombies or jumbies.

Another evil 'spirit' was called the 'ol' higue' in Guyana, *sukuyan* in Trinidad, and old hag or witch elsewhere. This 'person' was believed to have the capacity to change his (or her) form, fly through the air either as a bird or as a ball of fire, and suck the blood of his victims. This belief, too, had its origin in West Africa. There it was felt that a particularly evil wizard could deliberately exude his spirit from the body. This spirit then went out and attacked the kra of those persons who had left their bodies during sleep. (The kra had this particular penchant. In fact, dreams were held to be but the noctural adventures of the kra). Strictly speaking, the attack of the wizard or witch was an attack of spirit upon spirit, but the bodies of the victims wasted away as a result. In the Caribbean, the belief was that was 'ol' higue' actually sucked the blood of its victims. Maybe African beliefs combined with European notions of the vampire to produce this creole form of belief.

From the African religious view-point, life was a drama in which the processes of life were involved in a perpetual conflict with those of death. On the side of life were the divinities, the okomfo or vodu-no, the suman kwafo, the bonsam komfo, those plants with medicinal and curative powers, useful animals and minerals, the faithful mate, the family and the tribe. Allied on the side of death and destruction were the evil counterparts of the divinities like Sasabonsam and Nyankopon Kweku, the wandering spirits of people who had lived wickedly or died tragically, the spirits that belonged to the *aiye* (Yoruba) – the concentration of the power of evil in the world, the obayifo, plants with harmful qualities, and animals and minerals that could destroy life.

As a sign of his affirmation of life, a man was initiated into the society of those who made common cause against fragmentation, dissolution and death – the family and the tribe. At initiation, he accepted the divinities of his people and the tutelage and guidance of his people's spiritual leaders. He regulated his life in such a way that his actions would further the welfare of his family and tribe, or, at least, not threaten the welfare of those groups. When he met the obligations imposed upon him by the relationships in which he lived, he was adjudged to be good. The funeral rites and post-obituary ceremonies which attended his decease and on which his continuing life depended, indicated, both by the number of people that attended them and the degree of elaboration with which they were performed, the kind of esteem in which he was held.

In the Caribbean, the conditions under which the slaves lived must have made it difficult for them to affirm life. Indeed, the fact that some of them committed suicide, and that some mothers terminated their pregnancy or the life of many an infant, indicates that that affirmation was not readily made by some of the blacks. Many of them, nevertheless, did affirm life. That affirmation sometimes took the form of active and passive resistance to the authority of the plantocracy. Passive resistance involved the use of cunning at which the slaves became adroit masters. It is no accident that Anancy, the spider, the hero of Akan folk-tales who was notorious for his guile and craft, became the most enduring of African figures in Caribbean folk wisdom. The planters themselves were aware that the inspiration to such resistance (or from the standpoint of the slave, to the affirmation of life) was the religion of the blacks. In the British colonies, planter-dominated governments legislated against African religious practices. But the inability of the plantocracy to police the barracks and the cane-piece effectively, and the inability of the overseers, the result of apathy or fear, to curb the religious practices of the slaves, robbed the legislation of the power to put an end to slave religion, although that legislation did affect the development of African religious thought and practices in the Caribbean.

The affirmation of life, too, did lead the slaves to entertain hope for a change in their predicament. Those who did not seek to realise that hope by resistance, learned, nevertheless, to bear their plight with fortitude. Whatever the shortcomings of that kind of hope, it was responsible for preventing the blacks from yielding to despair and to personal and communal dissolution. In the quest for life, the slaves demonstrated a great capacity to adjust to their circumstances in order to cope with those circumstances. Thus, when the family unit was fragmented by the sale of husband-father or wife-mother, the slaves developed the institution of the Nanny, the grand-mother. This maternal and matriarchal figure not only provided waifs with training, home, and care, but, like Montejo's Ma Lucia, passed on to her charges the traditions and usages of her people as she remembered them. The Nanny's contribution to the preservation of 'African' religious ideas and practices in the Caribbean cannot be over-estimated, particularly since she sometimes functioned as akomfo and suman kwafo as well.

The Nanny's role in the preservation and transmission of these religious ideas considerably enhanced her status and influence on the Caribbean 'African' family. Henceforth, her mark would be left indelibly on the psychological and structural make-up of the family.

When tribal loyalties became meaningless in the context of the plantation, slaves arranged themselves in other groupings. Thus, in Cuba, they identified themselves as either Congolese or Lucumi. The criterion for distinguishing people came to be geographical rather than tribal origin. The same was also true of those slaves in Haiti who described themselves as Aradas whatever their tribal origins in the Gold or Slave coasts of West Africa. Voluntary 'secret' societies also made their appearance in the Caribbean. In Cuba, they were known as naniñgos. Membership in the group was regarded as important for a man's affirmation of his self-hood. The mutual recognition of many persons that they belonged together, amounted to a holy connivance for the affirmation of life of a wholesome quality, in opposition to the forces of *aiye*. In this way, the 'nation' (as the Aradas, Congolese, Lucumi and nañingos described their group) was essentially a religious group. And the worship ceremony of the 'nation' was a drama in which the life and death struggle of everyday life was symbolically enacted with the gods, the ancestral spirits, priests, men and women being the many participants. From the worship-drama, the human participants derived both the strength and the inspiration to continue the struggle in their day-to-day life with the malignant spirits and the obayifo, fortified with the knowledge that the gods as well as the groups were involved with them in this cosmic enterprise.

Meanwhile, at the level of the group, the development of traits of behaviour which were regarded as inimical to the integrity of the group, was strongly discouraged. Anti-group behaviour evoked severe reprimand in the form of those aphorisms which have come down to us as 'old people parables'. The aphorisms derived their force from a subtle combination of biting sarcasm, wit and irony. The thrust of the saying was usually to discourage a particular line of behaviour. Thus, a man who began to preen himself on his own importance and to fancy himself a cut above his peers might be reminded that: *"When cocobeh man han' tan' good 'e want fo' shake guvnah han'."* That is to say, in translation and exposition: When a leprous man thinks that his condition is improved to the point where he can now barely open his hand, he straightway aspires to be on such familiar terms with the governor as to shake hands with him. The heavy sarcasm of the statement itself was made all the more biting by the tone and subtle inflections of speech which the speaker normally used in order to ridicule his offending neighbour into desisting from a line of behaviour that went against the interest of the group. A precocious young man who questioned the authority of this elders might have his pretensions slapped with the rebuke that: *"Monkey tink him seed big; him na know ah goady 'e gat".* That is to say: The young fellow who thinks that he has attained maturity because he fancies that his testicles are fully formed does not know that the large size of his testicles is caused by an unnatural distension (caused by the strain of heavy manual labour) of those organs. In so far as many of these wisdom-sayings of the ancients were calculated to maintain the integrity of the group, and in so far as the group (family, 'nation', etc.) was important for the affirmation of life against death and dissolution, the wisdom-sayings were religious in nature.

In Chapter 7, we shall see how African ideas and beliefs influenced and shaped in a most profound way Caribbean people's perceptions and practice of Christianity, as they came under the impact of Catholic and Protestant missionary efforts.

Sometimes, the syncretism which resulted is very obvious; at other times, it is subtle enough to escape ready notice. But it is not too much to say that the most orthodox practice of Christianity in the Caribbean by blacks is affected by a spirit that is identifiably African. Not a few people who hold to orthodox Christian beliefs resort, in times of crisis particularly, to practices such as consulting the obeah man, for example, without too many qualms of conscience.

If African religious ideas as they evolved in the Caribbean did not lead to an open and joyous celebration of life generally, those ideas helped to sustain people in the struggle for survival under the harsh and oppressive conditions of life in slave and plantation society. 'African' religious practices became part of a people's survival mechanism — perhaps the most important part. The bliss of a better future was experienced in anticipation, as it were, in the ecstasy of the dance and other rituals involved in worship; but religious practices, generally, had to do with the anxiety to survive without too much trauma the crises of life.

Thus, 'African' religious ideas and practices shaped the perspective from which Caribbean people would perceive and receive the message of Christianity. In time, the pietism of Protestant Christianity with its other-worldly emphasis, and Catholicism with its marked preference to be non-engaging as far as society was concerned, would reinforce this perspective and would themselves be affected by it. In practical terms, this would mean that in pre-emancipation times Christianity would be an important agent of social control. In post-emancipation times, it would become an important criterion for social mobility.

Notes and References

1. R. Ligon, *A true and exact History of the Island of Barbados*, p. 47.
2. Long, *op. cit.*, ii, p. 353.
3. S. Gwynn, *Mungo Park and the Quest for the Niger*, p. 139.
4. *African Ideas of God*, ed. Edwin W. Smith, p. 253.
5. *Obosom* (god) is the singular of *abosom* (gods).
6. Esteban Montejo, *The Autobiography of a Runaway Slave*, p. 26.
7. E. Bolaji Idowu, *African Traditional Religion*, p. 183.

CHAPTER V

EVANGELICALISM IN THE CARIBBEAN TO 1838

The year 1732 saw the first evangelical missionaries in the Caribbean. These men, Leonard Dober and David Nitschmann, were missionaries of the Unitas Fratrum who were sent to the Danish island of St. Thomas by Count Nicholas Ludwig von Zindendorf, an influential Moravian pietist. In 1731, the Count met the Negro slave, Anthony Ulrich, in Copenhagen, and became interested in the evangelisation of Negro slaves in the West Indies.

Hitherto, the christianisation of the slaves had been undertaken in some measure in the Spanish and French islands by Catholic priests and missionaries. But in the Dutch, Danish and British colonies, apart from sporadic ventures by Quakers, no attempt was made to evangelise the blacks. Protestantism did not quite know whether non-Europeans were of theological significance. A Barbadian priest had unsuccessfully advocated the evangelisation of blacks as early as 1678. He had argued:

> In Acts VIII we read the Holy Spirit of God was no less than thrice particularly concerned and acting for the salvation of the Ethiopian treasurer, a condescension so amazing and so rare that few, either men or nations can boast of the like. And since God, who knoweth all hearts, bare him witness, and put no difference between him and other Gentiles, but purified his heart by faith, why tempt we God by detaining them in bondage to hell, no less than to ourselves, for when Christ died he redeemed them from hence.

The 1696 Jamaican slave code had stipulated that all masters and mistresses who owned or employed slaves were to endeavour as much as possible to instruct their slaves in the principles of the Christian religion, to facilitate their conversion and to do their utmost to fit them for baptism. But the stipulation was honoured only in the breach. In fact, to ensure that it would hardly ever be observed, the Jamaican Assembly a decade later set the fee for the baptism of a slave at a rate that was prohibitively high.

Earlier, the notion had prevailed in the British islands that the laws of England by which the colonies were governed forbade the enslavement of a Christian. Therefore, to make a slave a Christian was tantamount to emancipating him – an undertaking which was not in the interest of the plantocracy. Whatever the basis and influence of the notion, the fact is that in the understanding of English law as related to slaves, the slave was a kind of property. With the Spaniards, the slave was a person though of inferior status. As a person he could be christianised. But with the English the slave was merchandise. When he was bought by a planter, he became that planter's property. He was both chattel and real property. As chattels, slaves could be sold for debts; they could also be disposed of in accordance with the laws of inheritance as those laws related to real estate. People who regarded slaves merely as property in fact as well as by law were not likely to show an interest in christianising them, except, perhaps, if that process were to enhance the quality of the property. Edward Long, for one, was not unaware of the possible value of Christianity in this connection. He remarked:

> My observations have tended to confirm me in the opinion, that our Creole Blacks . . . may, with a very moderate instruction in the Christian rules, be kept in good order, without the whip.[2]

But Long would have been violently opposed to the baptism and admission of blacks into the Church of England, since this would have been tantamount to bestowing upon them the status and privileges of British citizenship. Long and the people whose views he represented would have thought this a foolhardy if not a dangerous thing since, as British citizens, the slaves would have been dissatisfied with their condition enough to seek to change it even if that entailed violence. It was with contemptuous amazement that Long noted that when a slave fled from English Jamaica to Spanish Cuba, he was admitted into the "bosom of holy mother-church, and straight becomes a *bueno catholico,* and a Spanish subject,"³ though he was still a slave.

British planters advanced several reasons for not evangelising the slaves. It was said that the number of clergymen was too small to minister to blacks and that the church buildings were too limited in space to accommodate them at worship. There were those who felt that the intellectual level of the blacks was too low for them to follow the most elementary sermon, and that to preach to them would have barbarised the purity of the gospel. There were those who felt that the Africans were not quite human. Edward Long, no doubt reflecting the attitude of his class, wrote:

> Ludicrous as the opinion may seem, I do not think that an oran-outang husband would be any dishonour to an Hottentot female; for what are these Hottentots? They are, say the most credible writers, a people certainly very stupid, and very brutal.⁴

The plantocracy, if not members of the Anglican clergy, might well have asked, how could such people appreciate the gospel?

It was only on the Codrington property in Barbados that an attempt of sorts was made to christianise slaves. Whatever the initial success of the Codrington experiment, the attempt was one of the earliest in the history of Protestantism to christianise non-Europeans. The Codrington property consisted of three sugar plantations which Christopher Codrington III bequeathed to the Society for the Propagation of the Gospel in 1710. The bequest was made with the stipulation that at least three hundred Negroes would be kept on the estates at all times. The bequest also made provision for the establishment of a college where "Physick and chyrurgery as well as divinity"⁵ would be studied and practised. The Society welcomed the Codrington bequest as a means of promoting the christianization of slaves in Barbados. The Society hoped that the Codrington property would serve as a model Christian plantation which would demonstrate that the plantocracy had no cause to fear the preaching of agents of the Society. The fears of the planters would be allayed when it was demonstrated that:

> The Christian slaves would be more docile and more diligent than the heathen Negro. Christianity would leave the established order of West Indian society undisturbed. The Christian slave would look for his reward in heaven, and his life would 'abide in the same calling wherein he was called.⁶

However, the Society's programme for the conversion of the blacks hardly got off the ground. Down to the time that the

103

first evangelicals came to the Caribbean, little, if anything, had been accomplished. Not least among the difficulties which frustrated the Society's plans was the opposition of Governor Lowther (1717-1720) to those plans. The Governor made out that the work of the Society was calculated to subvert the social order of the island. In 1726, the Rev. Arthur Holt became rector of the St. John's parish where the Codrington property was located. Holt was convinced of the spiritual equality of Negroes with whites: Under his supervision, it seemed that the evangelisation of the blacks might proceed apace. That same year, Thomas Wilkie was appointed by the Society to supervise its programme at Codrington. His approach to the task of making Christians of the blacks was to teach them (in English) the Creed, the Lord's Prayer and the Ten Commandments in order to prepare them for baptism. Wilkie insisted that the slaves observe the Sabbath and that they be monogamous. Opposition from the manager of the Codrington property, particularly when Wilkie undertook to teach the slaves to read and write, and the puzzlement of the blacks when presented with theological points of man's transgression and salvation made Wilkie's job very difficult. He died in 1733, having accomplished very little at Codrington.

If the incentive to christianise the blacks in Barbados was the Christopher Codrington bequest, other incentives to Christian missions among non-European people were beginning to emerge among Protestants in Europe. The discoveries of Captain James Cook (1728-79), the English navigator and explorer, forced European Protestantism to re-examine its belief that the *Corpus Christianus* (i.e. Christianised Europe and Christian Europeans settled in America and Australia) was identical with the world that concerned God. Hitherto, the notion had prevailed that Jesus' command to preach the gospel to all nations had been given to the apostles only, and that, in fact, the command had been fulfilled. Only a few individuals thought differently. These included John Campanius, a Swedish Lutheran, John Eliot who evangelised among American Indians in the 1640s, and Heinrich Plutzau and Bartholomew Ziegenbalg, again of the Danish-Halle Mission, who went to South India in 1706. A.W. Francke, the colleague and successor of the great German pietist, Philipp Spener, was largely responsible for Danish-Halle mission to India.

The belief that autochthonous peoples or aborigines were within the saving purposes of God did not come easily to the

Protestant churches. But, however slowly, the belief did come. When William Carey, an English Baptist minister, became aware of the existence of the South Sea islanders who had been discovered by Captain Cook, he pointed out to an assembly of his fellow ministers that it was clearly beyond St. Paul's missionary duty to evangelise the people of Otaheite since he would not have known about them. Consequently, Jesus' command must have been also given to ministers of the gospel who were the successors of the apostles. Carey was told harshly: "Young man, sit down: When God pleases to convert the heathen, He will do it without your aid and mine." Among those who thought Carey arrogant might well have been Primitive Baptists who held that since God had chosen those who were to be saved, missionary activity was superfluous. Nevertheless, under the compulsion that he had a missionary duty to fulfil, Carey founded a missionary society and, on the subscriptions raised, decided to go to India to evangelise the natives. It was probably on the advice of the Rev. Thomas Scott, who was later to become the first secretary of the Church Missionary Society, that Carey chose to go to India. But neither the Christian gentlemen who comprised the London-based East India Company (which, at that time, practically ruled India) nor their counterparts in the British Parliament shared Carey's missiological views or his convictions. The former refused him a licence to preach in India, and a member of Parliament declared that far from wishing to see one hundred thousand Indian natives converted, he would lament such a circumstance as the most serious and fatal disaster that could happen.

While the Protestant churches were pondering the theological significance of non-European peoples, the pietism of Count Nicholas von Zindendorf and the Herrnhut community, together with the Count's knowledge of the work of the Danish-Halle Mission and the Moravian tradition for missionary enterprise, had impelled von Zindendorf to send missionaries to distant lands. If the tradition for missionary zeal was brought to the Herrnhut community by the refugees from Moravia, the community learned its pietism mainly from Zindendorf, who, in turn, was deeply influenced by his godfather and teacher, Philipp Jakob Spener, the founder of German and European pietism. Describing the Count (and his belief), Gerald Cragg wrote:

> "He was a man of ardently emotional temperament. He believed that the mark of true Christianity is a simple and childlike faith:

it is enough to believe in the power of the blood of Jesus and trust wholly in the merits of the Lamb of God. In vivid, almost erotic, imagery he described the relation of the soul to Christ. Love, as a warm glow, lay at the heart of his religious life."[7]

In 1721, von Zindendorf bought the Berthelsdorf estate in Oberlausitz in Saxony. The following year, a small group of German-speaking Moravians[8] headed by Christian David settled on the estate with the Count's permission and the Herrnhut community was born. It became a centre of pietism and a refuge for exiles fleeing religious persecutions elsewhere. Von Zindendorf quickly became the dominant figure at Herrnhut. The understanding, at first, was that the members of the community would belong to the national (Lutheran) Church of Saxony and that its members would attend the church at Berthelsdorf where they would receive the sacrament of Holy Communion. In addition, however, the members of the community (who could not forget their old Unitas Fratrum links) held their own morning and evening prayers. Zindendorf himself prepared a special liturgy for these daily services. A daily watchword was read; this consisted of a Biblical text or a few lines from a hymn. Love-feasts and feet-washing which were believed to have been practised by the early church became part of the practice of the Herrnhut community.

What developed at Herrnhut was bound to spread. The faith of the Brethren was not only infectious; people who felt that they had had a pentecostal experience were resolved to share that experience with others. As a result of the activity of these itinerants, a network of societies modelled on Herrnhut developed in Protestant Germany and other European countries. This kind of religious renewal was labelled *Diaspora*. The impulse that gave rise to the diaspora in Europe inevitably sparked evangelistic activity in foreign lands. Once the movement had gone beyond Christian Europe to places where significant numbers of non-Christians lived, the Brethren felt that they could not aim merely at the renewal of religion among these peoples. The renewal of true piety among Christians had been their aim in christianised Europe. Among the 'heathen' they had to aim at the conversion of these peoples to Christianity. With nominal Christians, renewal was all that was needed; with non-Christians, conversion was vital.

The missionary enterprise of the Brethren spread to the West Indies (1732), Georgia in North America (1735), Surinam (1735), and Berbice in Guyana (1738). In the Caribbean, the missionary enterprise was bound to result in the establishment of a church organisation for those who were converted to the Christian religion, given the conditions of plantation society. In Europe, the 'renewed' people (i.e. the 'pietists' could be contained within the existing churches. In the Caribbean, however, it was hardly likely that the church of the planter-class would welcome into its midst the Negro converts of Brethren missionary enterprise. In fact, not a few planters were of the opinion that salvation (and by that token, Christianity) was for whites only. This, together with the antipathy with which the whites generally regarded the blacks, made it inevitable that a separate church organisation should be set up for the Negro converts.

The establishment of the Moravian 'church' in the Caribbean was almost contemporaneous with the establishment of the Brethren in Europe as the Renewed Moravian Church. Perhaps the need for a centralised authority to direct the work of missionaries was not without its influence on the formation of the renewed Unitas Fratrum as an independent episcopal church. The dating of this event varies. A convenient date is May, 1735. At that time, the episcopacy of the Bohemian Brethren was transferred to the Moravian community at Herrnhut. One of the first men of the Herrnhut community to be consecrated bishop was the Moravian David Nitschmann, who went to St. Thomas in 1732 as a missionary. With him went Leonard Dober, a Lutheran. Nitschmann was consecrated by Daniel Ernst Jablonski who held the ancient Moravian episcopal office, and who, at that time, served as a Reformed court chaplain at Berlin. In May, 1737, Zindendorf also was consecrated bishop after he had made an unsuccessful attempt to become a Lutheran pastor. The previous year, he had been accused of heresy and schism and expelled from Saxony. Zindendorf, however, was opposed to the idea that the Unitas Fratrum should become an independent religious community.

The missionary theology of the Herrnhutters was simple. The conversion of the world had to await the prior conversion of the Jews — an event that was not too far in the future. The wars of the sixteenth and seventeenth centuries were seen as signs that preceded the end-time. The fact that some of the Brethren could speak in tongues and attest to visions brought to mind the sayings of the prophet Joel that in the last days these things would happen. Meanwhile, Jesus Christ, through the Holy Spirit, had long been at work in the whole world seeking disciples for his Church. The purpose of missions, as far as Zindendorf was concerned, was to find those disciples and through the preaching of the gospel 'mark them' with the seal of the Lamb (i.e. Christ) which they, in fact, had already had. Zindendorf was not interested in the founding of churches. As he put it, "We are looking for 'first fruits' among the nations; and when we shall have found two to four of them, we shall dedicate them to the Saviour that he may act through them as he wills."

As we have seen above, the conditions of plantation society were to force the Brethren to establish churches for their converts. Evangelism became much more than a means by which those already marked by Christ were 'uncovered', so to speak. It became the means by which the 'heathen' might be saved from the wrath to come. It was for the purpose of rescuing souls from the unbelief that was tantamount to damnation that Dober and Nitschmann were resolved that for the sake of the Saviour they would gladly become slaves if by that means they could save be it no more than a single soul.

Zindendorf's *Catechism for the Heathen* gave directions as to the strategy that was to be used for teaching slaves the rudiments of the Christian religion. It also indicated what were considered to be the rudiments of that faith. It was to be assumed by missionaries that the heathen already knew about God. Since they did not know Christ, however, they were to be led to believe that God and Christ were the same person.

The catechism ran:

> Q: Who made men and women?
> A: The Lord God.
> Q: What do you call Him?
> A: Jesus Christ.
> Q: Do those words mean anything?
> A: Yes
> Q: What then?
> A: Jesus means Redeemer and Christ means King.
> Q: How did He obtain these names?
> A: That is a special story. [9]

The story of man's fall, the Incarnation and the Crucifixion was then recounted. Then the heathen was led to see how his salvation demanded that he should be baptised in the name of the Father, the Son and the Holy Ghost.

From about 1734, the preaching of Zindendorf became preoccupied with the theme of Christ's suffering. This theme
108

greatly influenced the preaching of missionaries. Emphasis was placed on the suffering of Christ. The details of the scourging, the crown of thorns, the crucifixion, the nail-prints and the wounded side, were dealt with at length as people were admonished to repose in the wounds of Jesus. Whatever the sentimentality of this kind of preaching, it was effective. It gained the Moravian missionary thrust thousands of converts in the Caribbean. But it was also responsible for entrenching at the very beginning a pious sentimentalism in the Christianity inculcated in the blacks in the Caribbean.

By 1790, the Moravians had established bases on the Danish islands of St. Thomas, St. John and St. Croix. Frederick Martin, who has been regarded as the real founder of evangelical Christianity in the Danish Caribbean, ran into opposition from Pastor John Borm of the Dutch Reformed Church which served the religious needs of the whites of those islands. Martin was accused of being grossly uneducated in theology, and of not being properly ordained since his ordination had not been confirmed by the king of Denmark. In St. Croix, there was, at first, opposition to the efforts of the evangelicals to instruct their converts in the tenets of the Christian faith and in the language of the missionaries. But by 1753, the planters of St. Croix were convinced that the christianised slave was much more useful than his 'heathen' counterpart. This led to a change in attitude to evangelical missionary activity on the part of some members of the plantocracy.

The Moravians had demonstrated (more unwittingly than wittingly) what the Society for the Propagation of the Gospel had hoped that the Codrington experiment would prove: that the Christian slave was more an asset than a liability on the sugar plantation. So well had they done this that their missionaries were actually invited by planters to go to Jamaica (1754), St. Kitts (1777) and Tobago (1790). Slaves in Antigua, who were said to be abnormally depraved, were by 1791, adjudged to be of a high moral standard primarily because they had come under the influence of the evangelical mission. Earlier, in 1749, an act had been passed by the British Parliament which allowed the Brethren to evangelise in the English colonies. This was done after Zindendorf had made representations to a parliamentary committee to the effect that the Old Bohemian (Hussite) Moravian Church had had the recognition of King Edward VI and King George I. In the late 1760s, Crommelin, the Governor of Surinam, besought the Brethren to undertake a mission among the Bush Negroes of that colony. The general feeling among the whites in Surinam was that without the gospel the Bush Negroes "would be a constant danger to the State."[10] In response to Crommelin's request, the Moravians began work among the Saramakkan (Bush) Negroes in 1765. A slave uprising in Berbice, in 1763, brought an end to the Moravian attempt to evangelise the Amerindians at Pilgerhut on the Wieronie river. That attempt had begun in 1738 when Moravian missionaries, prevented by the Dutch planters from christianising the black slaves, turned their attention to the Indians.

Converts recruited by the Moravian missionaries were grouped into 'bands' for Bible study and for instruction in their new religion. Helpers, who were recruited from among those slaves who had been Christians for some time, were sometimes appointed to superintend the bands. At first, the missionaries were expected to support themselves by their earnings from manual work. This proved very difficult. In the Danish islands, Frederick Martin bought a small plantation with money obtained from Herrnhut. He operated the plantation by slave labour. In Jamaica, when the New Carmel estate was given to the Moravians, they too operated it by slave labour. The mission-aries hoped to convert the plantations into self-supporting Moravian communities along the lines of Herrnhut. The success in this regard was only partial.

Methodist missionaries followed the Moravians into the Caribbean. Methodism in the region might well be dated from about 1760. That year, Nathaniel Gilbert a planter and the speaker of the Assembly of Antigua, returned from England where he and ten of his slaves had been baptised by John Wesley. The congregation started by Nathaniel was given new impetus by the arrival of John Baxter in Antigua in 1778. Five years later, the Methodist membership in Antigua stood around the two thousand mark. John Baxter, who was actually a wheel-wright by occupation, was eventually ordained by the American Conference. However, it was the Superintendent of that Con-ference, Dr. Thomas Coke, who was mainly responsible for the spread of Methodism in other parts of the Caribbean.

The Methodist movement itself arose out of the religious ferment that agitated England towards the end of the seven-teenth century and continued into the eighteenth. This ferment bred a number of religious societies which sprang up in London. Society members met for weekly prayers and discussion. They

Carib Indian women and children

Jordanite Elders

Jordanite women at worship

Muslims at Prayer

Alleluia (Akawaio) Indians dancing out their worship at a yam festival at Amakokopai

A Hindu wedding ceremony in progress

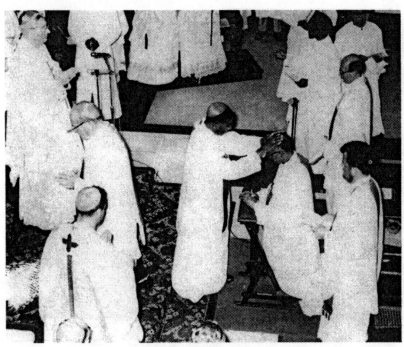

The consecration of a Roman Catholic bishop

Con-celebration at a Roman Catholic High Mass

St. Andrew's (Scots) Kirk, Guyana c. 1840

St. George's (Anglican) Cathedral, Guyana, c. 1840

Three Sephardic Jews

Interior of the Jewish synagogue, Kingston,

Revival table

Rastafarian drummers, Jamaica

A nineteenth century Hindu Temple dedicated to Shiva

attended the public religious exercises of the Church of England, but were also "careful withal to express due Christian charity, candour and moderation towards all such Dissenters as (were) of good conversation."[11] It was out of this ferment also that the Society for the Propagation of Christian Knowledge (1699) and the Society for the Propagation of the Gospel (1701) sprang. Early in the eighteenth century, evangelism became a prominent feature of this religious revival. Preachers such as Griffith Jones, a curate of the Church of England, Daniel Rowland and Howell Harris became convinced that Jesus Christ had died for them and that all their sins were laid on Him. Salvation through faith in Jesus Christ became the theme of their preaching.

John Wesley (1703-1791), the son of a rector in Lincolnshire, came under the influence of the revivalist movement. While at Oxford, he belonged to a 'Holy Club' of young men who imposed upon themselves a strict rule of life which included the practice of weekly communion. This strict rule earned for the Holy Club the nickname 'Methodists'. In 1735, Wesley, by then a priest of the Church of England, went on a missionary journey to Georgia in North America. On his return voyage, he came in contact with a party of Moravians who made a lasting impression on the priest. It was at a Methodist Society meeting at Aldersgate Street in London, in 1738, that he experienced what he felt to be his conversion. He felt relieved of the overwhelming sense of guilt for unpardoned sin with which he had been hitherto afflicted. From that time, he became an itinerant preacher with the dominant theme of his preaching being much in the vein of that of Jones, Rowland and Harris. Describing what happened on an occasion when he preached, Wesley wrote:

> "I preached at the Spen on Christ Jesus, our wisdom, righteousness, sanctification, and redemption: I have seldom seen an audience so greatly moved . . . Men, women and children wept and groaned, and trembled exceedingly; many could not contain themselves in these bounds; but cried with a loud and bitter cry."[12]

Those who responded to John Wesley's preaching were organised into a Connexion of Methodist Societies. The object of the Connexion was to fortify and supplement the work of the Established Church. Membership in a Methodist Society was open to those who were anxious "to flee from the wrath to come, to be saved from their sins." A Society was divided into classes of twelve which met for prayers, for the settlement of disputes, and for the study of the Bible. Membership tickets which later came to be called class tickets, were issued quarterly, usually on the payment of a fee of a shilling. Class leaders were appointed; Wesley was opposed to the election of these leaders on the ground that Methodists were "no republicans and never intend to be."[15] A class was further broken down into 'bands' according to sex and stage of spiritual development – a feature that was borrowed from the Moravians.

Itinerant preachers made rounds or circuits of a specified number of Societies preaching, teaching, and attending to matters of discipline. In time, the number of Societies covered by one such preacher was designated a circuit. From 1748, a quarterly meeting on the Quaker model was introduced to organise and discuss the affairs of the circuit. The first Methodist Conference was held in 1744. These developments notwithstanding, Methodism was still considered very much a part of the Church of England In fact, like all Anglicans living outside of Britain, the Methodists in America came under the jurisdiction of the Bishop of London.

The doctrines taught by John Wesley and embodied in the hymns of his brother Charles, combined the Reformed doctrine of justification by faith with the Anglican Arminian doctrine of grace. To this was added Wesley's teaching on sanctification. Methodist teaching ran: Man was in a state of sin as a consequence of Adam's fall. But he could be pardoned and his sins could be 'justified' by the grace of God. All that was necessary for his salvation was that he should believe that Jesus Christ died for his sins. The assurance of salvation came experientially. So far, Wesley was quite in keeping with the evangelical line of Martin Luther. But then he introduced the Arminian doctrine of grace. He held that God's grace was freely offered to *all* men; it was not restricted to a chosen few as John Calvin taught. Wesley held that once a man was justified, he was sanctified; that is, he was on the way to attaining Christian perfection. This peculiarly Methodist doctrine of sanctification was meant to awaken in Wesley's followers a deep desire for a state of God-like holiness, which was held to be realisable in this world. Methodism taught that this perfection was not attained by man's own powers, but that it was the work of the Holy Spirit. A man was not only sinless in the sanctified state; all his faculties were dedicated to God.

Wesleyans met for 'chapel' worship at five o'clock on

Sunday morning in order to avoid clashes with Anglican services. Wesley advised his followers to attend Church of England services at least every Lord's Day. In addition to these early morning services at which preaching was emphasised, the Methodists held 'watch-night' services. The first such service was held in London in 1742. As to the day when the watch-night service was held, Wesley wrote, "We commonly choose for the solemn service the Friday night nearest the full moon."[14] Such services began at 8.00 p.m. and lasted until after midnight. Thrice quarterly, the Methodists observed a love feast which followed a pattern set by the Moravians. The assembly feasted on cake and water while members related spiritual experiences which they might have had.

In spite of Wesley's insistence that the Methodists continue their relationship with the Anglican Church, a breach between the Methodist movement and Anglicanism was inevitable. This breach was complete in 1784 when the Methodist community in England was licensed as a person at law and, therefore, as an entity subject to the due process of law.

It was partly the spread of Methodism that brought about its eventual break with the Anglican church. When Methodist settlers in America found it difficult to obtain pastors, Wesley ordained several deacons and priests to serve societies in that land, much to the resentment of the hierarchy of the Church of England which was, at that time, preoccupied with the question of the orders of ministry in the church. It was felt that John Wesley had arrogated to himself the functions of a bishop. Dr. Thomas Coke, who had been appointed superintendent of the American Methodists, actually designated himself 'bishop.'

By 1824, Methodist bases (which were called Societies) had been established in St. Vincent, St. Kitts, Barbados, Dominica, Nevis, Tortola, Jamaica, the Bahamas, Anguilla, Haiti, Guyana and Trinidad. While the Moravians had no great difficulty in setting up missionary bases in the Caribbean, the Methodists, after a favourable start in Antigua, encountered problems in places such as St Vincent, Jamaica, St. Eustatius and Guyana. When Dr. Coke visited Jamaica in 1789, he preached on the text, "Ethiopia shall soon stretch out her hands unto God." He was rudely interrupted and mobbed by the whites in his congregation because of his favourable reference to the Negroes. The first Wesleyan missionary to Demerara (Guyana) went to that colony from Dominica. He arrived on September 30, 1805 and was interviewed by the Governor on October 2. When the Governor learned that the missionary was a Methodist and that he had come to the colony to teach the blacks the principles of the Christian faith he ordered him to leave by the next mail-boat. It was not until 1815 (i.e. after Guyana passed into the hands of the English) that the Methodists gained a foothold in Guyana.

The reasons for the hostility shown to the Methodist missionaries are discussed elsewhere in this chapter. But we may note here that this hostility was related to two factors: the activity in Britain of the Society for Effecting the Abolition of the Slave Trade, and the slave revolt in St. Domingue. The Society was founded in 1787 and the St. Domingue revolt erupted in 1791.

The Methodist missionaries recruited their converts primarily from among the free people of colour, free blacks and black slaves. As a general rule, very few whites joined the Methodist societies. In the Bahamas, however, where sugar plantations had not developed and where the Church of England had not been established, the Methodist movement attracted many white settlers. By the time Methodism took roots in the Bahamas (i.e. around 1800), the only Protestant religion that had reached the islands was the Baptist movement. The Baptists, who came from North America, worked among the black slaves and freedmen. Methodism became the religion of the whites. No doubt, the fact that Methodism was of English origin[15] and, for a good while, was regarded as very much a movement within the Church of England added to the attractiveness of the movement for the whites in the Bahamas.

Unlike the Moravians who campaigned mainly in rural areas, the Methodists, at first, tended to concentrate on the towns in much the same way that Wesleyan missionaries in England directed their efforts to the urban poor. This would account for that mission's recruitment of free people of colour and free blacks since these people tended to live mainly in and about the towns. While they were legally free, the free people of colour and the free blacks nevertheless suffered from political disenfranchisement and social ostracism from white society. This was particularly galling to the free people of colour. In terms of church membership, Methodism must have seemed to them the nearest alternative to the Church of England to which they would have liked to belong, but which they recognised as the church of the white folk.

Preaching was greatly emphasised whenever the Methodists met for worship. Preachers elaborated on the sins of their congregation, the punishment which such sins merited, and then proceeded to present Jesus Christ as the Saviour who had died to save people from the consequences of their sins. Failure to accept Jesus Christ as Saviour meant that unbelievers would have to reckon with him as dread judge. Commenting on the preaching of the Methodists, Matthew Lewis wrote:

> "These fellows harp upon sin, and the devil, and hell fire incessantly, and describe the Almighty and the Saviour as beings so terrible, that many of their proselytes cannot hear the name of Christ without shuddering."[16]

At first, Methodist congregations met for worship in private homes. Nathaniel Gilbert used his house in Antigua as a meeting place for his converts. Later, a house was procured in St. John's for that purpose. Because of the predominantly non-white composition of Methodist societies, it was unthinkable that these Christians would be accommodated in the Anglican churches in the several colonies. Thus, from the outset, Methodism in the Caribbean, unlike Methodism in England, was a movement that was recognisably separate and distinct from Anglicanism.

The year 1782 saw the establishment of the first Baptist base in Jamaica. A decade later, a Baptist missionary station was also established in New Providence, one of the Bahamas. In each case, the work was begun by a black American ex-slave. In the case of Jamaica, the man responsible for introducing the Baptist faith into the island was George Liele*; the pioneer of the Baptist movement in New Providence was Prince Williams. Before he was brought to Jamaica as the indentured servant of Colonel Kirkland, Liele had been the pastor of the Baptist churches at Brinton Land and Yamacrow in Georgia in America. It was his influence as a preacher that led to the formation of one of the first black congregations (Silver Bluff, South Carolina) in America in the 1770s. During the American War of Independence, Liele collaborated with the British. His fear of reprisals caused him to come to Jamaica in 1782. Incidentally, many white Loyalists also fled the United States. No sooner had Liele arrived in the island than he resumed his vocation as a preacher. He conducted his religious services at the Kingston Race course (now National Heroes Park) with such success that in seven years he had baptised about five hundred persons. By 1800, a second congregation was established in Kingston; this was in the care of Mr. Thomas Swingle, a member of Liele's church. By this time, Moses Baker, Liele's lieutenant, had gathered a congregation at Crooked Spring in St. James. It was Baker who suggested that the British Baptists might be invited to assist the Baptist cause in Jamaica. In 1814, in response to a number of appeals from Jamaica, John Rowe was sent out by the Baptist Missionary Society as the first English Baptist missionary to the island. Rowe was followed by Lee Compere and James Coultard. Two influential English missionaries to serve the Baptist church in Jamaica were James Mursell Phillippo and Thomas Burchell.

Prince Williams' early efforts were among the blacks who had settled in the area, in and about Nassau, which they had labelled 'Over the Hill' and which since 1821 had officially been designated Grant's Town. The black population of that area was greatly increased between 1776 and 1783 by the six thousand slaves whom Loyalists, fleeing from the American War of Independence, brought to the island. The presence of a number of Baptists among these slaves helped Williams' cause. Up to that time, the blacks in New Providence had been mainly the descendants of the slaves of those whites who had re-established a settlement in the island in 1666, after an earlier settlement had been demolished by the Spaniards.

The membership of the Baptist churches in both Jamaica and New Providence was predominantly black. Most of these blacks were slaves. The others would have been manumitted Negroes who earned their living as artisans and pedlars in the towns of Kingston and Montego Bay (Jamaica) and Nassau (New Providence). In Jamaica, a number of small peasant cultivators became members of the Baptist churches.

The responses of a candidate for baptism to a minister's interrogation give us an idea of what the blacks believed the Baptist faith was all about. The interrogation ran:

Minister:	Well, Thomas, do you know who Jesus Christ is?
Candidate:	Him de Son of God, Minister.
Minister:	What did Jesus Christ come into the world to do?
Candidate:	Him come to save poor sinners.
Minister:	Do you think he is able to save sinners?
Candidate:	Me know him able.
Minister:	How can you know that he is able to save them?
Candidate:	Because him make de world: and if him make de world, him able to do all tings: and minister

116

	no tell we often-time dis make him left him fader trone, and come into dis sinful world.
Minister:	What is necessary for us to know and feel before we can love and serve God as we ought?
Candidate:	We must know and feel truly dat me is great sinner – never do one ting good since me born – before me can sarve God in a right manner.

. . . .

Minister:	Do you think you have got a new heart?
Candidate:	Me hope so.
Minister:	What makes you think you have?
Candidate:	Because what me bin love before, me hate now; and what me hate before, me love now. Once me love to do de devil's work – blaspheme, carouse, and do all wicked tings: now me love precious Massa Jesus, who [s]pill him precious blood for me, poo[r] dyin' sinner.

. . . .

Minister:	What makes you wish to be baptised?
Candidate:	Because Jesus Christ, put under water, rise up again and we wish to pattern after him.
Minister:	Perhaps you think the water will wash away your sin?
Candidate:	No, no; water no wash away me sin: nothin' but precious Massa Jesus blood wash away me sin.

The candidate was further questioned by two or three members of the congregation into which he wished to be baptised. He responded as follows:

Question:	Who is the Holy Spirit, and what does the Holy Spirit do for you?
Answer:	The Holy Spirit is God too; and him change me sinful heart, make me fit for heaven.
Question:	Is there more than one God?
Answer:	No; three persons and one God.
Question:	Who are they?
Answer:	Father, Son, and Holy Ghost.[17]

The candidate indicated that if he died in his sin he would go to hell. If anyone should try to make him lose his temper and even to strike him, he would ask God to make him forgive his assailant. He would also ask God to change the heart of his assailant in order that he too might love God.

117

The Baptists in the Caribbean came into a tradition that had an interesting history. The claim has been made that the movement can be traced back to the Anabaptists, the radicals of the sixteenth-century European Reformation. Another claim has been made that the faith is a truly New Testamental one since the baptismal practice of the Baptists and their doctrines of the church and the sacraments are derived from the New Testament. Baptists hold the belief that the primitive (i.e. the New Testament) church practised the baptism of believing adults only, and that that church was organised along congregational lines. In addition, the church was not aligned to the state.

In about 1523, when the European Reformation was well under way, a group of priests and laymen in Zürich declared that believers should break away from the church there and form a community of believers or saints on earth. They were to elect their own pastor to guide them and to have nothing to do with the institutions of this world. In particular, they were to have nothing to do with the civil authority which was God's government for sinners. They would not bear arms, swear oaths, take part in government or carry out the duties of citizens. Among those who advocated this kind of religion were Conrad Grebel and the priest, George Blaurock. They advocated the rebaptism (dubbed anabaptism) of those believers who had been baptised as infants, charging that the practice of infant baptism was unscriptural and Satanic. The first rebaptisms were probably done in 1525. At Easter that year, a priest, Balthasar Hubmaier of Waldshut, had himself re-baptised; he then proceeded to rebaptise his entire congregation.

Persecution followed the act of Hubmaier. Anabaptists were imprisoned, exiled and drowned − the victims of unfounded alarms which caused the established order to panic. Hubmaier was imprisoned in 1527 and executed the following year. Not least among the reasons for the persecution of the Anabaptists was their denial of obedience to the civil authorities. Because of this known denial, rebaptism was regarded by many a state official as a declaration of treason. The persecution of the Anabaptists was a shameful episode in the history of European Christianity. It is true that some Anabaptists such as Jan Matthys and Jan Bockelson who tried to establish a theocracy at Münster, were given to excesses in violence and morals; but most of the adherents of the movement were pious, gentle people who believed fervently in much of what Luther, Calvin and Zwingli taught.

From Switzerland and Germany, the Anabaptist movement spread to the Netherlands where it came under the influence of Menno Simmons (1496-1561). In the Netherlands, the Anabaptists came to be known as Mennonites or *de Doopage-zinden*. From the Netherlands, the movement spread to England. The man responsible for the founding of the Baptist church in England was John Smyth (1554-1612) who identified infant baptism as the 'mark of the beast' in his book, *The Character of the Beast*. Smyth was uncompromising on the matter of church-state relationships. He declared:

> "The magistrate is not by virtue of his office to meddle with religion or matters of conscience, to force or compel men to this or that form of religion or doctrine."[18]

On Smyth's death, the leadership of the movement was assumed by Thomas Helwys (1550-1616) under whose guidance four congregations flourished in London.

Some English Baptists, following John Smyth, were Arminian in their theology. They believed that God's saving grace was available for mankind in general. They were dubbed General Baptists. The Particular Baptists, on the other hand, held to the Calvinist view of election. Prominent among them were Henry Jacob and John Lathrop, both of whom were eventually to migrate to North America. The first congregation of Particular Baptists met in Wapping in 1633; in 1641, they made baptism by immersion the rule of their church. In 1792, the Baptist Missionary Society was founded by William Carey. It was this Society that was responsible for sending missionaries such as Rowe, Phillippo and Burchell to Jamaica.

From England, the Baptist movement spread to North America almost with the first wave of English settlers. An important pioneer in the establishment of the Baptist faith in that part of the world was Roger Williams (1603-1683) who founded the colony of Providence in Rhode Island in 1636, after he was banished from Massachusetts. Williams was perhaps familiar with the opinions of the Mennonites and of Smyth and Helwys. He maintained that true churches could only be constituted of members who had experienced spiritual regeneration and who were baptised upon the profession of faith in Jesus Christ. Williams' church was made up of the men and women who had accompanied him from Massachusetts. Not only did that church practise the baptism of believers; it was also organised along independent or congregational lines.

In November, 1637, the First Baptist Church of Newport in

Boston was founded by John Clarke, a Baptist who had recently arrived from England. By the 1720s and 1730s, Baptist churches had been established in Virginia, North Carolina and Connecticut. The first black congregation was formed in Savannah, Georgia around 1788, although long before that time there were blacks in the towns and cities who were Baptists. It was from among these Christians that George Liesle and Prince Williams came to the Caribbean.

Congregationalism came to Guyana in 1808. That year, John Wray arrived in the colony in response to an invitation from Hermanus Hilbertus Post, the planter-owner of Le Resouvenir who had written the London Missionary Society requesting that a missionary be sent to instruct his slaves in the Christian faith. Earlier, the London Missionary Society (a Congregational body) had thought of sending missionaries to Jamaica. The Society was discouraged from doing so, however, by Dr. Coke, the Methodist missionary and superintendent of the Methodist church in Jamaica, who wrote to the directors of the Society indicating that the Methodist missionaries in the island were sufficient to man the 'openings' there.

Wray was to be followed by other missionaries to Guyana, the most notable among whom was the Rev. John Smith. These Congregationalists came to the colony with a single purpose: To save the heathen from "sinking into everlasting burnings" in the fires of hell to which unbelief consigned them. In this respect, the Congregationalists were no different from the Moravians, the Methodists and the Baptists. Wray's ministry was directed chiefly at the Negroes, although whites as well as free people of colour came to worship at Bethel Chapel, the centre of his missionary activities. The Congregational missionary preached to his hearers on Sundays and week-days, led them in singing from *Watts' Psalms and Hymns* and officiated at the sacraments of baptism and the Lord's Supper. In his preaching, Wray directed the attention of his congregation to the Lamb of God "who taketh away the sins of the world", and who is "the end of the law for righteousness unto all who believe" whether bond or free.

Congregationalism or Independency was born in England in about 1581 when some extreme Puritans broke away from the Established Church [i.e. the Church of England] and set up independent or separated congregations. The pioneers of the movement were Robert Browne and Henry Barrow. In 1582, Browne published his book, *A Book which showeth the Life and Manner of all true Christians; A Treatise of Reformation without tarrying for Anie,* in which he spelt out the central principle of Congregationalism, thus:

> "The Church planted or gathered is a company or number of Christians, which by a willing covenant made with their God, are under the government of God and Christ, and keep His laws in one holy communion, because God hath redeemed them into holiness and happiness for ever, from which they were fallen by sin of Adam."[19]

In their doctrine, Independents were Calvinists. It was in the manner of church order or organisation that they differed from Presbyterians. They repudiated the idea of an established church. Equally, they repudiated the hierarchical system of church government and emphasised the Reformation doctrine of the priesthood of all believers. Browne declared that every member of the church was made a king, a priest and a prophet under Christ to uphold and further the kingdom of God, and to break and destroy the kingdom of Antichrist and Satan. Each congregation elected its pastor, teachers and deacons. The pastor was ordained by representatives of the congregation by the laying on of hands. Each congregation was administratively independent although congregations often gave assistance to one another.

Before the English Civil War, (1642-1651), the Congregational movement made little progress in England. During the Commonwealth period, the Independents reached the height of their influence on church life in England. At that time, the Church of England was restructured along Congregationalist lines. But with the Restoration, Congregationalism fell into disfavour. It was not until 1689 that Independents were granted religious toleration along with other dissenters. The waning zeal of the Independents was quickened during the religious revival which sprang up in England towards the end of the seventeenth century and continued into the next century. It was as a result of this renewed zeal that the London Missionary Society was founded in 1795. The intention was that the Society should be interdenominational; but, in fact, it came to be a primarily Congregational concern.

In about 1814, a Scottish Presbyterian church, the Scots' Kirks, was established in Jamaica. It was regarded as an offshoot of the Church of Scotland. This was some 250 years after Scotland had adopted the *Confessio Scoticana,* and had, for all practical purposes, opted for Presbyterianism as the

121

recognised religion of the Scots, although the struggle against Catholicism was by no means over.

An earlier attempt in 1800 by the Scottish Missionary Society (founded in 1796) to conduct a mission in Jamaica had ended disastrously. Two of the three missionaries, the Rev. James Bethune and Mr. William Clarke, died shortly after their arrival in the island. In 1824, the Rev. George Blyth went to Hampden in St. James, Jamaica, at the invitation of two planters, Messrs. Archibald Sterling and William Stothert, to instruct their slaves in Christianity. Three years later, John Chamberlain arrived in Port Maria in St. Mary and in 1829, Hope Waddell began missionary activity at Mount Zion in St. James. The purpose of all three was to evangelise the blacks.

The Scots' Kirk in Kingston was meant to serve primarily as a chapel for Scotsmen in and around Kingston, although free people of colour were not excluded from church membership. Black slaves accompanied their masters and mistresses to services. An interesting side-light on the Scots' Kirk membership is provided by a letter written by the Baptist, James Coultard in August, 1817. It ran: "Many of the brown people are very excellent and respectable persons, though it is probable they that are most so will leave us when the Scotch Kirk is opened, for want of accommodation with us."[20] At that time, the Kirk was in the process of being erected. Although the letter suggests that the lack of accommodation in the Baptist church was the reason for the anticipated migration of the free people of colour to the Kirk, the matter of colour was undoubtedly another factor.

Like the other evangelicals that preceded them in the Caribbean, the Scottish Presbyterian missionaries were desirous of converting the Negroes by preaching Jesus Christ to them. The Rev. William Jameson, for example, was determined to bring before the minds of the Negroes the fact that they were "children of wrath", that through the love of God every believer in Jesus Christ, the Redeemer, was saved. Holiness in life was proof of salvation. Hitherto, the difficulty which Negroes had in believing and obeying Jesus Christ arose from the wickedness of their hearts — a condition which the Spirit of God alone could rectify. The theology of Jameson was uncompromisingly Calvinistic.

It can be safely assumed that the doctrines taught by the Scottish missionaries were Presbyterian in nature. But the congregations which developed in Jamaica as a result of the

122

Presbyterian missionary outreach were not organised along Presbyterian lines until after 1836. That year, ruling elders were elected and ordained for the first time in Jamaica. On February 10, 1836, the first local Presbytery was constituted in Montego Bay.

Meanwhile, a Presbyterian church had been founded in Stabroek, Guyana, in 1818. Strictly speaking, this church was neither the product of missionary enterprise nor was it interested in promoting missions among the blacks or free people of colour in Guyana. It was established by Scotsmen to serve their religious needs in much the same way that the English settlers in Demerara had built St. George's chapel to serve their needs. In this regard, the Presbyterian church in Stabroek (which was inevitably named St. Andrew's) was not unlike St. Andrew's Scots Kirk in Kingston, Jamaica, or the Presbyterian church in Bermuda which was established in the 1670s.

The site on which the church in Stabroek was established was originally donated by the government of Demerara to the Dutch Reformed Kerk for the purpose of erecting a place of worship. Work on such a building had in fact begun under the Predicant, the Rev. Gabriel Ryk, in 1811; but when Ryk died in 1812, the project was abandoned. The half-finished building was eventually bought by a committee representing the Scottish Presbyterian community in the colony, and, on September 27, 1818, the completed building was declared open for public worship. Ministers for the church were recruited from Scotland; the first minister was the Rev. Archibald Browne. Like the Dutch Reformed Kerk and the Church of England in Guyana, St. Andrew's Kirk was supported by public funds. From 1821 onwards, in true Presbyterian style, the affairs of the congregation came under the supervision of a Kirk Session. Although the Kirk catered primarily for Scotsmen and their immediate relatives, by 1821 a few descendants of slaves who were of good standing in the community had been admitted into the Kirk's membership.

A little more than a century had elapsed between the time that Dober and Nitschmann arrived in the Danish island of St. Thomas and the time that the first Presbytery was convened in Montego Bay. During that century, evangelicalism became established in the Caribbean from Surinam and Guyana in the south to the Bahamas in the north. That was an important century in the history of the Caribbean. The sugar industry in the British islands reached the peak of its development and then began its decline during the American War of Independence. The slaves in St. Domingue revolted in 1789 – an event that was not without its effects on the attitude of planters to missionaries in other islands. The British colonies were involved in such important issues as the abolition of the slave trade, amelioration, and the emancipation of slaves. These issues agitated public interest in Britain as much in the Caribbean.

One would expect that missionaries who had recognised the humanity of blacks enough to work for the salvation of their souls and whose work was primarily among slaves, would support the movements for abolition, amelioration and emancipation which so crucially affected the welfare of their converts. In fact, one looks in vain for a positive, uncompromising declaration on the part of the evangelical missionaries in the Caribbean against the institution of slavery. Whatever their personal views on slavery, the missionaries were hesitant to make those views public.

Zindendorf, who was responsible for sending Dober and Nitschmann to St. Thomas, did not see anything necessarily wrong with slavery. The Rev. Frederick Martin who was dubbed 'The Apostle to the Negroes' by Zindendorf and who was, in fact, the real founder of the Moravian movement in the Caribbean did not see anything wrong with the institution either. The Count advised the slave converts in St. Thomas on February 15, 1739:

> Be true to your husbands and wives, and obedient to your masters and *bombas*. The Lord has made all ranks – kings, masters, servants and slaves. God has punished the first negroes by making them slaves, and your conversion will make you free, not from the control of your masters, but simply from your wicked habits and thoughts, and all that makes you dissatisfied with your lot.[21]

The Moravian Church's acceptance of the *status quo*, its advocacy that slaves also accept it because it was of divine ordering, and its emphasis on industry on the part of slave children, were calculated to entrench slavery and thus provide the sugar industry with a reliable, highly manipulable and placid labour force. The fact that Moravian missionaries operated New Carmel (an estate in Jamaica of which they came into possession in about 1754) by the use of slave labour, demonstrated that they saw nothing incompatible between Christanity and slavery. Little wonder that Moravian missionaries were invited by planters to evangelise their Negro slaves.

The effectiveness of the teachings of the Unitas Fratrum in rendering slaves amenable to plantation life was demonstrated in Barbados on Easter Day, 1816. On that day, there was a slave revolt in Barbados. The Moravian missionaries were able to show that during the revolt not a single slave connected with the Moravian church was in any way involved in the disorders. What was more, the districts near Sharon, a base of Moravian operations, enjoyed a striking degree of immunity from disturbance — a fact to which Moravian evangelicals proudly drew the attention of planters. Further evidence of the effectiveness of Moravian teaching was given during the 1831 'Christmas' slave revolt in western Jamaica, instigated by Sam Sharpe, a slave and a Baptist deacon.

Moravian missionaries in Jamaica had consistently urged their converts to be loyal and obedient to their masters; and, according to J.E. Hutton, in 1831, "they had their legitimate reward."[22] At Fairfield, there was not a single sign of disorder; at New Eden, converts promised that much as they desired their freedom they would not use any illegal means to obtain it; at Fulneck, New Carmel and Mesopotamia not a single convert went on strike. It was in St. James, however, that Moravian converts displayed the 'finest' spirit. Speaking of the five 'native' helpers (presumably deacons or lay preachers), James Light, the missionary, declared that they "did their duty to their earthly masters."[23] Thus, at Williamsfield, the native helper, Robert Hall, defended his master's house so stoutly that his fellow blacks put a price on his head; at Tryall, the helper appointed a patrol to guard his master's property, and at Fairfield, the helper persuaded the slaves to be loyal to their master and not to revolt.

The notion that instruction in Christianity would make better slaves of the blacks made planters amenable to the idea that missionaries should be permitted to evangelise their slaves. Sometimes, the notion was ever advertised. Thus, *The American Baptist Magazine and Missionary Intelligencer* of January 7, 1818, carried a story which was meant to indicate the success with which Christian instruction "under divine blessing" might be attended. The story was related by a Mr. Marsh to an association in England. Marsh's friend was walking in his plantation when he saw some peas. A slave was standing nearby. Marsh's friend asked the slave why he did not take the peas, and the following ensued:

'They are not mine', answered the black.

'Oh, fellow', replied the master, in reference to the known propensity (to steal) of these people, 'Everything is yours that you can lay your hands on!'

'No massa', rejoined the slave, 'Negro who pray, no thieves!'

The planter was struck with astonishment. "What have I been about," exclaimed he, "not to let the missionaries come upon my estate?"[24] He immediately invited a missionary to evangelise his blacks.

Whenever planters suspected that the activities of a missionary were likely to lead to trouble, they could always investigate those activities. When John Lang, the Moravian missionary, was regarded as dangerous, his converts were interrogated regarding the teaching they had received from Lang. In this case the answers must have been very reassuring to the plantocracy. The questions and answers ran as follows:

> 'What sort of instruction do you receive?'
> 'We are taught to believe in God and Jesus Christ.'
> 'Well! what more?'
> 'We must not tell lies.'
> 'What more?'
> 'We must not steal from Massa'.
> 'What more?'
> 'We must not run away and rob Massa of his work'.
> 'What more?'
> 'We must not have two wives, for by-and-by they will get jealous and hurt one another, and Massa's work will fall back.'
> 'What more?'
> 'We must pray for buckra and everybody."[25]

In 1755, the Quakers came out in opposition to slavery. At this time, sugar was in its hey-day; the industry was bringing enormous profits to the countries involved in its production. One of the first written attacks on the slave trade was made by the Quaker, Anthony Benezet. John Wesley read Benezet's work and decided that slavery was a monstrous thing – albeit on grounds of natural justice rather than on religious or theological grounds. In 1774, he too attacked the institution. He wrote to Granville Sharpe deploring the traffic in slaves, and to William Wilberforce commending his 'glorious enterprise' against the trade. English humanitarians who came under the influence of philosophers such as Thomas Paine, John Locke and Jean Jacques Rousseau joined the attack against the slave trade as did the advocates of free trade. At about the same time that a

126

Christian writer under the pseudonym of Philalethes declared that slavery was inconsistent with the Christian religion, Adam Smith came out in condemnation of the institution in his *Wealth of Nations.* In 1787, the Society for Effecting the Abolition of the Slave Trade was formed.

As the campaign for the abolition of the slave trade mounted in Britain, the evangelical clergymen in the Caribbean, particularly the Methodists, came under the suspicion of the plantocracy. It was not unknown that Wesley was opposed to slavery. It was this suspicion that caused the governor of Demerara (Guyana) to order the Wesleyan missionary to leave that colony so speedily in 1805. Earlier (in 1791-93), because of this same suspicion, the Assembly of St. Vincent passed an Act forbidding missionaries to preach to slaves. Matthew Lumb, who disregarded the legislation was gaoled. Another missionary, Robert Gamble, was so badly beaten on the instigation of planters, that he died from the injuries which he received. The events which were taking place in St. Domingue at that time (1791-93) made the whites of the Caribbean islands fearful for their lives and safety. It was that fear that motivated the kind of legislation that was passed in St. Vincent.

It was also that fear that caused the whites among Dr. Coke's congregation in Kingston, Jamaica, to mob the missionary when in the course of his preaching, he referred favourably to the Negroes. The following year, 1790, the Methodist evening service was discontinued on the charge by the Grand Jury of Kingston that it was unsettling the "general peace and quiet of the inhabitants"[26] of Kingston. A nervous white community could not be too sure what would be the outcome of meetings where "wild extravagancies" were common, and where people gave vent to "indecent and unseemly noises, gesticulations, and behaviour."[27] It was better to be safe than sorry, hence the ban on the Methodist evening meetings. Methodist missionaries in Tortola in the British Virgin Islands came under suspicion when a slave revolt broke out in that island in 1799. An investigation by the Assembly proved the missionaries innocent of the charge that they were responsible for the rebellion. Nevertheless, the legislature thought it necessary to impose restrictions on religious meetings.

Meanwhile, events in Antigua demonstrated how little harm there was to plantation society in the religion preached by the missionaries. In 1795, in what was perhaps the first ecumenical venture between Methodists and Moravians on that island, those churches co-operated with the government of Antigua in raising a force of some one thousand volunteers from among their converts for the defence of Antigua against the designs of the French, led by Victor Hugues. Hitherto, the planter government had stuck to its policy of not arming Negroes nor recruiting them for the army lest they should consider themselves equal or superior to the whites. It was felt that "the moment the Negroes [should] lose their opinion of the superiority of white men, the authority of the white men [would] become precarious."[28] Another factor behind the policy was the very obvious one that an armed slave was potentially dangerous. In the crisis of 1795, however, the policy was waived. Black Christians were armed to defend the slave society of Antigua against possible invasion from the French who were fighting under the banner of 'Liberty! Equality! Fraternity!' The astonished Dr. Thomas Coke remarked:

> Nothing but the power of divine grace could induce the negroes to offer themselves for the defence of a country in which they were held as slaves and to protect their masters, many of whom, doubtless, had treated them with severity.[29]

The grace of God indeed. At precisely the same time, the blacks of St. Domingue, convinced that their *vodu* (spirits) made them immune to the musket fire and bayonetry of French planters and British soldiers, and convinced too that if they died in the cause of their freedom their spirits would find repose and reincarnation in Africa, fought with machetes, sticks, stones and their bare fists for that freedom.

Mounting panic caused the Jamaican Assembly to enact legislation in 1802 to prevent "preaching by persons not duly qualified by law." The reason behind the legislation was given thus:

> . . . there now exists in this Island an evil, which is daily increasing and threatens much danger to the peace and safety thereof, by reason of the preaching of ill-disposed, illiterate or ignorant enthusiasts to meetings of negroes or persons of colour, chiefly slaves, unlawfully assembled.[30]

Between the passing of the legislation and its disallowance by King George III, Baptist and Methodist missionaries were refused licences to preach; some were imprisoned for having preached without due authorisation to do so. According to Peter Duncan, not even the "ever-vigilant adversaries"[31] of the evangelical missionaries could prove that either the mission-

128

aries or their activities were subversive to the welfare of Jamaican society. But the authorities remained suspicious. To illustrate: When the Morant Bay chapel was re-opened in 1814, a ticket was found among the effects of a Negro woman. The Biblical text on the ticket declared: "The kingdom of heaven suffereth violence, and the violent taketh it by force." The ticket fell into the hands of the whites with astonishing results. Consternation reigned among them as they felt that the text was the watchword of a dark and sanguinary conspiracy. Even when a missionary showed that the ticket was identical to one issued to Methodists in England, the custos ordered the parochial militia to hold itself in readiness against possible revolt.

Evangelical missionaries were persecuted not because they actually advocated the abolition of the slave trade but because, as the counterparts of dissenters in England, they were suspected of being in sympathy with a cause advocated by some of their co-religionists there. The fact that blacks constituted the bulk of the membership of their chapels and meeting-houses lent weight to these suspicions. But the evangelical missionaries to a man observed the instructions given to them on their arrival in the colonies. According to those instructions, the missionaries were to pursue their sole business of promoting the moral and religious improvement of the slaves without interfering with the institution of slavery. Missionaries were not to pursue their activities without the permission of the planters or their representatives; nor were their times of service to infringe on the time the blacks were supposed to be at work. They were not to engage in disputes over civil matters or matters related to local politics either orally or by correspondence with persons in England or in the colonies. In the face of opposition, a meek and patient spirit and conduct was recommended.

The missionary theology of those days no doubt helped the evangelicals to promote their activities without questioning the propriety of the institution of slavery. It could well have been that even without the instructions which they received, the missionaries would have pursued a course of neutrality vis-a-vis the institution of slavery. Zindendorf had stated that theology at the outset of evangelical endeavour in the Caribbean: Salvation procured by the blood of Christ was for the souls of slaves; it did not affect the state in which the slaves lived.

What is remarkable is that the evangelical ethic which elsewhere advocated marriage and sexual chasity with puritanical

129

rigidity was in the Caribbean compromised without protest from the evangelicals. Until 1828, when legislation was passed by the British Parliament to regularise the unions of slaves solemnised by ministers of the Established Churches of England and Scotland, slaves in British colonies were not allowed to marry according to law. Instead, they could enter into a solemn agreement in front of witnesses, and live in what was called faithful concubinage. Missionaries accepted this position. Before 1824, when amelioration measures banned the separation of families by sale, evangelicals followed the line of the Moravians that:

> If by the sale of the Negroes, wives are torn from their husbands and husbands from their wives, and carried off to distant parts, though the Brethren (i.e. the Unitas Fratrum) cannot advise, yet they cannot hinder a regular marriage with another person, especially if a family of young children, or other circumstances, seems to make a helpmeet necessary.[32]

This line was perhaps the best that could be taken in a difficult situation. But, it amounted to little more than an accommodation to that situation.

In 1823, the attack on slavery was renewed in Britain. The attack came as much from the advocates of free trade as it did from the humanitarians. On May 15, 1823, Thomas Fowell Buxton called upon the British people to support the move to emancipate slaves in the British colonies. On May 22, East India traders began their assault on the monopoly hitherto enjoyed by West Indian producers of supplying sugar to Britain. From this time until the Emancipation Act was passed in 1834, humanitarians and free trade advocates cooperated in the effort to dismantle slavery. The Society of Planters and Merchants in Britain, representatives of the Caribbean sugar plantocracy, was aware of the danger which the plantocracy faced from the double attack of humanitarians and free traders. The Society declared:

> We cannot beat them [i.e. the parties hostile to the West India interest] by influence – we must trust to reason – and the only way of getting that weapon into our hands is by doing of ourselves, all that is right to be done – and doing it speedily and effectively.[33]

What the Society did was to propose ameliorative measures for slaves in the British Caribbean. It was no doubt felt that if the planters could demonstrate that they were interested in improving the lot of their slaves, the more drastic measure of

130

emancipation would be obviated. The ameliorative measures (which were, in fact, drawn up by the Society of Planters and Merchants), were incorporated in a circular and despatched to the several colonies for their consideration. High on the list was the proposal that religious instruction should be given to slaves. To ensure maximum attendance when such instruction could be given, it was proposed that Sunday markets should be abolished.

As a demonstration of their anxiety to bring religion to the blacks, the Society of Planters and Merchants, in 1823, helped to revive the Incorporated Society for the Conversion and Religious Instruction and Education of the Negro Slaves in the British West India Islands. The Planters and Merchants voted £1,000 per annum towards the Incorporated Society; people in Liverpool and Glasgow with trading interests and investments in the Caribbean made pledges of annual contributions of £100 each. Prominent figures of the London West India group of planters such as Sir Henry Martin, C.R. Ellis, George Hibbert, William Manning and Gilbert Mathison became members of the board of governors that managed the affairs of the Society for the Conversion and Religious Instruction of Slaves. Absentee proprietors living in Britain were approached for financial contributions; between 1823 and 1833 their contributions helped the total sum received to average about £3,500 annually. Clearly, the plantocracy did not regard religion as a factor that was calculated to undermine slave society. On the contrary, they felt that religion would guarantee the stability of that society. The planter Assembly of Antigua admitted that much in 1816 when it had sufficient confidence in the effect on the blacks of the moral and religious principles that were being inculcated by the missionaries to guarantee a stable society, to consider it unnecessary to introduce legislation against insurrection.

The plea of the Society of Planters and Merchants that the ameliorative measures be promptly adopted by their counterparts in the Caribbean met with little positive response. The planter-dominated legislatures in the British West Indies declared that Britain's recommendations for amelioration constituted an unwarranted and illegal interference in the domestic affairs of the colonies.

Meanwhile, the campaign against slavery was intensified in Britain. Religious journals such as *The Wesleyan Methodist Magazine, The Missionary Herald,* and *Missionary Notices* were

131

put at the disposal of the Society for the Mitigation and Gradual Abolition of Slavery. Dissenting churchmen fulminated against slavery from their pulpits. News of these events in Britain reached the Caribbean with every mail-boat. Evangelical missionaries in the area were regarded as the local agents of the anti-slavery party; in some colonies they ran into difficulties. It is to be doubted, however, that the evangelicals in the colonies were enthusiastic supporters of their counterparts in Britain.

When an Act was passed by the Jamaican Legislature authorising the Governor to deport any person from the island who was suspected of inciting behaviour that would disturb the peace and order of the society, four Methodist missionaries met in Kingston to review their position. They drafted a series of resolutions in which they sought to allay the fears that they were local agents of the anti-slavery movement. They refuted the charge that they held the belief that slavery was incompatible with the Christian religion and that their doctrines were calculated to produce insubordination among the slaves. The missionaries went on to declare that Christianity did not interfere with the civil condition of the slaves as slavery was established by the laws of the British West Indies. To make their case more convincing, the evangelicals made derogatory remarks about the 'emancipationists and abolitionists'. All this did not prevent the Colonial Church Union headed by the Anglican cleric, the Rev. George Bridges, from instigating acts of violence against the Methodists. In addition, a Sectarian Committee was set up to monitor the activities of dissenting preachers.

A slave uprising in Guyana in 1823 led to the imprisonment of the Congregationalist minister of Demerara, the Rev. John Smith. He died in gaol and because of this has been dubbed the Demerara Martyr. It was alleged that Smith had incited the slaves to revolt. In fact, he did no such thing. On the contrary, when the slaves first contemplated revolt because they believed that freedom had been granted by Britain and was being withheld from them, Smith advised them to be patient. He told the slaves that if there was anything for them they would soon hear of it, but if they behave insolently to their managers they would lose their religious character and provoke the government both in Guyana and in England. An indication of the extent to which Smith's Le Resouvenir chapel was involved in the revolt can be gauged from the fact that of about two thousand members under instruction for Holy Communion, only five or six were executed for their involvement in the revolt, and these were members who were of little importance in the congregation. On estates where Smith's members were concentrated, either no outbreak occurred or they behaved well during its continuance.[34] The only real connection between Smith and the revolt was the fact that it was his deacon, Quamina, who had led the insurrection. As another Congregationalist missionary, the Rev. John Wray, pointed out to Governor Murray, the London Missionary Society was entirely unconnected with any political party (and presumably uninterested in any political question such as emancipation), and that "with respect to the negroes obtaining any idea of freedom, it was not from the Missionaries, but from the colonists themselves."[35]

The slave revolt in Guyana caused panic throughout the British Caribbean. In Barbados, the Rev. Thomas Shrewsbury, a Methodist missionary, was run off the island. The reason for the persecution of Shrewsbury was partly the planters' reaction to the news of the violent revolt in Guyana and partly their anger at Britain for having introduced the Canning Resolutions which were intended to ameliorate the conditions under which the slaves lived. In Jamaica, the planters again became wary. When the free blacks and the free coloureds petitioned the Assembly for the recognition of their rights and privileges as British subjects, the indignation of the Assembly was excessive. Since the greater number of those free persons were members of the Methodist chapels, the wrath of the planter Assemblymen fell upon the Methodist missionaries who were suspected of being responsible for the agitation of the free people.

The slave revolt in Jamaica in December 1831 was blamed on the evangelical missionaries and particularly on the Baptist ministers, William Knibb and Thomas Burchell. In actual fact, the revolt was the work of one of Burchell's deacons – the slave, Sam Sharpe. It is significant that not even a plantocracy bent on proving the missionaries guilty in order to lynch them, could, with the resources available to them, find the ministers in any way implicated with the revolt. Burchell and Knibb were consequently acquitted. The responses made by Knibb when he was examined following the Christmas rebellion, are revealing. They ran, in part:

> What were the doctrines at all bearing on the temporal condition of the black population, which you inculcated?

133

I never touched upon the subject in my life.

In preaching to the slave population, have you not found it very difficult to keep altogether separate the spiritual concerns of that black population from their temporal situations?

It is difficult, but every good man would do it.

Is it possible, in addressing an unlettered audience, in inculcating doctrine of the freedom of the faith of Christianity, not to expose yourself to misrepresentation as to temporal freedom, as contrasted with spiritual freedom?

Whenever I have had occasion to speak on that subject, I have explained that when freedom is mentioned in the word of God, it referred to the soul and not to the body; that there were slaves in the times of the apostles as well as at present.

In preaching, you have touched on this subject?

On spiritual subjects I have preached the whole counsel of God.

Part of which is the freedom of the Christian?

Yes, the spiritual freedom; but it has been very seldom that I have touched on that point; I have never preached a set sermon on that; certainly I should not keep back anything in the word of God.

Illustrating that his charges could not have been misconstrued as to what he said in reference to spiritual freedom, Knibb said,

Since the rebellion, when I sent for my witnesses, and I sent for the head people from about seventy different properties, I asked them the question, if they ever understood by anything I had said that I had made any reference to their temporal condition; they all said, "No."

The interrogation continued:

You have said you thought it your duty to preach the whole counsel of God; is there not a text of this sort, 'The truth shall make you free'?

Yes, of that nature; but I never preached from it, nor would I preach from it, because the same doctrine might be conveyed from other texts. I never did quote such a passage of scripture in addressing a slave congregation.

Knibb went on to indicate that he thought it his duty to refrain from citing certain passages of scripture lest they should excite "any undue feeling in the mind of the negro on the subject of liberty." Further, they (i.e. the Baptists) had always enjoined the duty of obedience to masters on the part of slaves in such a way as "would lead them to suppose that (they) considered slavery quite compatible with Christianity."[36]

William Knibb was to become a champion for the cause of emancipation, but this was after he fled to England on his acquittal in 1831. Even so, when he was quoted by the

Edinburgh Evening Post as having said that Sam Sharpe deserved an imperishable monument for planning the Christmas rebellion, he promptly and publicly denied having made the statement. Meanwhile, the evangelicals in the Caribbean admonished their charges to be patient with their lot.

In the words of the Methodists, Bleby and Murray:

"We pointed out the hopelessness of any attempt on their (i.e. the Christian slaves) part to resist the authorities and the law; and advised the, whatever others might do, to go quietly and peaceably to work . . . and await patiently the time when the Lord, in his providence, would bring about a change in their condition."[37]

The Presbyterian Hope Waddell was no different. He told a group of disgruntled slaves who declared that Heaven had made them free and they would never be slaves again that they were taking the wrong way in redressing their grievances, that the burning of sugar estates was a crime which would do them no good and which would not have God's blessing.

On August 1, 1834, the Emancipation Act was passed by the British Parliament. The evangelicals in the Caribbean, unlike their counterparts in Britain, could claim little credit for that momentous legislation.

This chapter would be incomplete without a discussion of the efforts of the Church of England in the West Indies to christianise (if not to evangelise) the blacks. We have already looked at the efforts which were made on the Codrington estate in Barbados by the Society for the Progagation of the Gospel. Apart from the work done in Barbados, little effort was made to evangelise the blacks by the Established Church until about 1825, when Dr. Beilby Porteus became Bishop of London in 1787, and, by that token, diocesan of the Church of England in the Caribbean. He showed a lively interest in the conversion of the blacks. It was mainly through his initiative that the Incorporated Society for the Conversion and Religious Instruction and Education of the Negro Slaves in the British West India Islands was formed. The society soon became moribund, however, and Dr. Porteus' efforts were frustrated not only by the chronic shortage of staff, but moreso by the fact that his authority and influence in the Caribbean was greatly circumscribed by the local legislatures.

Meanwhile, individual proprietors of estates showed enough interest in their slaves to have their children baptised. This was more often the case after the abolition of the slave trade in

135

1807. After that time planters, sensitive to the fact that their stocks in slaves would not be replenished by new slaves from Africa, began to take increased interest in the welfare of those slaves which they owned. That interest sometimes led them to have their slaves baptised.. Sometimes parents were baptized along with their children. Usually the baptisms were done at home by the planters themselves; or, at least, under their supervision; the names were afterwards recorded in the register of baptisms kept by the parish church. Whenever 'Monk' Lewis, the Jamaican planter, performed such baptisms he modified the baptismal service. He tells us that instead of the required concluding prayer he substituted the prayer "that God would bless the children, and make them live to be as good servants to me, as I prayed him to make me a kind massa *(sic)* to them."[38]

In 1815, the Jamaican legislature recognised the right of the slaves to receive religious instruction. In order to implement the programme for instructing the blacks, special 'chapels of ease' were to be built and additional curates were to be employed to staff these chapels. But the general reluctance of the planters to admit the curates to work among their slaves put paid to whatever success might have been achieved by those curates. The Rev. George Bridges, ardent champion of the plantocracy in Jamaica, justified the reluctance of the planters to have their slaves instructed in religion on the ground that the planters could not spare the slaves any time off their work to attend classes. Bridges argued that the economic plight of the planters forced them to extract as much work as they could from their slaves. But the very spirit in which the 1815 legislation was enacted militated against any positive action to implement the programme for instructing the slaves. What the legislature was anxious to ensure was not the education of the slaves but the stability of the society. The Assembly regarded the legislation as the means of diffusing the light of a genuine Christianity

> "divested of the dark and dangerous fanaticism of the Methodists which has been attempted to be propagated, and which, grafted on the African superstitions and working on the uninstructed and ardent temperament of the Negro, has produced the most pernicious consequences to individuals, and is pregnant with imminent dangers to the community."[39]

Among the measures introduced by the British government in 1823 to improve conditions for the slaves was one for the establishment of two dioceses in the Caribbean for the better supervision of the work of the Church, particularly as it related to the slave population. The Duke of Manchester, the Governor of Jamaica, remarked on the occasion when he announced the appointment of a bishop to Jamaica that the bishop was entrusted with

> "the duty of reporting upon the state of the Ecclesiastical establishment particularly as it relates to the slave population, and upon the best means of diffusing the benefits of religious instruction to that part of the Community."[40]

From 1825 onwards, the Church of England in the Caribbean took up the task of evangelising the slaves as a matter of policy. Ably guided by the Rev. William Hart Coleridge, bishop of Barbados and the Leeward Islands, and the Rev. Christopher Lipscomb, bishop of Jamaica, substantially financed by the British exchequer, and staffed by men who had come under the influence of the evangelical revival in England and in contact with the Church Missionary Society, the Church made significant progress in evangelising the slaves. Not that progress came without opposition. In April, 1827, the Rev. W.M. Harte, the rector of St. Lucy in Barbados, was accused by his parishioners of inculcating doctrines of equality among the slaves; it was felt that this was inimical to the safety of the society. The Rev. Harte was found guilty of misdemeanour. In Jamaica, the Rev. George Bridges was a thorn in Bishop Lipscomb's flesh.

Unlike their counterparts in England, the evangelicals within the Church of England in the Caribbean kept silent on the question of the emancipation of slaves. In England, it was the evangelicals who worshipped under John Venn, the rector of Clapham, and who were dubbed the Clapham Sect, men such as William Wilberforce, Henry Thornton, Charles Grant, James Stephen, Zachary Macaulay and Fowell Buxton, who fought the cause of the slaves. It was these men, too, who campaigned successfully for Parliament to allow missionaries to go to India, against the opposition of parliamentarians such as Lord Teignmouth who argued that it was inimical to the security of the British Empire in India that missionaries "should preach publicly with a view to the conversion of the Native Indians, that Mohammed (was) an impostor, or should speak in opprobrious terms of the Brahmins, or their religious rites."[41] The evangelicals within the Church of England in England were as concerned that the Indians might remain "the slaves of the most cruel and degrading superstition,"[42] as they were that the blacks in the

137

Caribbean might remain slaves to the plantation system.

No doubt the Church of England evangelicals in the Caribbean were opposed to the slavery of the blacks; but they kept silent on the question. Perhaps they feared reprisals from the planter class; perhaps they did not want to jeopardise their mission. Strongly contrasted with their silence was the very articulate advocacy by the Rev. George Bridges of the planters' defence against the charges of the abolitionists. In 1831, that reverend gentleman was the co-founder, with the planter Hilton, of the Colonial Church Union in Jamaica. The Union was responsible for the active persecution of Baptist and Methodist missionaries and for the destruction of their chapels. While Bridges was not singular in his defence of the institution of slavery in the Caribbean, yet he cannot be regarded as representative of the Church of England's stance on the matter, in spite of the silence of other clergymen and, particularly, of the evangelicals within the Church. However, when emancipation came about, the Church of England evangelicals in the West Indies, like their noncomformist counterparts, could claim no credit for that momentous event in the history of the Caribbean.

Notes and References

1. *Barbados Diocesan History*, p. 11.
2. Long, *op. cit.*, vol. ii, p. 411.
3. *Ibid.*, p. 86.
4. *Ibid.*, p. 364.
5. *Codrington Chronicle*, ed. Frank Klingborg, p. 16.
6. J.H. Bennett, *Bondsmen and Bishops*, p. 19.
7. G. Cragg, *The Church and the Age of Reason* (1648-1789), pp. 102-103.
8. The Moravians, who called themselves the Unitas Fratrum, were followers of the Bohemian reformer and martyr, Jan Huss (1369-1415).
9. J.E. Hutton, *A History of Moravian Missions*, pp. 177-180.
10. *Ibid.*, p. 121.
11. Anthony Armstrong, *The Church of England, the Methodists and Society, 1700-1850*, p. 51.
12. *Ibid.*, p. 64
13. *Ibid.*, p. 66.
14. *Ibid.*, p. 76.

15. In fact, the first Methodist missionary to the islands came from the United States. He was the Negro, Joseph Paul. The Revs. Johnson and Turton who followed Paul to Nassau were responsible for erecting chapels there. Turton did effective work on the Out Islands as well.

16. Lewis, *Journal of a West Indian Proprietor*, pp. 145-6.

17. James M. Phillippo, *Jamaica: Its Past and Present State*, pp. 308-312.

18. Herklots, *op. cit.*, p. 81.

19. *Ibid.*, p. 76.

20. Quoted in Osborne and Johnson, *op. cit.*, p. 54.

21. Hutton, *op. cit.*, p. 44.

22. *Ibid.*, p. 214.

23. *Ibid*, p. 214.

24. *The American Baptist Magazine and Missionary* Intelligencer, vol. i, pp. 262-263.

25. Hutton, *op. cit.*, pp. 209-210

26. Peter Duncan, *A Narrative of the Wesleyan Mission to Jamaica*, p. 16.

27. *Ibid.*, p. 76.

28. *Minutes of the Meeting of the West Indian Planters and Merchants*, vol. ii, Minutes of the Standing Committee, 27th June, 1795.

29. Cited in E. Goveia, *Slave Society in the British Leeward Islands at the End of the Eighteenth Century*, p. 297.

30. Duncan, *op. cit.*, p. 51.

31. *Ibid.*, p. 83.

32. J.H. Buchner, *The Moravians in Jamaica*, pp. 44-45.

33. Cited in L.J. Ragatz, *op. cit.*, p. 414.

34. Thomas Rain, *The Life and Labours of John Wray, Pioneer Missionary in British Guiana*, p. 192.

35. *Ibid.*, p. 226.

36. Cited passages from J.W. Hinton, *Memoir of William Knibb: Missionary in Jamaica*, pp. 174-175.

37. Cited in Osborne and Johnson, *op. cit.*, p. 75.

38. Lewis, *op. cit.*, p. 108.

39. Alfred Caldecott, *The Church in the West Indies*, p. 85.

40. *Ibid.*, p. 90.

41. Eugene Stock, *The History of the Church Missionary Society*, vol. i, p. 102.

42. *Ibid.*, p. 100.

CHAPTER VI
HINDUISM AND ISLAM IN THE CARIBBEAN

The full emancipation of slaves in the British colonies came in 1838. Slaves in the French islands were also freed in 1838; those in the Dutch colonies in 1863. Freedom was followed by the movement of ex-slaves from the plantations and a general reluctance of the blacks to work on the estates except on conditions that were favourable to them. Ex-slaves were not wholly independent of estate employment; but where land was available either for purchase or for squatting their independence was greater. The degree to which the ex-slaves were independent of estate employment was the degree to which planters felt themselves denied a large and manipulable labour force — the kind of labour force that they felt was demanded by sugar cultivation. It was in order to secure such a labour force that natives from the Indian sub-continent were brought to the Caribbean. These Indians, in turn, brought their beliefs with them. The majority of them were Hindus; they were responsible for the fact that Hinduism took firm roots in Guyana, Surinam and Trinidad. A small percentage of the immigrants were Muslims. While they were not the first Muslims to come to the Caribbean, they were, nevertheless, responsible for the establishment of Islamic communities in those territories.

The following figures indicate the number of East Indians who came to the Caribbean:

TABLE 1

Guyana	239,000
Trinidad	134,000
Surinam	35,500
Jamaica	33,000
St. Lucia	4,000
Grenada	3,000

St. Vincent	2,700
St. Kitts	300
Guadeloup ⎱ Martinique ⎰	78,000
French Guiana	19,000

East Indian Migration to the Caribbean in the Nineteenth
Century

Those immigrants who came to Surinam and the British colonies did so mainly from the districts of Gorakhpur, Basti, Gonda, Fyzabad, Jaunpur, Azamgarh Ghazipur and Bali in the Eastern United Providences. They came also from the Saran, Muzaffarpur, Darbhanga, Shahabad, Patna and Gaya districts in the state of Bihar. Many of the immigrants to the French colonies came from these districts as well but some came from areas that were under French control in India.

Hinduism

The Hindu beliefs and practices that made their appearance first in the Caribbean were those of the Sieunaraini (or Sri Narayana) Panth. In Guyana, the Sieunarainis[1] were called Ramanandis or Kabir Panthis; in Trinidad, the three groups were regarded as three different sects. Whatever these sectarians were called, they held to certain common beliefs.

The Sieunaraini belief is that there is but one Supreme God who is all-loving. God is not to be identified with idols, nor is he to be found in temples, shrines or holy places ('neither in *Kaaba* nor in *Kailash*').[2] God is not impressed with the external forms of religion − the performance of rituals, the reading of scriptures, asceticism, pilgrimages, ablutions in the Ganges − unless the worshipper is truly devout and unless his devotion is matched by moral living. It is God alone who frees men from the Law of Karma and brings to an end the cycle of reincarnation in which a man might be caught. Freed from the karmic wheel, the soul is absorbed into the Absolute. This absorption or salvation comes to the man who has a simple, complete love for God.

As an act of loving devotion to the Supreme God, the sectarians were in the habit of repeating the formula, *"Namo Sri Narayan"* (Praise to Lord Narayana). It was this practice that gave the panth its name. Sri Narayana was the most venerated of the names used by the sectarians of Vishnu, the incarnation of the Supreme God. The Sieunarainis refused to believe that the Hindu scripture, the Vedas, had a special authority for belief which other sacred scriptures lacked. Their

141

holy book was called the Granth. Repudiating the pretensions of Brahmins to be leaders in religious activities, the Sieunarainis followed the leadership of *gurus* (teachers) whom they called *mahants*.

The Sieunaraini movement was essentially a *bhakti* sect. In order to understand this bhakti sect it is necessary to look at the development of Hindu thought, although its treatment here cannot pretend to be exhaustive.

The most ancient of Hindu scriptures, and, in fact, the most ancient of all sacred writings, are the four Vedas − the *Rg-Veda,* the *Sama-Veda,* the *Yajur Veda* and the *Atharva-Veda.* These writings were compiled by the descendants of people called Indo-Aryans who invaded India in about the middle of the second millenium B.C., and settled in the flood-plains of the three great Indian rivers, the Indus, the Ganges and the Brahmaputra. It was in the region between the Ganges and the Jumna which was called Aryavarta − the land of the Aryans − that Hinduism had its birth. The struggles between the Aryans and the dark-complexioned indigenous Dravidians are immortalized in the *Ramayana* and the *Mahabharata* − two great Hindu epics that are very much later than the Vedas.

The *Rg-Veda* gives us an idea of what the Aryans believed. Many of the hymns of this Veda are addressed to gods and goddesses who seem to be identified with natural phenomena. In fact, some of them are little more than natural forces that have been deified. Chief among the *devas* (heavenly ones) in whom the Aryans believed was Indra, the god of storms. It was Indra who brought the monsoon rains. It was he who slew the dragon Vritra, and who with his dreaded thunder-bolt led his people, like Yahweh of ancient Hebrew belief, into battle. If the Aryans adored Indra, they feared Rudra, the god who in disastrous storms swept down from the Himalayas to destroy men and crops. The Aryans prayed to him:

> Kill not our great or our small, our growing one or our full-grown man, our father or our mother. Injure not, O Rudra, our dear selves.

Other Vedic gods were Vayu, the wind, Ushas, the dawn, and Surya and Savitar, the sun at different stages of its diurnal run. Another god of the sun was Vishnu who in three strides covered the earth and the sky and dispelled the night. Then there was Yama, the god of the dead. Varuna was an important Aryan god. It was believed that he held the physical world together and caused it to operate by the principle of Rita − the principle of regularity. By association, it came to be felt that Varuna was responsible for helping men to maintain their integrity by obeying the laws of morality. Varuna was the judge between truth and falsehood. Associated with Varuna was Mitra, the god of loyalty. Other important gods were Agni, the god of fire, Soma, the divine presence in a drink used during worship by the Aryans, and Brahmanaspati, the prayer-word. Agni, Soma and Brahmanaspati were all associated with the Aryan worship services.

As the Vedic period came to an end, men began to probe after a unifying principle in their beliefs. The later hymns of the Rg Veda mention such a principle (or person) in Vishva-karman (He Whose Work is the Universe), Prajapati, Lord of Creatures, Purusha, the cosmic soul, and the indescribable That One Thing. It was said:

> They call him Indra, Mitra, Agni, and he is heavenly noble-winged Garutman.
> To what is One, sages give many a title: they call it Agni, Yama, Matarisvan . . .

By the end of the seventh century B.C., the *Brahmins* or priests were beginning to emerge as the most powerful of the Aryan social groups. Next in rank were the *Kshatriyas* or warrior-nobles; and, below them were the Aryan 'commoners' – *Vaisyas*, who were peasants and artisans. Much below the Vaisyas were the *Shudras*, the non-Aryan, indigenous, darker-complexioned peoples of India. *Varna*, or colour, now became an important criterion in social differentiation as the first three classes kept themselves aloof from the Shudras. Among the higher varnas there was a struggle for social prestige. The nobles and the priests declared that their claim to social privileges and prerogatives had divine sanction. In the end, the Brahmins emerged as the most powerful group. It was they, it was felt, who alone could utter the Brahmanaspati or sacred prayer word that made the gods function to keep the cosmos intact. In time, the Brahmins came to be treated as gods.

The Brahmins were responsible for the compilation of treatises which came to be called *Brahmanas*. These writings gave directions as to how sacrifices should be performed; they also sought to explain the inner meaning of rituals. Appended to the *Brahmanas* were the *Upanishads*. The period during which the Upanishads were written (700-300 B.C.) was the golden age, as it were, of Hindu religious speculation. The quest for a unifying principle in Hindu religious thought which was begun

143

in the late Vedic period, was pursued with vigour. The philosophical quest was after ultimate reality. "What is really real?" was the question for which answers were sought. The answer which the Upanishads presented is that That One Thing called *Brahman* is the substratum or ground of all that exists. In fact, Brahman is existence itself. Upanishadic thought runs:

> Verily, in the beginning this world was Brahma, the limitless One − limitless to the east, limitless to the north, limitless in every direction. Incomprehensible is that Soul, unlimited, unborn, not to be reasoned about, unthinkable − He whose soul is space! In the dissolution of the world He alone remains awake.

Brahman is not only all that is objective and exists outside of man; Brahman is also all that is subjective to man: his self-consciousness and his feelings. This inner self is sometimes designated the *atman*. But the atman does not exist of itself; it is but part of the *paramatman* (the universal atman). Better yet, the atman is identical with the paramatman. The major thrust of the Upanishads is to direct men to realise their identity with Brahman. This realisation, it is felt, will lead to man's release from imprisonment to karma and transmigration. Union with Brahman, it is held, is accompanied by a sense of mystical ecstasy. In union with Brahman, a man may achieve *turiya* or *caturtha*. This is a state of pure intuitive consciousness in which there is no knowledge of objects internal or external to the person caught up in it.

The Indo-Aryan doctrine of *samsara* (or transmigration of souls, or reincarnation) is closely related to what we have said above. If a man on dying does not achieve oneness with Brahman, his soul is reborn into another existence. This can recur in an endless chain. What is more, rebirth may take place in any of the many Hindu heavens or hells, or on earth in vegetable, animal or human form. It is the Law of Karma that determines the nature of a person's rebirth. This law signifies that a man's thoughts, words and deeds have ethical consequences for his future existence. Whatever a man sows in this life, so to speak, is what he shall reap hereafter. As the Chandogya Upanishad declares:

> Those who are of pleasant conduct here − the prospect is indeed that they will enter a pleasant womb, whether the womb of a Brahmin, or the womb of a Kshatriya, or the womb of a Vaisya. But those who are of a stinking conduct here − the prospect is, indeed, that they will enter either the womb of a dog, or the womb of a swine, or the womb of an outcast.

The karmic law came to be related to a person's social status. The fact that a man was born a Shudra or an Untouchable was explained on the ground that he might have been a Brahmin who had sinned in a previous experience. His low estate was the just punishment for his sins. Conversely, a privileged Brahmin or a Kshatriya could justify his position or privilege on the ground that he was but reaping the just desert of a life well lived in a previous existence. It came to be felt that any attempt to right social inequalities was both impious and wrong; it was to question the operation of the Law of Karma – a heresy if ever there was one.

The central question that came to dominate Hindu thought was: How to find release from karma and samsara? It was generally recognised that a man might legitimately seek pleasure *(kama)*, or power *(artha)* in this or any other life. It was better for him however, to follow the path of *dharma* – religious, moral and social duty. Best of all, he ought to seek after *moksha* (salvation or liberation) from samsara and all the attendant miseries of human life. Moksha would also result in *samadhi,* or absorption into Brahman.

Many people sought moksha by the Way or *Yoga* of Works *(Karma Marga* or *Yoga)*. The Brahmanas spelt out the requirements of this way to salvation. It was believed that men were indebted in several ways. They owed the gods sacrifices; they owed their teachers the obligation to study the Vedas; they owed offspring to the spirits of their ancestors and they owed their fellows hospitality. It was felt that if a person met the obligations imposed upon him by the number of relationships in which he was involved, he would acquire enough merit to pass into the heavens or be reborn as a Brahmin at death. In the new state, he would be so much nearer final union with Brahman. Later, *dharmashastras* or law codes were compiled to direct men as to how they could meet their several obligations. The best known of these has been the *Code of Manu,* which was compiled about 200 B.C., The dharmashastras placed great stress on the ceremonies which ought to be celebrated at the crisis points in life – birth, name-giving, the first hair-cutting, initiation into manhood, marriage and death. The Code of Manu also prescribes a way of works for women which, in essence, demands little more of them than obedience and subservience to their men-folk. The Code runs:

> In childhood a female must be subject to her father, in youth
> to her husband, when her lord is dead to her sons; a woman must

145

never be independent.

A more superior way of seeking salvation is the Way of Knowledge *(Jnana Marga)*. This has been the path to moksha that the more philosophically-minded have found congenial. Jnana Marga assumes that at the heart of the human dilemma is ignorance *(Avidya)*. It is felt that man is grossly ignorant about his own nature. His problem is not moral transgression, but mental error. Man's avidya consists of his thinking of himself as having an existence that is independent of Brahman. He fails to realize that the world and the self do not exist apart from the paramatman. As long as man lives on the ignorance-fostered illusion of separate selfhood he is bound to the karmic wheel of samsara. Salvation can only come with right understanding. When that happens:

> The knot of the heart is loosened,
> All doubts are cut off,
> And one's deeds (karma) cease.

The Way of Knowledge is followed mainly by Brahmins and Kshatriyas. It is a lifelong programme that embraces four stages or ashramas. The first *ashrama* is that of the student of religion. Once the young Brahmin has been invested with the badge of his caste at an initiation ceremony, he is taken to the home of a *guru* (teacher) where he begins his study of the Vedas. His study may last until his twenty-fifth year. When he has acquired a sufficient knowledge of the Vedas, the Brahmin enters the second stage of his 'pilgrimage.' He becomes a householder; he marries and raises a family. Then, when he has met all the obligations laid upon him by virtue of the fact that he has been the head of a household, the Brahmin leaves his home and becomes a hermit. As a hermit, he concentrates on the development of a sense of complete indifference to the world as he ponders the Upanishads. When he becomes wholly 'spiritual,' the Brahmin enters the stage of the *sannyasin* – the holy man. In this stage, the Brahmin seeks the final goal of Jnana Marga – union with Brahman. The sannyasin spends his time in meditation. In this regard, the Code of Manu advises:

> By deep meditation let him recognise the subtle nature of the supreme Soul, and its presence in all organisms . . . He who has in this manner given up all attachments reposes in Brahman alone . . . He attains the eternal Brahman . . .

The masses of the Indian people were not impressed by the philosophical speculations of the Upanishads. For centuries

146

they worshipped their gods in their own way. While the upper-caste members sought salvation by the ways of works and knowledge, the ordinary man sought that salvation in the worship of his gods and goddesses. It is to the credit of the Brahmins that they were able to accommodate the ordinary man's way of salvation within the philosophical and theological framework of Hinduism. This way to salvation came to be known as *Bhakti Marga* (the Way of Devotion).

Bhakti Marga receives recognition in the famous *Bhagawad Gita* or *Song of the Blessed Lord*. More than that, the Gita spells out the doctrine of bhakti which is articulated in the book by the hero-god, Krishna, to Arjuna. In the story, Arjuna, the great Pandava warrior, hesitates to lead his brothers and their allies into battle against his kinsmen, the Kurus. Krishna, his charioteer, urges Arjuna to follow his caste duty and to fight without any thought of reward or consequence. Having by this advice exalted the way of duty or works, Krishna goes on to indicate to Arjuna that another way of exerting oneself is to meditate. Meditation, according to Krishna, will lead to that wisdom which is self-identification with Brahman and which is a necessary condition if one is to act rightly. Thus, the Gita exalts Jnana Marga as well. In fact, Karma Marga and Jnana Marga merge in the estimation of Krishna, since, as he puts it, "no one can ever rest (in meditation) even for an instant without performing action."

Krishna, who is in fact the incarnation of Vishnu, leads Arjuna to realise that the person whose greatest wish is to be absorbed in the paramatman, may find that salvation through meditative absorption in a Person. That Person may be Vishnu himself, or Krishna, the incarnation of Vishnu. In a theophany which astounds and terrifies Arjuna, Krishna reveals himself as Vishnu, the eternal World Spirit, Brahman, in god-form. Once more in the form of Krishna (which the god assumes at the request of Arjuna), the charioteer articulates the heart of the Gita's message thus:

> Cling thou to Me!
> Clasp Me with heart and mind!
> So shalt thou dwell
> Surely with Me on high. But if thy thought
> Droops from such height; if thou be'st weak to set
> Body and soul upon Me constantly,
> Despair not! Give Me lower service!
> Seek to read me, worshipping with steadfast will;

And, if thou canst not worship steadfastly,
Work for Me, toil in works pleasing to Me!
For he that laboureth right for love of Me
Shall finally attain!

The salvation that Bhakti Marga offers is for everybody, regardless of sex or caste or state. All that is required is in the words of Krishna addressed to the devotee:

Fix heart and thought on Me! Adore Me!
Bring Offerings to Me! Make me prostrations!
Make Me your supremest joy! And, undivided,
Unto My rest your spirits shall be guided.

Worship is simplicity itself. As for the offering, Krishna declares, "Whosoever offers to me with love a leaf, a flower, or fruit or even water, I appear in person before that disinterested devotee of purified intellect, and delightfully partake of the articles offered by him with love."

In time, many a local village or tribal god came to be recognised as the avatar or incarnation of Vishnu. Similarly, many village goddesses came to be recognised as the consorts of the local avatars. Suitable myths and legends evolved by way of explanation as to how *grama-devatas* (village deities) came to be avatars of Vishnu. This kind of development took place as more and more regions in India came under the religious and cultural influence of Hindustan. It was the development and spread of the doctrine of bhakti that made this kind of religious accommodation possible. In this connection, the writings of Tulasi Das (1532-1623), one of the greatest and most famous of India's poets, were very important. Soon after its completion early in the seventeenth century, his *Ramacaritamanasa (The Holy Lake of the Acts of Rama)* became, as far as northern India was concerned, the most authoritative guide to religious life and conduct. Verses of his poems were as widely quoted among Hindus as were verses from the Bible in Europe. The over-riding motive of Tulasi Das was to inculcate bhakti by emphasising the moral example of Rama. But the assimilation of local cultic beliefs into the bhakti movement was never quite complete. Millions of people managed to combine the practice of that kind of Hinduism which they hoped would lead to moksha, with the worship of local gods and spirits that were never quite identified with Vishnu or with his avatars.

Meanwhile, in popular religious thought, three great gods emerged — Brahma, the Creator; Shiva, the Destroyer; and Vishnu, the Preserver. The Brahmins have explained this phenomenon by saying that the Brahman atman (or paramatman) has revealed itself in the three-fold function of creation, destruction and preservation. This three-fold function has been personified and deified in terms of *trimurti* (literally, three faces of deity), or three personal deities, or deity in three forms.

Little worship is accorded Brahma. Shiva, on the other hand, has grown to be the great god of India and of Asia. He has been dubbed *Mahadeva* – the Great God. Shiva is, in fact, the dread Rudra of the Vedic period whose worship had not ceased in spite of the speculations of the Upanishadic period. Although Shiva has been associated with destruction, he has also been identified with the reproduction of animal, vegetable and human life. The male and female sexual organs, the *lingam* and the *yoni* respectively, have been traditionally recognised as his symbols. The thinking has been that Shiva destroys only in order to make room for new life. Associated with Shiva are his consorts, Parbati, Uma, Durga, Chandi and Kali. Ganesha, the elephant-headed god, is regarded as the son of Shiva by Parbati. Generally, Shiva's spouses have been regarded as his *shakti* or power, but in some parts of India (notably the northeast) they have been worshipped in cults of their own. Kali, the black mother, has been particularly popular.

Vishnu, the preserver, has been traditionally regarded as benevolent to mankind. He is responsible for the preservation of moral values. It is believed that whenever evil threatens to overcome the good, Vishnu intervenes for the preservation of goodness. To this end, he has come to earth in avatars or descents. Thus, he came as Rama, the hero of the epic *Ramayana,* as Krishna of the *Mahabharata,* and as seven other avatars. He will come a tenth time at the end of this *yug* (world period), as Kalki with flaming sword on horse-back to destroy the wicked and to usher in the new era of truth and goodness. Meanwhile, devotion to Rama or Krishna may result in moksha for the devotee. Rama's consort is Sita, the ideal of Indian womanhood, Krishna's favourite mistress is Radha. Associated with Rama has been the monkey-god, Hanuman.

The worship of Vishnu in any of his forms has been described as Vaishnavism. The Sieunaraini panth was a Vaishnavite sect. It was founded by Kabir (1440-1518) who was himself a disciple of Ramananda who lived in the fourteenth century. Both men were reformers; both taught that salvation was to be found in the love of God alone. Kabir's favourite name for Vishnu was Sri Narayan. It was to Narayana that Kabir called men to bhakti.

The Sieunaraini movement took early roots in the Caribbean for a number of reasons. In the first place, it was the religion that was most widely held by Chamars and other lower caste groups in Northern India. It was from among these groups that labourers were recruited for the Caribbean plantations and many of these labourers were Sieunarainis. The panth did not require the leadership of high-caste men or of 'professional' priests in order to function. Because of this, its leadership did not suffer from the policy of the Caribbean plantocracy not to recruit too many Brahmins and other high-caste people. Because Kabir-panthis disregarded caste pretensions, they would not have been demoralised into religious inactivity by the fact that they had crossed the *kala pani* (black waters) — an act that led to the loss of caste for other people and with that loss, a kind of temporary spiritual malaise.

Sieunaraini beliefs and practices were suited for life on plantations in distant lands in a way that other systems of Hindu beliefs and practices were not. To Sieunarainis, no place or building in India or elsewhere was particularly sacred; they could worship anywhere. Their religion did not place any dietary restrictions on them or any ban on their mingling with other people of whatever caste. They could eat whatever was available in the estate barracks and rub shoulders with whomsoever they met in the cane-brake or on the barrack range without doing violence to any religious scruple. Above all, they could (and did) proselytise; this was unheard of among 'orthodox' Hindus.

Not all the Indians who came to the Caribbean were Sieunarainis. Towards the end of the nineteenth century, temples dedicated to the worship of Rama and Krishna began to appear in Trinidad and Guyana. These were erected mainly in those villages and settlements which were established by the immigrants on the expiry of their indentureship. The appearance of prayer flags *(jhandi)* testified to the fact that many Hindu gods had survived the crossing of the kala pani and the rigours of estate life. These flags were put up as part of the *puja* (worship) of the gods. The red jhandi indicated that Hanuman, the monkey-god and faithful friend of Rama, was worshipped; white ones showed that pujas were held in honour of Vishnu himself in the form of Suruj Narayan, the solar deity and god of truth. Yellow flags indicated that Krishna and his consorts were worshipped.

Meanwhile, the avatars of Vishnu were honoured in the

names which immigrants gave to their children. Such names included Ramcharran, Ramlall, Ramlakhan, Krishna and Krishnadath. Their consorts were remembered in the names of girls – Sita, Radha and Radika. At the festival of *Holi* or *Phagwah* which commemorated the burning of the demon Holika and marked the beginning of the Hindu year, the youthful pranks of Krishna were re-enacted. This festival was celebrated from almost the beginning of immigrant life in the Caribbean. Estate managers found it prudent to allow their labourers to celebrate the festival although Phagwah day was not recognised as a holiday. Excessive drinking of rum became a feature of Phagwah celebrations.

Another festival to make an early appearance in the Caribbean was the *Dasserah* or *Durga Puja.* In Guyana, it was popular in the 1890s. The festival was held in honour of Durga's victory over the demon giant, Maghisan. A Christian missionary in Guyana described an aspect of the festival thus:

> "An image of the goddess made of straw and clay represents her as possessed of ten arms, each grasping a weapon, with one foot on a lion and the other on the prostrate giant. This terrific idol is worshipped for three days and then cast into Demerary, or Essequibo, or Berbice river . . ."[3]

The worship of Kali Mai, the consort of Shiva, was very much in evidence in the early 1900s. It was in times of crisis, the failure of crops or the occurrence of sickness, that pujas to the Black Mother were celebrated. Thus, in 1919-20 in Guyana, there was a Kali Mai revival on the Essequibo Coast. That period saw the outbreak of an influenza epidemic in the colony in which, in Essequibo alone, about a thousand East Indians died. Hindu priests said that this was because the gods, in particular Kali, were angry with the immigrants for having forsaken the faith of their fathers. Great pujas were held at which sacrifices were made to Kali Mai. The worship of Kali or Durga was not unlike the worship of Shiva's consorts which was well known in north-eastern India. Whenever a puja was held in Kali's honour, a black jhandi was set up.

In the very late nineteenth and the early twentieth centuries, festivals normally celebrated by the higher castes in the villages in India began to gain in popularity in Trinidad and Guyana. These included *Ram Naumi, Chauti, Shiva-ratri* and *Divali.* By this time, many immigrants had settled away from the barrack and logie lines and many had acquired some wealth from rice-farming, cattle rearing, ground provision cultivation and shopkeeping. Their new residential and economic status gave them that respectability which they felt qualified them to celebrate high-caste festivals. Not a few of them arrogated to themselves caste pretensions that had little relationship to their lineage or pedigree.

Distinct Vaishnavite and Shivite cults were late in developing in Surinam. In the first half of the twentieth century, however, Shiva was worshipped along with his more attractive consort, Parvati. If anything, Parvati was the more popular of the two. She was regarded as Adi Bhavani (The first power of Shiva) and as Mahamaya who had power to restore sight to the blind and wholeness to the leper. As Gauri Parvati, the goddess of girls, she was worshipped at the *maktor* ritual which was part of the wedding ceremony.

By 1890 or so, the question surrounding the status of Brahmin priests had been satisfactorily settled by the Hindus in the Indian immigrant communities in the Caribbean. That question related to the loss of caste which Brahmins were believed to have suffered because they crossed the kala pani and mingled and ate with people of inferior castes on board immigrant vessels. The informally held consensus was that the caste pollution incurred by migration did not interfere with the ability of Brahmins to function as priests in the colonies. In addition, the immigrants respected their status and desired their ministrations. The immigration agent, Henry J. Gladwin, who was stationed in Guyana, summarised the priests's position thus:

> "The priest . . . is in the same position as a Christian Dissenting Minister whose orders are not valid but who derives his office from the people."[4]

Once the question surrounding their status had been satis- factorily settled, Brahmin priests could pursue with more vigour the task of imposing some organisation of Hindu beliefs and practices in their several territories. Two incentives spurred the Brahmins to this task In the first place, they felt that it was necessary to curb the tendency on the part of some Hindus to convert to Christianity. Secondly, and more important, events in India were stirring up in Caribbean Indians a tremen- dous sense of 'national' pride and racial consciousness. In the southern Caribbean, Brahmin priests in the first and second decades of this century mounted a campaign against apostasy from Hinduism. That campaign resulted in the proliferation of Hindu religious exercises. The importation of Hindu literature

152

and religious pictures into the southern Caribbean no doubt aided the Brahmins' campaign.

In India, the Indian National Congress was conducting a campaign of its own – that of *swaraj* (independence for India). The most outstanding personality in the campaign for swaraj was Mohandas K. Gandhi. The strategy which he employed – satyagraha – involved him in long periods of fasting and canonised him as a saint. His imprisonments won for him the reputation of a martyr and the cause of the campaign itself made him a hero in the eyes of Indians at home and abroad. He was dubbed *Mahatma* or Great-Souled and was represented as the Exemplar par excellence of the dharmic man. Among Hindus and other Indians in the Caribbean, his fame was sung at weddings and festivals. The Mahatma became an object of veneration for Hindus. There were even those who claimed that Gandhi was the Kalki avatar.

The reputation of Gandhi and the writings and speeches of the leaders of the Indian National Congress engendered in East Indians in Trinidad, Guyana and Surinam, a strong sense of racial and 'national' consciousness, which, in turn, gave a great stimulus to the 'national' religion, Hinduism. The visits of Arya Samajist missionaries to the Caribbean were also responsible for sustaining the sense of 'national' pride among the immigrants. The Arya Samaj movement was founded in India in 1875 by Swami Dayanand. It was essentially a reform movement within Hinduism, anti-Christian in bias and strongly opposed to Western culture. Its watch-word was: 'Back to the Vedas.' Important also for the development of the strong 'Indian' sentiment among the immigrants were the visits of Indian officials to the colonies.

In 1927, the *Sanatan Dharma Sabha* (Eternal Religion Society) was formed in Guyana. Similar sabhas were formed in Trinidad and Surinam as well. They were all modelled on the Sanatan Dharma Maha Sabha of India. Local priests, who were almost all members of the sabha in their own colony, made out that the local sabha had the patronage of important Indian princes. This enhanced the status of the local sabhas. By 1930, the sabhas were becoming influential in determining what Hindu orthodoxy was in relation to religious beliefs and practices. The Brahmin emphasis at this time was on *dharma*. William de Bary has defined dharma thus: "Dharma is in fact a key word of Hindu culture, and Hinduism itself is sometimes designated as Sanatan Dharma, the Eternal Dharma."

153

It might well be said that Hinduism in the Caribbean came to be understood in terms of dharma. Generally speaking, dharma was regarded as the right course of action for men appropriate to their caste, their age and their station in life. In the Caribbean, caste took on racial overtones. It was propounded by Brahmin priests and Arya Samajist missionaries that the man of Indian origin ought to follow the religious traditions of his ancestors. This duty was demanded by dharma. Among themselves, East Indians distinguished between Brahmin and Chamar, and between Kshatriya and Dosadh. This was done mainly for ritual and ceremonial purposes. In relation to the larger society, the immigrants distinguished between themselves as Indians and the rest of the society as non-Indian. Needless to say, the rest of society was fragmented into several racial groups which were readily identifiable and which seemed anxious, in varying degrees, to maintain their identity. In Trinidad and Guyana, where a degree of cultural homogeneity was taking shape around social values which included literacy in English and membership in the Christian church, the 'illiterate' and 'heathenish' Indian immigrant was often assigned a place on the fringes of society.

Orthopraxy (i.e. dharma) demanded that a man meet his obligations to his family, his fellows, his religious superiors, the gods and the spirits of his ancestors. If he was faithful in these things then he might merit *swarga* (heaven) or, at least, qualify for rebirth in comfortable circumstances. Thus, for all practical purposes, the goal of dharmic striving was not unlike that of Karma Yoga except that not many people seemed preoccupied with the desire to escape samsara and attain moksha. Perhaps people equated the attainment of heaven with moksha. There were always those few souls, however, who sought through meditation and discipline in the manner required by the Jnana Marga to attain absorption into Brahman. Such a soul was Kohalal Das, the saint and mystic of Caroni in Trinidad.

In whatever way they understood Hindu orthodoxy, however, the vast majority of immigrants believed in the existence of spirits which they called *bhuts* (ghosts). Some of these were supposed to haunt queerly formed trees. A feared bhut was the *chureil,* the ghost of a woman who had died during pregnancy. Chureils and 'tree' bhuts were known in North India. Not known there, however, was the peculiarly Negro spirit called 'ol' higue' in Guyana, and 'sukuyan' in Trinidad. This spirit was credited with the ability of being able to shed its skin, fly through the air and suck the blood of its victim. Many Indian immigrants quickly came to fear this Creole spirit. East Indians in the Caribbean came to believe too in the powers of the obeah-man — a figure from the world of Negro folk beliefs. It was not long before they began to credit Brahmin priests, mahants and Muslim imams with the powers of the Negro obeah-man, and to solicit from them charms, amulets and potions against the mischief of real and imaginary enemies. This combination of beliefs in spirits with Vaishnavism, Brahmin orthodoxy and shaktism indicated that Caribbean Hindus were not unlike their counterparts in India.

Islam

Every ship-load of Indian immigrants that came to the Caribbean contained a few Muslims. The following list showing the number of immigrants that sailed from Calcutta to Guyana in 1892, gives an indication of the number of Muslims (Mussulmans) that came to the colony during a year of regular recruitment.

TABLE II

CASTE AND RELIGIONS	MALE	FEMALE	TOTAL
Brahmans and high castes	113	76	189
Agriculturalists	1,533	585	2,118
Artisans	242	110	352
Low Castes	949	553	1,502
Mussulmans	373	185	558
Christians	4	–	4
TOTAL	3,214	1,509	4,723

Immigrants sailing from Calcutta to Guyana – 1892.

Islam was first taken to Northern India by Muslim Turks from the kingdom of Ghazni (now Afghanistan). In about the year 1000 A.D., Mahmud, the ruler of Ghazni, raided the Punjab. Mahmud justified his raids on the Punjab on the ground that his purpose was to rid the land of infidels and idolators. By 1030, when Mahmud died, a Muslim governor was established at Lahore and the surrounding territories were incorporated into the Ghaznavid kingdom. Towards the end of the twelfth century A.D., new waves of Turks under the Ghuris invaded India once more. By 1206, when Muhammad, the last of the Ghuris, was assassinated, most of Northern India, from Sind to Bengal, had passed into the hands of the Turkish invaders. Effective rule was exercised by Muslim soldier-rulers among

155

whom was Kutbuddin Aibah who established the sultanate of Delhi.

The Muslim Turks intermarried with the conquered Indians, many of whom converted to the religion of Islam. The missionary enterprise of the Sufis, Muslim holy men and mystics, resulted in the spread of the new religion among the Hindus and Buddhists of north-western India. The missionary strategy of the Sufis was simple. They stated that the name of their god, Allah, was but another name for the supreme God in whom the Hindus already believed. They further affirmed that Muhammad, the founder of the faith, was an avatar of the supreme God, Brahma.

The fall of Persia and the destruction of Baghdad under the impact of Genghiz Khan's Mongols in the mid-thirteen century, led to the influx of many Persian Muslims into the sultanate of Delhi. Delhi itself became one of the most important centres of the Asian Muslim community. But it was under the Moghul rulers that Islam was to reach the peak of its influence in India. Moghul rule in India may be dated from 1526, when Babur overthrew the Afghan sultanate in Delhi and defeated a Hindu army at Panipat. Earlier (1405), the Turkish Muslim, Tamerlane, alleged successor to Genghiz Khan and ancestor of Babur, had sacked Delhi but his rule there was short-lived. Babur was succeeded by a number of famous emperors who were deeply religious Muslims. These included Akbar (1556-1605), Jahangir (1605-27), Shah Jehan (1627-1658) and Aurangzeb (1658-1707). Under these emperors, Islam made significant inroads into Hindu India. It engendered a number of Hindu reform movements such as the Kabir panth; but, more important, it won over considerable numbers of Indians to Allah and his prophet, Muhammad. It was from among the descendants of these converts to Islam that Muslims or Mussulmans were recruited for labour on the Caribbean plantations.

The conversion of Hindus to Islam did not seriously affect the life-style of many of the converts. In the villages of Northern India, there was little to distinguish the Muslims from the Hindus. Not only were the former of Hindu descent, but their conversion to Islam did not prevent them from observing Hindu festivals and customs and even from worshipping at local Hindu shrines. In addition, most Muslim villagers observed the rules of caste to which their Hindu forebears belonged. These rules related to social intercourse, group endogamy and occupation. The conversion of some Hindus was facilitated by

156

the fact that they understood Islam in bhakti terms – a phenomenon made possible by the spread of the bhakti movement in Northern India at an earlier period. Thus, people saw Allah as a personal expression of impersonal Being, and not a few of them believed that Muhammad was an avatar of Brahma in much the same way that Rama and Krishna were. If Muhammad was not an avatar, he was at least an important guru who taught men how they could find moksha by devoting their worship and attention to Allah.

The most powerful appeal of Islam must have been its simplicity both in its doctrines and in its demands on its adherents. By the time Islam reached India, its beliefs and practices had achieved their definitive form.

Central to Islamic belief is the doctrine of the unity of God. God (Allah in Arabic) is one; beside him there is none other. The faithful remind themselves of this belief by repeating the *shahada* (confession) as often as they can: "There is no god but Allah, and Muhammad is his apostle." In Arabic, the shahada runs: *"La ilaha illa Allah Muhammad rasul Allah."* Allah is omnipotent; he is the creator of all things and of man, whom he created from "a blood-clot." Allah communicated his plan for humanity to Adam and his descendants. The message is simple: Happiness and peace are to be found in submission to and worship of Allah. The word 'Islam,' which means both peace and submission, contains this message in its most succinct form. Disobedience or the refusal to submit to Allah will be punished by the Almighty.

Throughout history, Allah has reiterated his will through prophets among whom have been Adam, Seth, Enoch, Abraham, Moses, David and Jesus. In every case the message has been changed and distorted by perverse men. In the case of Jesus, for example, his disciples chose to worship the messenger rather than to heed his message. At last, Allah sent down his final revelation through Muhammad. This time, the revelation was written down in the form of the *Qur'an*, the Word of God for Muslims. What was more, Muhammad was responsible for forming an Islamic community that was pledged to live in submission to Allah and to spread the message of Islam far and wide.

Muhammad was born in about 570 A.D., at Mecca, in what later came to be called Saudi Arabia. He belonged to the Quraysh tribe. When he was about forty years old (i.e. 609/610) he received the call and command from Allah:

157

Recite: In the Name of thy Lord who created, created Man of a blood-clot.

Recite: And thy Lord is the Most Generous, who taught by the Pen, taught Man that he knew not.

Having overcome his initial hesitation over the call, Muhammad preached Allah's message of warning and judgement with the result that a few converts were made to the new faith. These included the prophet's wife, Khadijah; his uncle, Abu Talib and two of his staunchest comrades, Abu Bakr and Umar. Persecution at Mecca at the hands of the Quraysh caused the Muslims (submitters) to migrate to Yathrib. The migration which took place in 622, has been called the *Hijra* and it dates the beginning of the Muslim era. Yathrib became a Muslim centre; it was renamed Madinat-al-Nabi ('the City of the Prophet'), or, more simply, Medina. The peaceful conquest and conversion of Mecca, which took place later from the base at Medina, was followed by the conversion of the better part of the Arabian peninsula. By the time of the prophet's death in 632, the Arab tribes were practically organised into a theocracy governed by the will of Allah. And already the Muslims were beginning to burst into the surrounding lands in military and missionary conquest.

Allah has also made his will known through angels, principal among whom is Gabriel. It was Gabriel, in fact, who made the initial revelation to Muhammad. In Islamic understanding, Allah sits in splendour in the seventh heaven, surrounded by angels who serve him and do his every bidding. The Devil, or Iblis, or *Shaitin*, is an angel, who, because of his pride, fell from Allah's grace. Iblis is now the tempter who, along with his assistants, obstructs Allah's will and tempts men to disobey him. Of those who disobey, the Qur'an says:

After this sort will be recompense the transgressors. They shall make their bed in Hell, and above them shall be coverings of fire! . . . And the inmates of the fire shall cry to the inmates of Paradise: "Pour upon us some water!"

Bliss awaits the faithful in Paradise. According to the Qur'an:

But the pious shall be in a secure place,
Amid gardens and fountains,
Clothed in silk and riches robes, facing one another . . .
On inwrought couches
Reclining on them face to face:
Aye-blooming youths go round about to them
With goblets and ewers and a cup of flowing wine;

158

Their brows ache not from it, nor fails the sense:
And with such fruits as shall please them best,
And with flesh of such birds as they shall long for:
And theirs shall be the Houris, with large dark eyes, like pearls
   hidden in their shells,
In recompense for their labours past . . .

· It is on the Last Day, the Day of Judgement, that men will
be bodily resurrected to reap their just deserts of either the
bliss of paradise or the terrors of hell. On that day, the last
trumpet will sound and the dead will rise to face the judgement
of Allah. Meanwhile, people are well-advised to perform the
duties prescribed by the 'Five Pillars (al-Arkan) of Islam.'
They must repeat the shahada; they must pray five times daily,
at dawn, mid-day, mid-afternoon, sunset and before retiring
to sleep, with the face turned in the direction of Mecca. On
Friday, adult male Muslims are expected to attend prayers at
the mosque. Public prayers are conducted by the *imam*. The
Muslim is required to perform *zakat*, that is, he is required to
give alms to the poor and needy. During the holy month of
Ramadan, all Muslims, except pregnant women and the sick,
are obliged to fast. Finally, every Muslim is expected, unless it
is impossible, to go on a pilgrimage (hajj) to Mecca at least
once in his life-time. It was, of course, impossible for the
Muslim immigrants in the Caribbean to go on hajj to Mecca. It
was not until well into the twentieth century that a few of
them were able to do so. Presumably, they observed the other
pillars of their faith.

In 1891, when D.W.D. Comins visited the Caribbean on a
mission from the Government of India, Muslim mosques were
to be seen in Surinam, Guyana and Trinidad. By this time, the
Tadjah (or *Tazia*) festival had become well-known not only in
those three colonies but in Jamaica as well. Tadjah was celebrated in South Trinidad as early as the 1850s. In 1884, Tadjah
celebrations led to riots in San Fernando. Violent clashes also
took place in Guyana between those who celebrated Tadjah
and those Hindus who celebrated Dasserah. Both festivals
tended to be celebrated at about the same time in Guyana;
both involved processions and both became so secularised that
their celebration involved excessive rum drinking. The following
is a late nineteenth century description of the celebration of
the festival in Guyana:

> The name Tadjah is derived from the taj (temple or tomb) of
> which a representation in gaudy coloured paper and tinsel is

carried in procession to be thrown into the river when the play is over. The women following a band of men with drums, who come behind the great model tomb, which is sometimes fifty feet high, keep up a pathetic wailing for Hassan and Hosein, the last descendants of Mohammed, and give the whole procession the appearance of a funeral pageant. . . . At intervals they visit the manager's yard and go through a series of sham fights, single stick combats and gymnastic exercises.[6]

The Tadjah was actually a *Shi'ite* festival that was celebrated on the tenth of the Muslim month of Muharram to mark the culmination of ten days' mourning for Hassan and Hossein, the sons of Ali and the grandsons of the prophet Muhammad, who were slain in the seventh century struggle over the succession to the Islamic Caliphate. Ali and his sons lost the struggle but their followers refused to recognise the leadership of the Umayyad caliphs. They came to comprise a sect (by no means the only one) within Islam and were known as *Shias* or Shi'ites. The Sunnis or orthodox Muslims held the celebration of Muharram in contempt. In Trinidad, in the 1880s they tried to get the government to ban the celebration of the festival.

Tadjah was popular on the sugar plantations. But as soon as Muslims settled in villages they began to observe the feasts of *Id-al-adha, Id-al-fitr* and the festival of *Mawlid an Nabi. Id-al-adha* is celebrated on the tenth of the Muslim month of *Dhu-al-Hijja.* It is supposed to commemorate the sacrifice of a sheep by Abraham in substitution for his son, Ishmael. This was done on the instruction of Allah. Because the animal slaughtered on the occasion of the commemoration of this sacrifice in the Caribbean at an earlier period was the goat, the feast is popularly known as *Id-bukri* or *Bukri-id* (the ceremony of the goat). *Id-al-fitr* which marks the end of the fast of Ramadan is an occasion for great rejoicing. The festival of *Mawlid-an Nabi* marks the birthday of the prophet Muhammad.

A Muslim practice that has grown up in the Caribbean is that of the *kitab.* This is the reading of the Qur'an in the homes of devout Muslims. On this occasion, relatives, friends and neighbours are invited, gifts are made to the poor, *sherni* is distributed, and the guests are treated to a meal. The kitab might well have developed in imitation of the Hindu puja.

By 1930, Muslims in Surinam, Guyana and Trinidad had organised themselves at village and district level into voluntary organisations called *jamaats.* Later, colony-wide associations would be formed such as the Anjuman Sunnat-ul-Jamaat of Trinidad. The village and district jamaats were responsible for erecting mosques, organising schools for the teaching of Arabic, determining what was orthodox behaviour in line with the teachings of the Qur'an, and for imposing sanctions on those Muslims in the community who erred in relation to Islamic orthodoxy in belief and behaviour. Muslims of the peasant class felt that they met the obligations of their religion if they prayed regularly, attended the mosque on Friday, gave alms, fasted during Ramadan, celebrated the festivals, abstained from eating pork and drinking liquor, married their children and buried their dead according to Muslim rites, circumcised their young sons and gave an occasional kitab. That was enough to merit paradise. In case it was not enough, the consolation was always there that Allah is compassionate and merciful and could be trusted to do his best to save the faithful from the burnings of hell.

Hindus and Muslims did not usually come to the Caribbean in family or caste groups. These social groups had traditionally served as the matrix of Hinduism. They were also important for the practice of Islam insofar as the Islam of the Indian villages from which the immigrants originated was highly Hinduised. And Hinduism was so rooted to the Indian soil that its transplantation away from home seemed impossible.

Yet Hinduism and Islam survived the crossing of the kala pani to find new homes in the Caribbean. That they were able to do so is testimony to the liveliness of the beliefs of the Indian immigrants, and to the capacity of those beliefs to adapt themselves to the conditions of life first of all on the sugar plantations and then later in the larger host societies of Guyana, Trinidad, Surinam and Jamaica.

The evolution of a distinctive Caribbean Hinduism (and of a Caribbean Islam which was, in the earlier period, regarded as a Hindu sect) was due to a number of factors. Not least of these was the tendency of the plantocracy not to interfere with Hindu and Islamic religious practices as long as these did not adversely affect the performance of the 'coolies' in the cane-brake or in the factory. At first, there was a reluctance on the part of plantation owners and managers to recruit Hindus of the priestly caste to work on the plantations. It was felt that the priestly disdain for manual labour would lead to the kind of disaffection that would disrupt life in the logie lines and work in the fields. The fact that Brahmins (priests) were in the early days of indentureship, involved in strikes in Trinidad and Guyana, would seem to indicate that the fears of the plantocracy were not unfounded.

161

In spite of the plantocracy, however, Brahmins did come to the Caribbean. They were to help in the process of Hindu social and cultural reconstruction which we can conveniently date to about 1920 or so. By that time, Hindus had come to terms with caste snobbery and pretensions sufficiently for marriage to take place across caste lines (although caste snobbery was to be very much in evidence, particularly among members of the higher castes, for a long time to come). Fictive kin relationships that had hitherto sustained social life were giving way to the relationships of the extended family with which the Indians were familiar. The question of the status of priests had long been settled by popular demand for the services of men whose credentials would have been questioned in India. The annual cycle of Hindu and Muslim festivals had been fixed.

The shape of the reconstruction was affected by the physical conditions which prevailed on the estates and by many factors which were related to indentureship. But the reconstruction was definitely influenced by religious notions and beliefs. In this regard, low caste religious ideas dominated. Low caste influences were at work in the ceremonies marking the important *rites de passage* of marriage and funeral and in the choice of festivals which the immigrants celebrated. The preponderance of lower caste folk among the immigrants was, no doubt, responsible for the prevalence of lower caste religious motifs. But ideas and practices which were traditionally associated with the higher castes surfaced as well, affecting, for example, the shape of the marriage ceremony that was to become popular. This ceremony now combines lower caste rituals with those traditionally practised by people of higher castes.

Perhaps this process of social and cultural reconstruction began spontaneously in the early days of indentureship as immigrants tried to order their social life along the lines of 'remembered' tradition. The memory of these traditions was strengthened and augmented by every new wave of immigrants from India. Once estate life had developed its own ethos and tenor, newer immigrants found it convenient to subscribe to this peculiar 'Indian-Hindu' life style. Not a few people would remain critical of that life style, not being altogether convinced that it was the same as that of the village in India. This ambivalence, in turn, would help to create that cynicism which characterises Caribbean Hindu society.

In time, increasing numbers of immigrants moved off the plantations into villages sandwiched between those settled by

162

African ex-slaves. As they came into wider contact with people of other races and religions, their own religions, Hinduism and Islam, became important criteria by which their claims to an identity that was different from other groups in the host society would be strengthened.

By that time, the larger society had already identified membership in the Christian church as one of the more important marks of civilisation. From that perspective, the non-Christian Indians were perceived as barbarous aliens. This perception among other things, together with the Indians' own tendency towards cultural encystment, would make their assimilation into the host society very difficult. It would lead as well to the development of the plural society in places such as Trinidad and Guyana.

From the viewpoint of the larger society, Islam was at first perceived as a sect within Hinduism. This was due in part to the ignorance of the larger society regarding these matters, and in part to the fact that like the Hindus, the Muslims were Indians. Doubtless when it came to matters relating to racial and cultural identity, Muslims identified with Hindus. But as the Islamic communities in the Caribbean became larger, as they became more knowledgeable in their faith, and as news of the problems between Hindus and Muslims in India began to reach the Caribbean, the Hindus and Muslims in these parts began to become aware of their distinctiveness. That distinctiveness was seen as almost exclusively religious in nature.

These developments took place without any significant effect on the rhythm of plantation life. That life was disrupted from time to time by strikes and work stoppages but religion had little to do with these disruptions. In fact, it is felt that the reverence with which Hindus held the god Hanuman, the apotheosis of self-surrender, total obedience and unswerving loyalty, predisposed them to accept the indignities of estate work life without much complaint. The argument is sometimes adduced, too, that many indentured labourers saw their station and lot on the plantation as the will of their god or as their destiny which had been determined by the Hindu notion of *karma*. As such, they were not likely to protest overmuch against the conditions under which they lived and worked on the plantation.

Notes and References

1. *Sieunarainis* is an anglicised way of pluralising.
2. The Kaaba is a Muslim shrine found in Mecca, Kailash is a Hindu holy mountain.
3. Bronkhurst, *British Guiana and its labouring population*, pp. 356-7.
4. Quoted from D.A. Bisnauth, *The East Indian Immigrant Society in British Guiana, 1891-1930.* p. 223.
5. *Sources of Indian Tradition*, ed. W.I. de Bary, vol. ii, p. 206.
6. James Rodway and James H. Stark, *Rodway and Stark's Guide-book and History of British Guiana*, pp. 56-57.

CHAPTER VII
THE AFRICANISATION OF CHRISTIANITY

No doubt many of the African slaves and freemen who became Christians under the impact of Catholic and evangelical missionary effort turned out to be completely orthodox in their understanding of the new religion. Others, however, had only a partial grasp of the new faith, while not a few understood Christianity in terms of religious ideas that had their roots in Africa.

The Spanish Catholics were the first to teach Christianity to the blacks. Their programme for christianising the Negroes could not be thorough. There were never enough priests and friars to conduct an adequate mission among the slaves. The result was that, in Cuba, many blacks learnt enough of Catholic saints to identify them with their gods or to include them among their pantheon of divinities. The accommodation was facilitated by the belief that the saints functioned as intermediaries between the Supreme God and mankind, in much the same way that the African divinities were believed to function as intermediaries between Oludumare, for example, and the Yoruba tribesmen.

The cult that grew up around the worship of the saints and African divinities in Cuba, was called *Santeria* (Saint worship). In the estimation of Esteban Montejo, Santeria was the worship of the Yoruba god Ogun in the form of San Juan (St. John). Santeria cultists worshipped Ogun as Ogun Arere, the warrior, Ogun Oke, the hunter, and Ogun Aguanille, the metal worker. While Ogun might have been the chief divinity of Santeria belief, doubtless the cultists combined the worship of this Yoruba divinity with that of other gods. In this respect, as will be seen later, the Cuban Santeria would not have been different from Shango as it came to be practised in Trinidad.

Catholicism was also taught to the blacks, in the colonies of

St. Domingue (Haiti) and Trinidad, and it was there that the accommodation of Christian ideas and practices within the framework of African beliefs was greatest. In St. Domingue, the cult that developed as a result of this accommodation was facilitated because of the resemblance (in the eyes of the blacks) between the saints of Catholicism and the divinities of African religions.

Haitian Vodun:

The Haitian vodunist retained the African belief in a Supreme God whom he called *Le Bon Dieu* or *Le Grand Maitre*. Like 'Nyame or Mawu, *Le Bon Dieu* (The Good God) was believed, as the name signifies, to be well-disposed to man. Consequently, there was no need to worship him. Worship, however, was directed to *loas* (spirits or divinities) which were sometimes referred to as *vodous, z'anges, z'espwits* or *mysteres*.

The loas numbered hundreds. Many of them were identifiably African in origin; these included Ogun, Damballa, Shango, Legba, Obatala and Sousou Pannan. Other were identifiably Catholic saints. There were for example, St. Anthony, St. Patrick, Papa Pie (St. Peter) and Mater Dolorosa (Mother of Sorrow, i.e., the Virgin Mary). In the understanding of some Haitian peasants, the saints were identified with the divinities. Thus, Damballa was said to be St. Patrick, Legba was identified with St. Anthony, and Erzilie was said to be Mater Dolorosa. What might have happened is that the peasants, at first, added the Catholic saints to the host of African spirits which they worshipped. Then, as some saints came to be perceived as resembling some spirits in function and in other characteristics, the former were identified as the latter.

Some vodunists however, felt that the spirits 'under the water' (i.e. the African divinities) were nearer man, while the saints were nearer heaven. It was felt by these people that the loas conveyed to the saints the wishes and desires of man which were, in turn, relayed by the saints to the Supreme Being. Yet another opinion was that the loas were fallen angels. This opinion might well have been held by those peasants who were more catholicised than their fellows. One thing is certain, the Catholic saints had been given the status of divine intermediaries between Le Bon Dieu and the vodunists.

Quite in keeping with African practice, the saints-turned-loas were ascribed certain attributes and qualities. These were not derived from Biblical sources or from Catholic tradition. For example, St. Peter, or Papa Pie was regarded as rather military in appearance; he was not given to laughter and he was supposed

166

to have his abode at the bottom of rivers and ponds. St. John was regarded as a rather stern, nervous loa, who was always on the move. This saint was credited with a thirst for champagne and fine liqueurs and an appetite for the meat of black cattle and white sheep.

The paraphernalia arranged on or about the vodun altar included a number of objects from the world of Catholic worship — crucifixes, rosaries, holy water, candles and chromo-liths of Catholic saints. These were mingled with thunder stones, flags, flowers, and foods and liquors that the gods specially liked. Altars were to be found in *humforts* (temples), but some-times an altar was set up either in a private house or in a tent set up near to such a house when the service was arranged by a family to urge the gods to desist from persecuting members of that family. The persecution of the gods might take the form of the destruction of crops or the prolonged illness of children.

Elements of Catholicism were integrated into the vodun ceremony. After the *vever*[1] of the principal god to be invoked was made and the twins[2] were duly summoned, fed and dis-missed, the service continued with the consecration of those places (trees, springs, cross-roads) where the spirits were believed to reside. For the ritual of consecration, holy water obtained from a Catholic church was often used. The sprinkling of the holy water was invariably accompanied by the intonation of formulas which were Catholic in origin. After the general salutation *(sagwe)* to the gods, prayers were said either by the presiding *houngan* (priest), *mambo* (priestess), *badjican* (assistant priest) or by some-one who was familiar with Catholic prayers. A prayer said on such an occasion might run:

> O Mary, Mother of Mercy, take pity on these poor, abandoned souls. Mary, Mother of God, Mother of mothers, Mother of Grace, pray for these converted souls, these souls of purgatory. All the Saints, all the angels, angels of the heavens, gods of the water, gods of the forest, gods known and unknown, all the gods, all the twins, come and deliver this poor brother from tribulation. Do not permit bad spirits to spoil the service. And you, the dead, stop persecuting him, make him prosperous, give him peace, repose, complete understanding. Save him, for he has never refused you. Times are bad, but he offers you a great sacrifice. Do not let him be shamed by the devil. Fervently pray God that he may be victorious over his enemies, that he may triumph over Lucifer and his demons. Grace! Mercy! Pardon!

The gods were then summoned to the service. Legba was invariably the first to be invited by chanting and dancing to the

167

accompaniment of drumming. During the dance, a *serviteur*[3] would become possessed by Legba. She would go through a set of violent contortions and then walk about with the limp that was believed to be characteristic of Legba. The god would then give the 'salute' which would be repeated by the worshippers in song. After Legba had spoken again through the person possessed, he would be presented with a black chicken. The chicken would be washed and perfumed then its neck would be wrung by Legba. All the while, the singing and dancing would go on. Finally, the chicken would be given to the cooks. Other gods were then summoned; they possessed serviteurs and the ceremonies continued. The climax of the service was reached when the time for the sacrifice of the goat arrived. The animal was given in sacrifice to the principal *z'ange* that was invited to the service. During the ritual involving the sacrifice of the goat, the Catholic hymn, "There is a King of the Angels" might be sung. After the arrival of the principal z'ange, dancing continued until the food was cooked. Serviteurs and *fideles*[4] and z'anges participated in this to the point of exhaustion.

Next morning at six, the food was sprinkled with holy water, Catholic prayers including the Magnificat were chanted, and then the gods were fed. The participants in the service were also given food as were the drummers. When the gods dispersed, the priest concluded the service by chanting:

Thanks to God
Thanks to the Saints,
Thanks to the Z'anges,
Thanks to the dead,
Thanks to the twins,
Mercy for the master of the service,
Mercy for his wife,
Mercy for his children,
Thanks to all the Z'anges!

The purpose of the vodun ceremony was to summon the gods in order to put to them the requests of those who organised the ceremony. These requests were made as gods and worshippers danced and feasted together. The fact that the gods deigned to attend the ceremony was interpreted as an indication that they would meet the requests of the suppliants.

Most vodunists were also members of the Catholic church. Their houngans advised them to attend mass regularly. But their Weltanschauung, their understanding of the world around them, was provided by vodun. In addition to the loa-saints their universe was believed to be peopled with the spirits of their departed ancestors and by the 'dead' generally. In this respect, the beliefs of the vodunists were almost identical with those of their African forebears. The vodunist 'dead' fell into several categories. There were the zombie errants − the spirits of those people who died in accidents and thus, unnaturally. *Diablesses* were the spirits of women who died as virgins; these spirits were regarded as evil. Zombie errants had to live out their allotted life-span on earth before they could qualify for heaven; diablesses had to make expiation for their omission (probably of not bearing children) before they could be similarly qualified. *Lutins* were the ghosts of children who died before they were initiated (i.e. baptised), while the *marassa-jumeaux* were the spirits of dead twins who were held in awe by *vodunists.*[5]

Both Catholic and African ideas influenced the vodunists' beliefs concerning the soul after it had left the body at death. Among the more Catholicized, it was felt that 'natural' death was occasioned by God's recall of a person's soul. The soul then went to its judgement and to receive its reward or punishment as the case might be. A good soul might remain with God in the sky or it might return to earth as a good loa or it might become incarnated in a new-born baby. The bad soul might spend an eternity of suffering in hell.

Where African ideas prevailed, it was felt that it was necessary to perform the appropriate death rites in order to speed the spirits of the deceased to their proper places. It was believed that a person was composed of a body, a *gros-bon-ange* or spiritual double of the body, and the *ti-bon-ange* or spirit. In addition, a person was possessed of a loa *mait-tête* which was master of his head. The death rites were meant to dissociate the gros-bon-ange (the soul) and the loa mait-tête from the body. The departure of the ti-bon-ange (or conscience) for heaven was marked by little ritual since it was believed that it was automatically freed from the body at death, although it hovered over that body for nine days before ascending to heaven.

The main death ritual was that of the *dessounin* or 'degradation'. The dessounin accomplished the liberation of the loa who might return to its permanent home, the abysmal waters. The ceremony also freed the gros-bon-ange from the material body. Freed of the now defunct matter, the gros-bon-ange became an independent spirit and part of the general spirit world. It was, however, held to be specially related to the family of the now deceased person. In time, it might even become the loa mait-tête of one of that person's descendants.

Sometimes, while a person was alive, his gros-bon-ange was

ceremonially put in a receptable, a govi or a canari. If the receptacle was stolen and magic worked upon the body through the gros-bon-ange, the belief ran that the person could not properly die until body and gros-bon-ange were reunited. To bring about this reunion, the gros-bon-ange had to be reclaimed from the abysmal waters where it was temporarily confined. The rites of reclamation were performed a year and a day, after the person had died.

The development of vodun was no doubt facilitated by the provision made by the Code Noir (1685) that the African slaves were to be baptised and instructed in the Catholic religion. That same code outlawed the meeting of slaves for any other purpose save that of Catholic worship. Nevertheless, the slaves did meet surreptitiously for the practice of religious rites and ceremonies which they brought with them from Africa. Knowledge of these practices was transmitted from generation to generation. Over the years, the traditions of other tribes became merged with the predominantly Dahomean ones to form the African bases of the vodun cult. The 'Dahomean' rites came to be called Rada after the Dahomean township of Allada.

In addition to the Rada rites, there evolved rites of a more aggressive and violent nature among many vodunists, particularly those who lived in the more inaccessible hill country. By 1751, some 3,500 blacks had fled to the hills of St. Dominque to escape the rigours of plantation life and the brutality of slavery. The rites which developed among these blacks came to be identified as those of the Petro 'nation'. Some of the Petro deities were of New World origin. These included Dan Petro, Baron Samedi, Simbi and Azacca. Simbi was originally the local Amerindian god of rain and Azacca the Indian deity associated with the maize. Samedi and zombie might well have been derived from the Arawak *zemi;* both were related to the spirits of the dead. Obviously, Indian ideas were assimilated into the African framework of beliefs.

While the Rada deities were regarded mainly as the protectors and guardians of their serviteurs and of the fidèles, the Petro deities were looked upon as sources of inspiration for aggressive action, particularly against oppression. The Petro was born in protest against slavery, and long after the successful slave revolt in St. Domingue at the end of the eighteenth century, the theme of revolt, "Vive la liberté," was dominant in Petro ceremonies. 'African' loas that in Rada rituals were more dignified in character became distinctly aggressive in Petro ceremonies.

170

Thus, Ogun, the dignified and chivalrous warrior of Rada, became in Petro, Ogun Ge-Rouge, the epitome of the ruthless fighter, and Erizilie, the gentle Goddess of Love (Rada), became Erzilie Ge-Rouge, the raging termagant of Petro.

Vodun achieve definite form between 1750 and 1790 Cultic beliefs inspired slave revolts against and resistance to the French plantocracy.

Macandal, who ran riot in northern St. Domingue in 1757-8, claimed that he was the representative of a divinity who was presumably African. Jean-François, Biassou and Hyacinthe Ducoudray claimed inspiration, not possession by African gods, while Romaine Riviere, who led a revolt at Trou-Coffi, stated that the Virgin Mary was his special patroness. Boukman, who led the slaves of the Turpin plantation in revolt in August 1791 and thus precipitated the St. Dominigue revolution, was undoubtedly a worshipper of African divinities. He might even have been a houngan. It was at a Petro ceremony which he conducted on the night of August 14, 1791, that he inspired the slaves to revolt. The vodun, leaders invariably asserted that their gods made them invulnerable to the weapons of their enemies. The militant faithful were sometimes assured that if they died in the cause of their freedom their spirits would return to Africa.

The accommodation of Catholic elements into the cult must have begun in the period before 1790, although there was greater degree of accommodation after that date. After the Revolution, the Haitian rulers Toussaint, Dessalines and Christophe tried to suppress vodun. They imposed a ban on vodun ceremonies and were ruthless in their punishment of those people who were caught practising vodun rituals. At the same time (1800-1815), Catholicism was practised with freedom. This, no doubt, helped to determine the extent to which Catholic elements were absorbed into the vodun cult. The mid-nineteenth century marked the turning point in the development of the cult. Under Emperor Soulouque, cultic ceremonies could be publicly celebrated without let or hindrance from the authorities. From about 1860, the Catholic Church sought to combat vodun, and occasionally a Haitian ruler might try to suppress it but vodun has not declined in its influence or its attraction for many Haitians, some of whom are members of the elite class of that society.

Shango
In its early development in Trinidad, shango combined

171

African religious ideas with those of Catholicism. While the African ideas which predominated in the formation of vodun were Dahomean in origin, those that were most influential in the development of shango were of Yoruba origin. The beliefs and practices of the shangoists as they developed, say to 1930 were remarkably similar to, if not identical with, those of vodun. Not only was the 'common' African background responsible for this; so too was the 'common' influence of Catholicism which Trinidad shared with Haiti.

Nineteenth-century observers in post-emancipation Trinidad noted that the blacks met at nights, sang and danced to the accompaniment of drumming. Sometimes, they worshipped what has been described as a 'fetish.' At such worship ceremonies, people exhibited all the marks of spirit possession. It was noted, too, that the practice of obeah was widespread among the blacks. It is possible that the shango cult achieved a definite form even before emancipation. By that time, religious ideas held by slaves and free blacks in the one-time Spanish island might have merged with those brought by the slaves of those French (Catholic) colonists who migrated to the island from St. Vincent and Grenada between 1783 and 1797, and from the French islands of Guadeloupe and Martinique. The result of the merger was the system of beliefs and practices that came to be called shango.

The name of the cult can be misleading. While in Nigeria the Shango cult is dedicated solely to the worship of the Yoruba divinity of that name, in Trinidad, shango is only one of many 'powers' that are worshipped by shangoists. The people, incidentally, refer to themselves as 'Yoruba people' or 'Orisha people' or 'African people' and not as shangoists.

Olurun, the supreme god of Yoruba belief, is not worshipped by the Orisha people. He is not even known among them. He might have failed to survive the Middle Passage because – in common with other African tribal supreme beings – his worship was too attenuated to survive the rigours of that passage. Two Yoruba gods, Elephon and Obalufon, are regarded as 'Eternal Father' and Jesus respectively. But it is to be doubted that either of them is held in the same regard as Olurun is held by the Yorubas. For all practical purposes, Eternal Father and Jesus are just Christian names that have been assigned to Elephon and Obalufon who, in spite of those names, retain their 'African' characteristics. Thus, Elephon is regarded as the 'head man' in shango ceremonies and rituals.

172

Like the vodun loas, the shango powers are sometimes identified with Catholic saints. Thus, Shango is identified with St. John, Shakpana with St. Francis or Moses, Obatala with St. Benedict, and Ogun with St. Michael. But there are also those Catholic saints that are regarded as 'powers' purely on their own merit. No attempt is made to identify them with African divinities. Such saints or powers include St. Agatha, St. Lucy, St. Luke, St. Rose and the Virgin Mary. Some of the powers are of local origin; others like Bogoyana and Samedona are said to have originated in Guyana.

Again, like the loas of vodun belief, the powers have their special characteristics and their peculiar tastes in food and clothing. Thus, Oya, the mistress of wind and rain, is hot-tempered; her preference is for offerings of female goats or hens and her favourite colour in clothes is green, Ogun, the god of iron and war, is given to violence. His preference in offerings is for rams or cocks and puncheon rum; his colours are red and white. When a person becomes possessed by a power at a shango ceremony he manifests the characteristics of the power thus making it possible for an identification of the spirit to be made.

Ceremonies are usually held at cult centres. The buildings at a centre are usually the *palais,* the *chapelle* and the house of the *amombah* (priestess). The paraphernalia which usually occupy the altar in the chapelle are almost identical with those to be found on a vodun altar. The annual shango ceremony follows a pattern that is similar to the vodun ceremony outlined above.

The palais having been incensed, the four-day annual ceremony begins with prayers that contain obvious Catholic elements. Shango prayers, however, are more recitative than intercessory. A favourite prayer runs:

> Blessed Martin was called the Father of the Poor. He saw in the poor, the sick and the dying the children of God, and he helped them in a thousand practical ways. He studied medicine so that he might know how to cure the sick. Every day he distributed alms to the poor. He built an orphanage for children. Let us imitate the charity of Blessed Martin that God may bless us as he blessed him.

Eshu, who, because of his proneness to commit pranks is identified with Satan, is suitably summoned, fed and dismissed in much the same way that the twins are. Then the gods are summoned, beginning with Ogun (St. Michael). They indicate their presence in their presence in the same way as Legba at a vodun ceremony and are welcomed and given offerings. The power may, in turn, bless the worshippers. Shango Abacuso, for example, may put his hands on the heads of the worshippers who kneel before him and bless them. In addition, he may wipe the faces of the devotees with a piece of white cloth *(adado)* and give those who wish it a sip of olive oil. Meanwhile, drumming goes on incessantly.

Throughout the ceremony, sacrifices of chickens, pigeons, doves, agoutis, goats and sheep are made. Sometimes bulls are sacrificed as well. Later in the ceremony, the worshippers eat the flesh of the sacrificed birds or animals, but not before heaped platters of cooked meat are placed on the floor of the chapelle or on stools dedicated to powers as offerings to the divinities.

Another important shango ceremony is that of "feeding the children." The *rationale* for this ceremony is often stated thus: "When you feed the children, you feed the saints." Some of the prayers said on this occasion are: The Hail Mary, the Lord's Prayer and the Twenty-third Psalm. At every important point in the ceremony the formula is repeated: "In the name of the Father, the Son, and the Holy Spirit." Incensing forms an important part of the ceremony and so does the throwing of handfuls of parched corn in the direction of the powers' stools.

Another ceremony that shows the blend of African and Catholic influences is that which is held on All Saints' Night (November 1). On that night, lighted candles are placed on the stools of the powers, on the altar in the chapelle, and in the palais, in honour of the saints and powers. A song sung on that occasion runs:

> Here is All Saints' night
> Here is All Saints' night
> Here is All Saints' night
> Ogun we want; All Saints' night
> Osain we want; All Saints' night.
> Shakpana we want, All Saints' night.

In common with other lower class Trinidadians, shangoists hold to a lively belief in *sukuyans* and *legawus*. The sukuyan is a woman who is credited with the ability to fly through the air and attack her victims by sucking their blood. The legawu is the male counterpart of the sukuyan. Amombas are said to be able to protect people from the attack of this Caribbean version of the African witch. The shango beliefs regarding the dead are

174

similar to those held by vodunists.

Syncretism and accommodation in the ex-British colonies

Many blacks in the British colonies displayed an early interest in Christianity for several reasons. For example, Richard Ligon knew a slave in Barbados who wanted to be made a Christian because he felt that that would endow him with the knowledge which he lacked and which he suspected the whites had because of their religion. Matthew Lewis, who encouraged his slaves to be baptised, made the observation that Christianity was regarded by the blacks as "a superior species of magic."[6] Some of them felt that baptism made them safe from the machinations of the obeah-man. Others felt that baptism (or 'christening' as they called it) enabled them to take oaths upon the Bible — something which they regarded as a bit of 'buckra' superstition and a qualification which made what they said credible to the ears of the whites. Sometimes, when a baptised slave suspected that his lie might not be believed by his master he would make some remark such as:

> "And now, massa, you know, I've been christened; and if you do not believe what I say, I'm ready to buss the book to the truth of it.[7]

With the coming of evangelical missionaries to the Caribbean, Christianity was preached to the blacks of the British islands. Converts to the Christian faith were baptised. Archibald Monteith, a Moravian black lay preacher of Jamaica, noted that baptism was regarded as a form of magic by some blacks and that the baptism service was sometimes followed by a dance. To correct this tendency, missionaries generally instructed their charges in the proprieties of the faith before baptising them. Believers were discouraged from attending feasts, dances and games arranged by blacks who were not converted. Converts who betrayed a hankering after the practices of their unbaptised forebears were regarded as backsliders from the Christian faith. If they persisted in their backsliding, their membership of the Christian congregation was terminated.

James M. Phillippo, the British Baptist missionary to Jamaica, tells of an interesting development which took place in that island towards the end of the eighteenth century. According to Phillippo, some blacks came to Jamaica from America at the close of the American War of Independence. The immigrants assumed the role of teachers and preachers and disseminated a form of Christianity which blended important truths with

175

'extravagant puerilities'. Phillippo does not identify the purveyors of these 'pernicious follies,'[8] but the Presbyterian missionary, William Jameson, did. They were Moses Baker and a Mr. Gibb, Baptists, who, Jameson said, were "sincere and zealous men; but their knowledge of Christianity was most imperfect, and their minds were filled with the most absurd superstitions."[9]

The converts of Baker and Gibb placed great emphasis on dreams and visions. It was felt that while God had given the Book (i.e. the Bible) to the whites, He had given dreams to the Africans. Dreams, then, were a source of revelation, in much the same way that they were in African religious beliefs.

In order to qualify for membership in the congregations established by these men, aspirants had to testify to some supernatural revelations which they had received in dreams. Accordingly, some blacks slept under trees and in bushes in order that they might have the necessary revelation. The nature of their dreams indicated whether or not they were 'fittin'' to be baptised. Baptism was by immersion. Baker and Gibb authenticated their ministry by claiming the ability to foretell the future (perhaps by way of prophecy) and to speak ecstatically in strange languages under the inspiration of the Holy Spirit.

Meetings were held regularly; these lasted far into the night. It was at these meetings, that the worshippers prayed with their arms extended and their bodies transfixed. Sometimes, they prostrated themselves on the ground where they remained in prayer for a long time "manifesting the most violent muscular contortions, and uttering the most discordant sounds expressive of internal anguish and agonizing supplication."[10] It was as if they sought that kind of assurance of God's favour and forgiveness that in African (or vodun) religious practice they would have had by being possessed by the god.

At Christmas, the teachers or shepherds of the several groups of converts who followed the teachings of Baker and Gibb went with their groups to the woods or among sheep (if these were around), hoping to be favoured by an angelic visitation similar to that which the shepherds outside Bethlehem had on the night of Christ's birth. It was believed that the angels made an annual appearance at Christmas. At other times, individuals went to secluded spots to seek the Saviour, in the manner in which it was believed John the Baptist did.

Members of the movement who became sick were usually ceremonially anointed with oil by the shepherd or father *(tata)* of their group. This was supposed to be in imitation of Jesus anointing by Mary Magdalene, before his crucifixion. This ceremony was accompanied by singing in which the tata led. The anointing of the sick in order to effect healing was known in the early Christian church; it was also a common practice among Africans. Members of this religious fraternity claimed that they knew the whereabouts of those people that had died. What was more, they claimed to be able to communicate with the 'dead'. This communication took place in that general medium of revelation — the dream.

The followers of Baker and Gibb were not the only people who believed that revelations in dreams were necessary to corroborate men's testimony regarding their faith in the Christian's God and in that God's acceptance of them. When the American evangelist, George Lewis, came to Jamaica in about 1800, many slaves had 'the convince' as a result of his ministry. 'The convince' (i.e. the conviction that they were really saved) came to them in dreams after they had undergone periods of fasting.

While some people relied on dreams for revelation, others relied on possession by the Holy Ghost. Among these were the myalmen who seem to have been the Caribbean counterpart of the West African priest (Akan: *okomfo*). While it was only in Jamaica that the priests were called myalmen, such men were to be found throughout the Caribbean. One thing that they all had in common was their hatred of obeah. The myalmen of western Jamaica in the 1840s claimed to be possessed by the Holy Spirit expressly for the purpose of combatting obeahmen, who, they asserted were under the influence of the devil. The myalmen claimed to be Christians — a claim that the Moravian missionary, John Buchner, was prepared to accept as sincere as far as many of them were concerned. Their evening services were held under silk cotton trees. Dancing was part of those services as was the drinking of rum. Myalmen had little patience with Bible study. Some of them were reported to have said: "Let us not rely on books, let us rely on the Holy Ghost; and thereby we shall see how misguided the missionaries are."[11]

Before he was exposed to the influence of Christianity, the myalman (okomfo) received his inspiration from the world of the African spirits. As he became increasingly christianised, he came to rely more and more on the inspiration of the spirit from the world of Christian beliefs — the Holy Spirit. This is not to say that he forgot the African spirits completely. With

177

his African instinct for a more intuitive and dynamic experience of spiritual realities, he preferred direct revelation under the inspiration or possession of the Holy Spirit to mediated revelation through the reading of the Bible. His inability to read the Bible no doubt made him much more dependent on 'spirit' revelation. In any case, he probably felt that the direct revelation by the Spirit was much more authentic than that which came by way of the Book.

The observation has been made that a more modern Jamaican movement, revivalism, is myalism under a new name. If that is the case, then myalism has assimilated more Christian elements over the years. But, that assimilation has taken place within the structure of African traditional beliefs. In this regard, revivalism is not unlike vodun or shango, except that while vodun and shango represent the Africanisation of Catholicism, revivalism represents the Africanisation of Protestantism.

Revivalists believe in a high god who is the creator and ruler of the universe. He is God the Father. But God the Father, like Le Bon Dieu or 'Nyame, is not involved in worship services. He does not leave his throne in the high heavens to attend a revivalist 'trumping,'[12] nor does he ever possess a revivalist worshipper, although that worshipper may believe that in the final analysis trumping is "to worship God and serve Him forever." Jesus Christ, who is God the Son, comes to the service, but he too never trumps. God, the Holy Spirit, however, not only comes to every service, but he is the chief spirit in the revival and he trumps.

The important trumpers at a revival service are Biblical characters – prophets, evangelists, archangels and apostles. These include, Elijah, Moses, Daniel, Isaiah, Mark, Luke, John, Michael, Gabriel, Peter, Paul, James and Matthias. The divinities of West African religions, the powers and saints of shango, and the loas and saints of vodun are replaced by the Biblical characters of Protestant preaching and Bible reading. But they are not the only spirits that possess the revivalist worshippers. Important shepherds and shepherdesses of revivalist bands, who, on dying, enter the spirit world, also come to labour and trump. Father Levas, Shepherd Blair and Shepherd Bendigo are among these spirits.

The revival service begins with the singing of hymns (taken mainly from the hymn-book edited by Ira Sankey) and the recitation of psalms and prayers. The Holy Ghost and the four evangelists, Matthew, Mark, Luke and John, are invited first,

178

since their presence is vital for the service. Their presence is necessary for the consecration of the booth in which the service is held. Then, as the worshippers continue to trump and 'labour' as they circle the altar in a counter-clockwise direction, other spirits arrive and possess the faithful.

The whole purpose of the revivalist service is to induce the spirits to possess the worshippers. Possession itself is held to be desirable because it is by this means that the worshipper comes to apprehend the truth of spiritual realities. The initial possession is felt to have a cleansing effect on the individual; subsequent possessions help him to grow into spiritual maturity. These possessions will take place as a person stays with the revivalist band. The spirit-filled person will also receive revelation through dreams and visions. The emphasis of revivalism is clearly on personal spiritual growth and development. The movement, therefore, shares the ethos of the Protestant thrust in the Caribbean up to recent times.

When revivalists seek the cure for some sickness which may afflict a fellow band-member or friend, they feel themselves to be involved in a spiritual matter since illness is more a matter of the spirit than of the body. When a cure is being sought from the spirits, revivalists wear white gowns. Blue gowns are worn when members desire a conference with the spirits and with 'departed' officers of the cult.

Revivalist practices surrounding death betray the influences of both African retentions and Christian ideas. Since the spirit of the dead is believed to affect the living for good or ill, it is imperative that the dead be treated with respect. A wake ('setting up') is held on one or two nights before the body is buried. It is believed that on the third night, the spirit or soul, following the pattern of Christ's resurrection on the third day, is resurrected. On the ninth night, the spirit of the dead returns to its former home. On this occasion, a service of remembrance may be held at which the departed soul is admonished to continue to serve God — the greatest of all spirits. A mourning service (or 'table') is held three months after the death of a person; a second such service is held after the lapse of another three-month period. At this second 'table', the departed soul is commended to Jesus Christ and, a year later, another service commends the soul to the Holy Spirit. At this service, the Holy Spirit comes to trump and so does the departed soul who is now at peace.

Revivalists believe in the effectiveness of obeah; but while the revivalist shepherd may practice healing and provide charms against diseases and duppies (ghosts), he cannot be described as an obeah-man. Obeah-men are invariably private practitioners. They do not, like shepherds, lead congregations. In a real sense, the shepherd is like the Akan *okomfo;* he is a priest, not an obeah-man.

Kumina, another Jamaican cult, differs from revivalism in that the Christian influence is not so great in this cult as it is in revivalism. The spirits who come to dance 'myal' at Kumina are described as sky gods, earthbound gods, and ancestral spirits. Prophets, archangels, evangelists and apostles are conspicuous by their absence. Sky gods include Oto, Judee, Goomba and Fayah. It is generally felt that these gods are African in origin. Their names have probably been creolised beyond recognition. Goombah is the most popular of these spirits; he has given his name to the drum whose resonant 'voice' is said to have the ability to evoke Goombah. Some earthbound gods are Fata, Wilmott, Darcos and Ajax. These "gods" were probably one-time leaders of the cult. Most of these gods are believed to be strong; earthbound gods however, are unable to leave the earth. Ancestral spirits are the deceased members of families that belong to the cult. In life, they would have been kumina drummers and men and women who became possessed frequently. Some ancestral spirits are powerful. They are identifiable, like other spirits, by the style of their dance and their known propensity to respond to certain drumbeats and songs. Deceased ancestors on whose behalf memorial ceremonies are not held, are likely to become wandering ghosts. These ghosts are generally a menace to the living.

The Spiritual Baptists of Trinidad share many of the beliefs and practices of the revivalists of Jamaica. The Spiritual Baptists, however, place a greater emphasis on baptism for which candidates undergo instruction before they are immersed in a river. It should be pointed out here that in Bedwardism – a variation of revivalism in Jamaica – baptism by immersion is also emphasised. In both the Spiritual Baptist and Bedward cults, baptism is followed by anointing. Like the revivalists, the Spiritual Baptists emphasise spirit possession but they limit their spirits to the Holy Spirit, although it is quite possible that a Baptist may become possessed by a shango power.

The White-Robed Army (Jordanite) Movement

The Jordanite movement is peculiar to Guyana, yet its

beginnings can be traced to Trinidad, if not to Grenada. For all practical purposes, conversations begun around 1882 between a young Grenadian working in Trinidad and an East Indian immigrant residing on that island led to the birth of the new religious movement that was to develop into the White-Robed Army[13] in Guyana.

The Grenadian was a Joseph MacLaren. He worked as an overseer or supervisor of Indian labourers and was probably coloured. This latter factor would explain his employment as an overseer at a time when there was a general reluctance on the part of the plantocracy to appoint blacks to supervisory positions. This factor would also partly explain why he was either nicknamed or baptised Lallu Das.[14] MacLaren's interest in Hindu practices − no doubt encouraged by the fact that he worked with Indians − led him to cultivate the friendship of the immigrant, Bhagwan Das. MacLaren was an Anglican by religion; but the dialogue between Das and himself led him to think of starting a new faith which was probably to contain some elements from Hinduism as that religion was popularly understood and practised by East Indian labourers. Bhagwan Das who was also called Chattoo Maraj (a name which indicates that he might have functioned in a priestly capacity among his countrymen) probably taught MacLaren some of the tenets of popular Hinduism. In any case, MacLaren was sufficiently impressed by Das to receive baptism at his hand.

In 1895, MacLaren came to Guyana to propagate his faith which boasted the name, The Church of the West Evangelical Millenium Pilgrims (WEMP). He worked in Berbice with the result that in a short time sixty- five persons were converted to the new faith. One of his converts was a Barbadian named Bowen who was appointed elder of this new gathering of members of WEMP. Bowen later migrated to Chateau Margot on the East Coast, Demerara.

Little is known of the fortunes of the fledgéling movement down to 1917. In that year, however, Nathaniel Jordan, a field làbourer of Buxton on the East Coast Demerara, became a member of WEMP. For the next ten years, Jordan laboured in the cause of his new faith on the East Coast in the Chateau Margot area; he also preached on the East Bank, Demerara, around Agricola. Such was Jordan's impact on the movement that by the time he died in 1928, people had begun to identify the movement by his name.

Though illiterate in the English language, Jordan was undoubtedly a gifted man and a charismatic leader. In this regard, he was not unlike Bedward of Jamaica. Jordan was dubbed by Elder Bowen a 'seeing' man after the Buxtonian had identified the elder as the bearded man of a dream-vision which he had had. In addition to revelation which he received in dreams, Jordan also heard 'voices' from time to time. One of his most remarkable predictions was that of the day, date and time of his death – an event which took place on April 7, 1928.

By the time Jordan died, the beliefs and practices of the movement had reached their definitive form. The movement was sufficiently well-organised to survive the death of the man who had led it for some twelve years; it survived as well the ridicule and persecution of the larger society. The leadership of the 'Jordanites' devolved on Elder James Klein. Under Jordan, he was commissioned a 'captain' and sent out to preach. He was also designated 'Defender of the Faith' and in that capacity functioned as an apologist of the beliefs and practices of the movement. Before Klein joined Jordan's movement, he was a member of the Guyana chapter of the Universal Negro Improvement and Conservation Association (UNIA). The UNIA was founded in Jamaica in August, 1914, by that great Jamaican, Marcus Mosiah Garvey. The Guyana chapter of the UNIA flourished in the 1920s and the early '30s, but declined in importance after that period.

Because the UNIA withered in importance at precisely the period during which the White-Robed Army was gaining in popularity, and because many erstwhile members of the UNIA became members of the Army, one is tempted to think that the Jordanite movement superseded the UNIA in the estimation of the lower class blacks as the movement that was more likely to promote racial pride and love among blacks and, at the same time, to offer them spiritual strength and inspiration with which to cope with their state of social, economic and political deprivation. No doubt the ideas of Garvey influenced the thinking of the Jordanites through Klein and those ex-Garveyites who joined the movement.

After the death of Jordan, splinter groups arose within the White-Robed Army. Doctrinal differences and personal conflicts were responsible for this schismatic development. All the 'gatherings' however, continued to recognise Jordan as their founder. It is difficult to assess with precision the numerical strength of the White-Robed Army. According to Elder Klein, "God doesn't number his children." By 1970, there were some

182

fifteen 'gatherings' (congregations) of Jordanites in South West Georgetown alone in such districts as Charlestown, Albouystown, La Penitence, Alexander Village, Ruimveldt and Lodge Village. While the members were predominantly Afro-Guyanese, a few white and East Indian admixtures were to be found among the Army membership.

Persons desiring to be members of the White-Robed Army must be at least fifteen years old. They must be able to attest to dreams or visions which they have had as signs of their fitness for baptism. In traditional Christian fashion, Jordanites believe that baptism symbolises spiritual rebirth or resurrection. The devout Jordanite abstains from eating meat, onion, garlic, shallot, and on certain occasions, from salt. He does not drink tea, coffee or alcoholic beverages; his preference is for bush 'teas' and wine made from local fruits. He worships on the Sabbath (i.e. Saturday), observes the appearance of the new moon, and believes that contrary to the teachings of the 'big churches,' Jesus Christ was born at the new moon in October, crucified on Thursday of Holy Week and resurrected on the following Monday.

As its earlier name, the Church of the West Evangelical Millenium Pilgrims, suggests, the movement is strongly millenarian. Ever since the Army took root in Guyana, its members have been on the look-out for the Last Day. On that day, the 'law-keepers' (i.e. Jordanites) will be abundantly rewarded while the wicked of this earth will be punished. Meanwhile, the Jordanites nourish a strong 'African' sentiment and seek to regulate their lives in keeping with their accepted scriptures[15] and the teachings of Nathaniel Jordan.

Their emphasis on regulations as these relate to the Sabbath, modes of dress and dietary habits makes them more akin to Jews than to Christians. So too does their observance of the Passover. They, however, hold Trinitarian views in that they believe in God the Father, God the Son, and God the Holy Spirit. Jordanites are adamant that God is black and that Jesus had black antecedents through Ruth, the Moabitess. They hold that the Holy Spirit communicates with them by entering their bodies. 'Possession' by the Spirit induces convulsions in the possessed and enables them to speak in tongues.

'African' ideas are not without their influence on the beliefs and practices of the White-Robed Army. The service for the spirit of the departed held on the fortieth day of a person's death, reminds one of the 'second burial' of African practice.

183

Jordanites hold that the spirit ascends to heaven on that day. They believe, too, that wicked spirits that cannot gain entrance to heaven remain on earth to haunt people. African notions of reincarnation persist. It is believed that when God feels that a soul is ready for rebirth He sends it back to earth in much the same way that Elijah was 'sent' back in the form of John the Baptist Reincarnation can take place across racial lines. The notion (often associated with the Hindu view of reincarnation as it relates to *karma*) that if one lives a morally upright life he will be reincarnated in a better position is widely held among Jordanites.

The early influence which popular Hindu thought must have had on the shaping of the beliefs of the West Evangelical Millenium Pilgrims through the conversations of Joseph MacLaren and Bhagwan Das was never eroded. If anything, it was strengthened by Jordan's association with Hindus. Jordan was baptised by the Hindu priest, Bhagwan Das Maraj.[16] Many Jordanite weddings are performed at night. In Hindu fashion, they are performed under the ceremonial bamboo and, more often than not, by East Indians who are recognised by Jordanites as Hindu priests.

The Jordanites call their seven-day feast a *bhagwat*. The term is derived from popular Hindu usage. Among Hindus, a bhagwat is a religious ceremony which may run into several days. At this ceremony, Hindu scriptures are recited and expounded, *bhajans* (hymns) are sung to the accompaniment of Indian musical instruments, offerings are made and the devotees are fed. According to Elder Klein, the taboo against the eating of onion, garlic and shallot is derived from the Hindu holy book, the *Bhagavad Gita*. The claim is made by Jordanites that the food given by God mentioned in Ezekiel 16:19, is the *neivoddya* or *parsadan*[17] that is often offered to the deities invoked by Hindus in their worship. Jordanites, who like devout Hindus are vegetarians, are particularly fond of parsadan. Indian influence is also to be seen in the turban and the *kurtah* (skirt) that are worn by male Jordanites, particularly on ceremonial occasions.

The beliefs and practices of the White-Robed Army then are traceable to a number of sources. It was the genius of Nathaniel Jordan that wove an identifiable and coherent system of beliefs and practices from different strands of thought and practice. That system provides the white-robed believers, who are recruited in the main from the more depressed classes, with a

184

faith by which to survive.

The Rastafarian Movement

The Rastafarian movement is indigenous to Jamaica. The inspiration which led to its genesis in the 1930s was Messianic or millennarian in nature. In its short history, the movement has been sustained and pervaded by a sense of African triumphalism. These two factors justify our discussion of Rastafarianism in this chapter.

The Rastafarian doctrine that Haile Selassie is God, was first preached by Leonard P. Howell in Kingston, Jamaica. Howell had travelled to Africa where he allegedly fought against the Ashanti chief, King Prempeh, in 1896. He spent several years in the United States where he had first-hand experience of black and white racism. Another early preacher of the Rastafarian doctrine regarding Selassie was Joseph Nathaniel Hibbert, who returned to his native Jamaica from Costa Rica in 1931. In Costa Rica, Hibbert had joined the Ancient Mystic Order of Ethiopia and had become a Master Mason. Yet another early exponent of Rastafarianism was Archibald Dunkley, who had worked as a seaman on the Atlantic Fruit Company boats which plied between the United States of America and the Caribbean. Meanwhile, people such as Paul Erlington, Vernal Davis and Ferdinand Ricketts, concerned over the social conditions in Jamaica, were discussing the possibility of social reform in the island and of repatriation to Africa as an alternative for black Jamaicans. When Haile Selassie was crowned Emperor of Ethiopia in November, 1930, they recalled the words of that great Jamaican Marcus Garvey, that when a king was crowned in Africa, the time of Africa's resurgence was near. Under the influence of Robert Hinds, Erlington and his fellows came to believe that Selassie was the Living God. This was in 1934.

Howell, Hibbert and Dunkley had no doubt come under the influence of ideas that were current in Pan-African circles in the United States and Costa Rica. Erlington, Davis and Ricketts would have absorbed those ideas from Marcus Garvey who was himself an important and influential exponent of the same ideas both in the States and in Jamaica. In any case, many of the ideas which inspired Rastafarianism were popular in Pan-African circles.

Many themes that were to become important to the Rastafarians were explored by black writers. They were later made popular by Afro-Americans. Ottobah Cugoano, for example, a

185

Fanti who was kidnapped and taken to Grenada as a slave while still a child, prophesied the reversal of Africa's fortunes when he wrote in 1786:

> Yet, O Africa! Yet, poor slave! The day of thy watchman cometh, and thy visitation draweth nigh, that shall be their (i.e. the white nations) perplexity.
> Therefore I will look unto the Lord: I will wait for the God of my salvation; my God will hear me.[18]

Nearer our own time, the African, P.K. Isaka Seme, in a prize-winning address delivered at Columbia University on April 5, 1906, spoke of the resurgence of Africa thus:

> The giant is awakening! From the four corners of the earth Africa's sons are marching to the future's golden door bearing the record of deeds and valour done.[19]

Meanwhile, another theme had been articulated by Martin R. Delaney. It was spelt out to the National Emigration Convention of Colored People which met at Cleveland, Ohio, in August 1854. Delaney proposed a programme of repatriation of coloured people to Africa declaring that "Africa is our fatherland and we are its legitimate descendants." Delaney's formula was: "Our policy must be . . . Africa for the African race and black men to rule them."[20] Later, W.E.B. DuBois and Marcus Garvey would echo Delaney.

Another development was the growth in importance of the symbolic value of Ethiopia. For Cugoano, Ethiopia was synonymous with Africa. For the Afro-American, Robert Alexander Young, the Ethiopian stood for the black negroid African. Blacks such as H. Easton and J.C. Pennington lauded the greatness of ancient Ethiopia in the same breath as they did that of ancient Egypt. W.W. Brown and Isaka Seme touched on the theme of Ethiopia while Casely Hayford, the author of *Ethiopia Unbound,* dreamed of a future 'Free Ethiopian Empire'.

Throughout these developments, the religious motif was always present. Cugoano looked to God to bring about the reversal of Africa's fortunes. Gustavus Equiano (b. 1745) had remarked on the strong similarity between the Africans and the Jews before the latter entered the Promised Land. He even argued that the Africans were descended from the Jews. Pennington, addressing himself to the myth that blacks were cursed because they were the descendants of Ham, remarked that Noah's curse could not apply to Africans since they were the descendants of Kush and Miriam and not of Canaan. The black evangelist, James M. Webb, declared around 1906, that Jesus had curly hair and Ethiopian blood in his veins and that he would have been classified as Negro in America. The theologian, Henry Garnet, quoted Psalm 68:32 to the effect that 'Ethiopia shall soon stretch forth her hand to God'. The passage was to become the text of many a sermon to be preached by blacks; it was regarded as a Biblical prophecy that Africa would soon be redeemed.

It is more than likely that Howell, Hibbert and Dunkley were aware of these ideas. These themes were canvassed at Pan-African conferences and congresses down to their time; they were the watch-word of the many Pan-African Associations that were formed in the period down to 1930. They were the topics of discussion whenever and wherever black men met to discuss the social, economic and political inequalities from which their race suffered. Above all, they were the subjects touched upon by Marcus Garvey. It was in London between 1912 and 1914 that Garvey imbibed notions of African 'nationalism'. When he returned to Jamaica in August 1914, he founded the Universal Negro Improvement and Conservation Association and the African Communities League.

Among other things, Garvey's objective was to establish a Universal Confraternity among the African race; to promote the spirit of racial pride and love; to reclaim the fallen; to minister to and assist the needy; and to assist in civilising the backward tribes of Africa.

In 1916, Garvey went to the United States where he made contact with Afro-Americans such as John Edward Bruce,. W.E.B. DuBois and William Ferris He founded branches of the U.N.I.A. in Harlem and New York. His main objective, to liberate Africa, came to nought but his impact on blacks in Jamaica, the States, England and even Africa was phenomenal. Among the blacks of Western Kingston, he assumed the status of a prophet in the mould of Elijah or John the Baptist. When Ras Tafari was crowned in November 1930 as Emperor Haile Selassie of Ethiopia, King of Kings, Lord of Lords, Conquering Lion of the Tribe of Judah, many blacks saw in the coronation the fulfilment of Garvey's prophecy that one day someone would arise in Africa who would unite the people of that continent into one nation. Biblical support for this point of view was found in such texts as Revelation 5:2, 5. "And I saw a strong angel proclaiming with a loud voice, 'Who is worthy to open the book and to loose the seals thereof?' . . . And one of the elders saith unto me, 'Weep not: behold, the Lion of Judah, the Root of David, hath prevailed to open the Book and to loose the seven spirits of God sent forth unto all the earth'. "

It followed that if Haile Selassie (which means 'Power of the Trinity') was the one of whom Garvey spoke, then the resurgence of Africa was at hand. What was more, the scattered sons and daughters of Africa would return to that land to share in its glory. For those sons and daughters in Jamaica, it meant that their exile in 'Babylon' would be over with all the deprivation that went with that exile. The millennium was about to be born.

For people such as Hibbert, Howell, Dunkley, Erlington and Davis, both the historical and the Biblical evidence was overwhelming. It could not be a coincidence that the Ras Tafari (Prince of Peace) was elevated to Haile Selassie (Power of the Trinity) nor could his titles, King of Kings, Lord of Lords, Conquering Lion of the Tribe of Judah, be purely honorific. After all, these names and titles are not only soundly Biblical, their reference in the Bible is to the Saviour-God who would redeem Israel and gather the remnants of the children of Israel who are scattered among the nations of the earth. It was no coincidence also that the Ras Tafari was of the Davidic line through King Solomon.

It was not difficult for the Rastafarians to find Biblical passages to support their Messianism. The Messianic theme runs throughout the Old Testament. The term Messiah, ('The anointed of Yahweh') is used in the Old Testament of Saul and, more important, of David. It was used in Old Testament times of that king who stood before the Israelites as the representative of Yahweh and who, in fact, governed in his place. Through him, as it were, Yahweh ruled the whole world from Mount Zion. Yahweh's anointed was supposed to be the unconquerable and virtual Lord of all the earth (Psalms 2, 72, 110. In the estimation of the prophets, the lofty ideals held out for Yahweh's anointed and his government were never realised. The more this was the case, the more the realisation of the ideal was pushed into the future (Isaiah 1:2ff, 4:2ff). One thing remained constant: the future glory of Israel was bound up with Mount Zion and with the house of David. This note recurs in the literature of the post-exilic period. The Messianic hope in the Old Testament could be summarised: The anointed of the Lord

188

will be raised up that he may vanquish the wicked rulers of the nations, purify the desecrated land of Judah, gather the dispersed members of his people, and bestow on them all over again their nationality, while the nations do him homage Psalms 72, 110.

The hopes of Jewish Messianism are expressed in political terms. Peace and well-being are to be experienced in a kingdom established on earth. While the more transcendental side of Messianism is taken up in the New Testament, there is enough material in that part of the Bible to sustain a political interpretation of the kingdom (or rule) of God. The millenarian motif of Revelation lends itself to this kind of interpretation. That motif can be summarised thus: Christ will return to earth at the close of the present dispensation, vanquish the devil and his allies, and inaugurate a glorious age of peace and joy. This age will last for a thousand years or more. During the millenium, God's elect will dwell in bliss under the immediate personal rulership of Christ.

The Rastafarians used their spiritual genius to translate the dreams of Garvey and the Pan-Africanists into the Messianic and millenarian terms of the Bible. This gave the political utopianism of Garvey and the others all the force and dynamism of a religious movement. At the same time, the Messianism of the Rastafarian was expressed in political terms that were not unlike those contained in the Old Testament. The Rastafarians appropriated the Messianic promises for themselves simply by regarding themselves as the reincarnation of the scattered children of Israel. Israel itself was transposed, in Rastafarian thinking, into Ethiopia.

The expected liberation of the Rastafarians which was construed in terms of repatriation to Ethiopia has been postponed. The Messianic hope still finds expression in such slogans as 'Africa for the Africans — At Home and Abroad,' and in such songs as 'Oh! Africa awaken, the morning is at hand' and 'Ethiopia, the land of our Fathers.' Meanwhile, Rastafarianism manifests the marks of a full-blown millenarian cult. It preaches the overthrow of the present power structures and the reversal of the present social order. In the new order of things, the present disinherited and disadvantaged — 'the sufferers' — will occupy positions of ease and power. Those who occupy such positions now will become slaves and servants.

Because Rastafarians share the same scriptures, the Bible, with the larger Jamaican community they have been forced, consciously or unconsciously, to justify their interpretation of the Bible. Their strategy has been a three-fold one. They ignore or dismiss the traditional rules of Biblical exegesis, claiming that the traditional interpretation of Biblical passages reflects the wicked distortion of Jah's (i.e. Yahweh's) word by white men and black traitors. They heap scorn on those who have been traditionally responsible for interpreting the Bible – ministers of religion and priests. Their claim is that these church officials are ranged on the side of Babylon – the symbol of wickedness and oppression. Finally, Rastafarians claim that they know the truth intuitively. This, they make out, is possible since, as the ancient Israelites reincarnated, they have been with God from the beginning of creation. In these ways they have, to their own satisfaction, neutralised the canons of traditional authority. In their places, the Rastafarians offer a new interpretation of scriptures.

By claiming to be the elect of Jah and the 'insiders' to esoteric religious truth, people who had hitherto felt themselves to be at a disadvantage in a society where social status was also determined by church affiliation reversed, to their own satisfaction, the categories of religious worthiness and unworthiness. The traditionally pious came to be classified as hypocrites while the religious outsiders became the chosen few. Similarly, in true millenarian fashion, a people who had been economically (and politically) deprived in a country where money was an index of economic, political and social status, created an ideology of poverty and suffering which helped them to cope with their condition of being deprived. Wealth came to be regarded as the symbol of corruption and oppression (or 'downpression', to use a Rastafarian category) while the 'sufferer' became, like the poor in the Gospel according to St. Luke, 'blessed'. As the not so underprivileged and the discontented sons of the privileged joined the movement, they exaggerated and idealised a poverty which they, in fact, did not share.

The satisfactory reversal of the value system in religious affiliation, social status, economic worth and political power in a society where these things mattered greatly, liberated the Rastafarians from a preoccupation with the traditional values. The gap between what might have been their expectations for themselves and the extent to which they were able to satisfy those expectations, given the circumstances in which they lived, now became irrelevant. The result was that Rastafarians as a group experienced a tremendous release of emotional energy

190

which expressed itself in all kinds of creative activity in the visual and plastic arts, handicraft and music.

The larger society reacted to the Rastafarian movement in the manner that larger societies have traditionally responded to seemingly heretical or revitalising movements which question by their very genesis, the legitimacy of the traditional order. Attempts were made from the 1930s until recently, to destroy the movement either by eliminating it by force or by ridiculing it into non-existence. These attempts have failed. What may not fail is the neutralisation of the dynamism of the movement as it becomes incorporated in the larger society. Some of the factors that may bring about this incorporation are the overt sympathy shown to Rastafarians by churchmen, the acquisition of wealth by some of them made possible by their creative genius, a growing sense of their political power engendered by the fact that politicians recognise and seek to exploit their power of the vote, the levelling of social inequalities which the movement itself engendered and which makes the Rastafarian less unacceptable than he was a decade ago, and the acceptance which the Rastafarian style in dress and language receives in the larger society.

Like the holders of millenarian beliefs generally, the Rastafarians live according to the ethics of the anticipated millenium. They observe the food taboos of the ancient Hebrews; many of them are vegetarians. Many of them live by what they consider to be the Nazarite vow regarding shaving the face and consuming alcoholic beverages: they grow their beards and abstain from drinking alcohol. While they hold the institution of marriage in contempt, Rastafarian couples hold to a high standard of fidelity. Infidelity and promiscuity are abhorred as deadly sins. Status distinctions are severely restricted among Rastafarians. The Nya Binghi or Locksmen, who claim to be priests, regard themselves as being of the Aaronic line; women are generally regarded as subordinate to men. Apart from these distinctions, Rastafarians regard one another as brothers. A Rastafarian sometimes addresses another as Jah.

Unlike the vodunists, shangoists and revivalists, Rastafarians have no truck with the dead[21] or with the ancestral spirits. Rastafarians do not believe in the existence of ancestral spirits. Death for them is the result of sin; as the Bible says: ". . . the wages of sin is death, but the gift of God is eternal life." They believe in their own immortality. When a member of the movement dies, they attribute this to sin and in keeping with

191

what they believe to be the Biblical injunction, they leave 'the dead' (non-Rastafarians) to bury the dead member.

The most important religious ceremony for Rastafarians is the 'Grounation'. Men and women share in this activity which has been described by them as grounding in the spirit. At the grounation, several cultic beliefs are symbolized and celebrated and are by that token, sustained and renewed. In many respects, the grounation is for Rastafarians what the Eucharist of Holy Communion is meant to be for Christians. The bliss of the new life in the Promised Land is anticipated as the brethren, clad in their flowing 'African' robes, sing their songs of praise to Jah and share a common meal of 'ital'[22] food. A state of euphoria is induced by the smoking of the herb (i.e. ganja or cannabis). The smoking of ganja on this occasion is done with the elaboration and formality of a ritual. Indeed it is a ritual with every act – lighting the chillum pipe, the addition of water to the herb, inhalation, exhalation – being pregnant with symbolism for the initiated. The pipe is smoked communally. This has the effect of strengthening the bonds of the community. In addition, the act of sharing serves to focus on the ethics of the community since the pipe is not passed to anyone who is regarded as being out of perfect love and charity with the brethren. Thus, if a Rastafarian should leave his woman or 'queen' temporarily, and another one should begin a relationship with her, the latter would be excluded from sharing the communal pipe.

It is at the grounation ceremony that Rastafarians assert and re-affirm their beliefs, values, truths and understanding of history. The grounation is, in effect, part of the process of Rastafarian world-building. By the process of mutual reasoning, the 'brothers' think aloud as it were, on events which take place in the larger society and in the world at large. They seek to rationalise those events in terms of their Weltanschauung. This 'grounding in the spirit' takes place under the influence of ganja which no doubt sharpens the sensitivity of some Rastafarians while it makes the shy more prone to share their thoughts. All in all, ganja-smoking produces the atmosphere in which relaxed reasoning and sharing can take placè.

The Rastafarian movement has survived the crisis posed by the death of Haile Selassie. The detractors of the movement who have always ridiculed the belief that Selassie is God have argued (if we may express it in the form of a syllogism):

All mortal men die
Selassie has died

Therefore Selassie was mortal.

To this line of argument, the Rastafarian rebuttal may be expressed thus:

God cannot die
Selassie is God
Therefore, Selassie is not dead.

As for all the news concerning the death of Selassie (and the alleged corruption of his regime, for that matter), the Rastafarian sees this as pure fabrication on the part of imperialists and other agents of Babylon.

The Rastafarian movement has spread from Jamaica to other parts of the Caribbean. Small groups of Rastas are to be found in Grenada, Trinidad and Guyana. Whether the movement in these countries will achieve the importance it has in Jamaica remains to be seen. But few will now doubt that, in Jamaica, Rastafarianism has had a great influence on the life of the total society.

Notes and References

1. The *vever* was a symbolic design made on the ground with wheat or maize flour or ashes. The purpose of the vever was to invoke the presence of the loa.
2. The twins, called Marassa, were believed to be half human and half divine. They were regarded as the first humans and also as the first dead; as such they became the ancestral loas. The twins, who were also conceived of as children, were saluted first at vodun ceremonies. The sentiment ran: 'Papa Marassa is the one who must be fed before all the gods.'
3. The *serviteur* was someone who served a particular loa.
4. *Fidèles* – the faithful, who, as a rule, did not become possessed.
5. Twins were believed to be endowed with supernatural powers.
6. Lewis, *Journal of a West Indian Proprietor*, p. 309.

193

7. Ibid. To 'buss the book' was to swear on the Bible.

8. Phillippo, *Jamaica: Its Past and Present State*, p. 270.

9. Alexander Robb, *The Gospel to the Africans*, p. 34.

10. Phillippo, op. cit., p. 271.

11. Hutton, *A History of Moravian Missions*, p. 222.

12. The term 'trumping' is used of the laboured, rhythmic dancing associated with revivalist worship.

13. The name is derived from the fact that white clothing is characteristic of members of this movement.

14. Lallu is the diminutive of the Hindi word *lall* which means red. Lallu is often used in the sense of 'My little fair one.'

15. The accepted scriptures include the King James Version of the Bible (Old Testament especially), the Apocrypha. The Lost Book of the Bible, The Antiquities of the Jews, The Aquarian Gospel, The Book of Common Prayer (Church of England).

16. It is not clear whether or not Bhagwan Das Maraj was the priest who baptised MacLaren.

17. They would, however, call this sweetmeat *parsad* or *mohan bhog*.

18. Cited in Imanuel Geiss, *The Pan-African Movement*, p. 39.

19. Ibid., pp. 118-119.

20. Ibid., p. 165.

21. In this regard, Rastafarians are like the Jordanites who do not take the bodies of the dead into their church. This, for them, is defiling. Those who handle dead bodies must undergo a period of purification before they can resume attending services. Like the Jordanites, the Rastafarians hold to the Biblical adage that advises: 'Let the dead bury the dead.'

22. *Ital* foods are strictly vegetable and herbaceous.

CHAPTER VIII
CHRISTIANITY IN POST-EMANCIPATION CARIBBEAN SOCIETY

1. Church and Society

Full emancipation of slaves was effected in the British West Indian colonies in 1838, in the French colonies a decade later, in the Dutch colonies in 1863, and in the Spanish colonies in 1885. All the colonial societies in post-Emancipation times were segmented along racial and colour lines. In the British West Indies, this segmentation was reflected in the churches where denominationalism was related to the social and economic conditions of church members. Because these conditions were related to people's skin colour, denominationalism was also related to race and skin colour.

The segmented nature of Trinidad society around the middle of the nineteenth century led the governor of that island, Lord Harris, to remark that whereas "a race had been freed . . . a society had not been formed."[1] Commenting on the situation as it existed down to about 1914, the late Chancellor of the University of the West Indies, Sir H.O.B. Wooding, indicated that the society was still very much fragmented: the French in Trinidad represented an urbane and distinguished segment. They were a people who were ever mindful of their aristocratic origin and ever watchful to preserve their cultural and economic dominance. The British saw themselves as benevolent administrators. They remained aloof from the rest of Trinidadian society. The Africans had not forgotten the humiliation of slavery; they chafed under the disadvantage of social inferiority to which that institution had doomed them. The Portuguese and Chinese (who came originally as immigrant labourers) and the Syrians and Jews (who came as traders and entrepreneurs) contented themselves with their associations and showed little concern over the difficulties of others. The coloureds pirouetted upon the stage and convinced themselves, but nobody else, that they were *'la crème de la crème'*. The East Indians lived as outcasts in their new home.[2]

The cultural segmentation which characterised Trinidadian society was repeated in every other British Caribbean colony. The only variable was the degree of that segmentation. To use Jamaica as an example of the state of affairs that existed in the British West Indian colonies: In that island, the elite of the society were the descendants of the plantocracy and members of the civil service who came out from England to administer the affairs of the island after it had become a Crown colony in 1865. At the base of the society were the ex-slaves and their descendants. Separating the base from the apex of the society, so to speak, were the children of miscegenation – the offspring of members of the white managerial class and black slave and ex-slave women. The most important criterion of social worth and status in that society was skin colour. In a real sense, therefore, in spite of the fact that slavery had been dismantled, the social stratification of the colony remained much the same as it had been in pre-Emancipation Jamaica. The difference was that the slaves were now free. Given time, education and the attainment of some of the status symbols – among which was religious affiliation – which the society prized, a few might reach the lower rungs of the middle class ladder or, at least, the upper levels of the lower class gradations. Beyond that, social mobility was impossible since elitism was associated with white skin pigmentation.

The distribution of church membership in Jamaica showed a race and colour bias as well. Whites were Anglicans although Scotsmen, not surprisingly, showed a preference for the Presbyterian Kirk. As the Established Churches of the British realm, the Anglican and Presbyterian churches enjoyed great prestige. The urban membership of the Methodist church in the island was almost exclusively coloured. This may be explained by the fact that the early Methodist missionaries concentrated their efforts in and about Kingston where there was a heavy concentration of free coloured people. Nevertheless, the coloured nature of the Methodist congregations contrasted sharply with the urban membership of the Baptist church which was almost exclusively black. The membership of the Baptist church was responsible for that church's reputation that it was a 'poor man' church. The reputation, in turn, might have helped to make the Baptist church attractive to the blacks who knew themselves to be a poor people.

The race and colour pattern of church membership seen in Jamaica might not have been as neatly drawn in all the British colonies, but the pattern itself was repeated from colony to colony. It was the peculiar missionary thrusts and emphases of the several churches in the pre-Emancipation period that were responsible for the development of the pattern. Those emphases themselves were, in the first place, determined by the very nature of the plantation society. In places such as Bermuda, the Bahamas and the Cayman Islands where the sugar plantation did not develop and where there was no white plantocracy to serve, the Anglican Church was tardy in establishing a footing. Meanwhile, the substantial numbers of whites there joined the Presbyterian, Independent (Congregational) and Methodist churches. Even so, the race and colour bias in church member- ship developed. Thus, in New Providence, the Methodist church became the church of the whites and near-whites, while the Baptist church membership was almost exclusively black. In Bermuda, the Presbyterian, Independent and (later) the Anglican churches served the white islanders, while the Methodist church served the blacks. Patterns that were established during slavery, continued in the post-Emancipation period although there was one very significant change to be discussed later.

What remained practically unchanged during the nineteenth century was the concentration of the effective leadership of the churches at the level of the clergy in the hands of white expatriates. The only exceptions to this rule were the Baptist churches in Jamaica, the Bahamas and Trinidad, which had black leadership from their earliest establishment. To pro- vide for the continuation of native leadership, the Baptists in Jamaica began training men for the Christian ministry as early as 1843. Their training centre, Calabar, was at Rio Bueno. The Methodists did develop indigenous leader- ship at lay level; these lay leaders were the class leaders. Most of these class leaders were recruited from among the coloured members of the congregations. By 1850, the Methodists had about a dozen local men, most of whom were either black or coloured, on a staff of some ninety ministers in the Carib- bean. But they were regarded as lacking in quality, and they served as assistant missionaries. As for the Presbyterians,

197

although the Rev. William Jameson undertook as early as 1840 to train a number of catechists for the ministry, the trainees were all Scotsmen. At Codrington in Barbados, Richard Rawle set out to introduce theological education seriously around 1846. The tradition was continued by his successor, but the relatively few men who were ordained to the West Indian clergy after being trained at Codrington, were mainly West Indian whites. Rawle himself had thought seriously of recruiting men in England for training at Codrington for the West Indian ministry.

It has been suggested that the extremely slow development of black church leadership was due to the fact that the blacks were not educated enough to assume that leadership. The thinking of those days — so the suggestion runs — was that an educated ministry was a *desideratum*. Unfortunately there was little incentive for the descendants of slaves to acquire a sound education, particularly when that education was so costly. The suggestion is not without validity. It must be noted, however, that the Baptists did fairly well at the task of recruiting local leadership, although the Rev. E.B. Underhill, a British Baptist, thought that the academic attainment of the black Jamaican ministers left much to be desired. The tendency on the part of the Presbyterians in Jamaica and the Anglicans in the Caribbean to recruit whites for training for the ministry must have been a great disincentive to those blacks who might have considered taking the cloth as a vocation. There might have been reasons other than the lack of education why white missionaries who sat on the administrative bodies of churches were reluctant to recruit and train local men for leadership in the Caribbean churches. Whatever these were, the fact that the clerical leadership of the churches was concentrated in the hands of missionaries was calculated to convey the impression that an important criterion of worth in the church was white, expatriate status. A prevailing notion in those days was that metropolitan origin and white skin pigmentation were important criteria of status in post-Emancipation British colonial society.[3] The state of affairs that existed in the churches (except among the Baptists) would have helped to perpetuate that notion.

As far as social segmentation went, matters were no different in the French islands of Martinique and Guadeloupe. The whites who were economically worse off than some coloureds were regarded as socially superior to those coloureds. Clubs and societies at Basse-Terre and Point-a-Pitre catered for whites almost exclusively. At public festivities, a female creole white, whether wealthy or not, would not dance with *gens de couleur*. As in the British colonies, the negroes formed the base of the social pyramid. Between the blacks and the whites were the *gens de couleur* some of whom were the light-complexioned *mulâtres blancs*. Not even the whites held the negroes in greater contempt than those people of colour who were economically well off. The anxiety of the members of the *haute bourgeoisie mulâtre* was to maintain their colour. Marriage between themselves and blacks, therefore, was discouraged. A poorer mulatto who was just a shade superior to blacks and, in fact, a wealthy negro could, however, find acceptance among these *gens de couleur*. Whenever this happened the mulatto or the negro was dubbed a *gros-mulâtre!*

The three social classes in the Spanish colonies of Puerto Rico and Cuba were the whites, coloureds and negroes, in that order of social importance. There was a small degree of mixing between people of the first group and some of the lighter-complexioned people of the second group with the result that a few upper-class people came to possess negroid features. The physical ideal of the upper-class however, remained white caucasoid. Social interaction between the coloureds and the negroes was severely limited. Mulattoes avoided marrying blacks because it was generally felt that while the possession of caucasoid features increased a person's chances of upward social mobility, the possession of negroid features had the opposite effect.

The official religion of the French and Spanish islands was Catholicism. The attitude of both the Spanish and the French governments, as reflected in *Las Siete Partidas* and the *Code Noir* respectively, encouraged the christianisation of negro slaves. Almost from the time blacks were first brought to the Spanish and French islands, Catholic missionaries were as active as they could be among them. This was in direct contrast to what happened in the British colonies. No doubt the 'national' character of the Church of England led that church to confine its activities only to those who were considered nationals. Not only were the blacks in British colonies not nationals, they were also chattels. A 'universal' Catholic church, however, could embrace anybody in its ministry, and in Catholic thinking, the Negro was somebody; although in the heyday of sugar

199

the Catholic planters in the French islands and those in the Spanish colonies of Puerto Rico and Cuba forgot that aspect of Catholic thought.

In spite of the universal, all-embracing nature of Catholicism, however, French and Spanish colonial societies were no less segmented than those of the British colonies. Whatever the status of men in the sight of God, in the sight of white Catholics, blacks were certainly not their equal. A state of affairs that existed in a place like pre-Emancipation Martinique, where blacks and whites sat in different sections of the church building and were even buried in different parts of the cemetery, was not likely to change with the coming of Emancipation. It might well have been that Catholicism which held to a hierarchical view in social theory, helped to entrench the cleavages in the French and Spanish islands. These cleavages, because of the nature of plantation society and because of the influence of social Darwinsim which affected much of European thought in the nineteenth century, ran along racial and colour lines. Catholicism might have helped to perpetuate social cleavages in yet another way. Blacks and whites shared the same religion, worshipped in the same places, and because some whites served as god-parents to black children, a friendly social atmosphere was created in Catholic colonial societies. This atmosphere helped to neutralize any striving for real social equality on the part of the blacks.

There were variations on the theme of cultural (and ecclesiastical) segmentation along racial and colour lines in the Dutch colonies. In Curaçao, the socially dominant segment comprised white Dutchmen. Most of these were members of the higher civil service and scions of the prominent mercantile and military families that settled the island. A mark of elitism in Curaçao was membership in the Dutch Reformed Church. Lesser whites belonged to other Protestant churches or to the Roman Catholic Church. The Sephardic Jews who first came to the island in about 1650 acquired much wealth. In fact, the Jews as a body were wealthier than the Dutch Reformed Protestants, but the latter regarded the former as alien and inferior.

At the base of the Curaçao society were the negroes who from the beginning of the importation of slaves into the island outnumbered the whites. The blacks of Curaçao were evangelised by Catholic missionaries. The dominant white group that was traditionally unfriendly to Roman Catholicism, overcame its

200

unfriendliness to the point of permitting the Catholics to evangelise the blacks. This was preferable to the risk of having the social barrier which existed between blacks and whites breached by promoting evangelism among blacks by Dutch Reformed missionaries. Such evangelism would have led to blacks becoming members of the 'white' church.

2. Religion and the Development of a Social Consensus in the British West Indies

The churches did not create social segmentation in the Caribbean although they helped to perpetuate that state of affairs. What they helped to create was a social consensus that cut across social and colour lines without seriously affecting those lines. It is now our business to demonstrate this.

Emancipation was followed by a heightening of missionary activity in the British Caribbean. The Anglican bodies, the Church Missionary Society and the Society for the Propagation of the Gospel, were mainly responsible for the increase in the Church of England staff in the Caribbean. In 1835, there were only 56 priests in the West Indies; by 1844, there were 90. In 1833, the Methodist missionaries in the Caribbean numbered 54, in 1840 that number had grown to 85. The London Missionary Society, which had established bases in Guyana, sent missionaries to Jamaica for the first time in 1835. The missionary activity of the Baptists resulted in a leap in the Baptist membership from 10,000 in 1830, to 27,600 in 1842. This heightened missionary activity was aimed primarily at the blacks and the coloureds.

The churches' programme of christianising the blacks and coloureds by preaching and teaching had an interesting effect on Caribbean society. By the mid-nineteenth century, it came to be felt − even by those people who did not have formal membership with any church − that to be Christian in religion was an important criterion for social worth in the society. The fact that the important people in the society (government officials, school-teachers, ministers of religion) were Christians, helped to strengthen that feeling.

Meanwhile, in the schools which operated under the patronage of the churches and were staffed by people appointed by the churches, the importance of English cultural values was stressed. The values were recognized by those lower class negroes who came under the influence of the schools. For the coloured people and the professional negroes, these values became part of the criteria of excellence. In the final analysis, the values inculcated in schools were not unlike those shared by the white elite class in the several colonies. In fact, it may be argued that those values were derived from that class. By the end of the nineteenth century, a 'greater tradition' of cultural values had developed in the British West Indies. The churches and their schools played a vital part in this development.

Caribbean society still remained segmented, but a social consensus had developed around such values as an education in English, adherence to the Christian religion, the correctness of speech in English, the identification of the self with the superior British race and the possession of a light or fair complexion. The degree of a person's civilisation was determined by the extent to which he possessed all or some of these qualities. The significant thing is that many churchmen subscribed to those criteria of worth and status. In fact, it can well be said that the shaping of the consensus was the work of the Christian church leadership in the Caribbean. That leadership (except in the case of the Baptists) was concentrated almost wholly in the hands of missionaries who, almost to a man, came from Britain. The assumptions of many a nineteenth-century missionary were that baptism was an act of civilisation and that Anglo-Saxon civilisation was the finest expression of Christianity.

Given the above, one would expect the Church of England to prove attractive to British Caribbean peoples. It did. Some forty years after Emancipation, the Church of England in the Caribbean boasted a membership of about one hundred thousand. By that time, that church was "the leading body in these colonies; even among the Negroes themselves (it) held an honourable and promising position." Between 1871 and 1890 — the heyday of British colonial expansion — the membership of the Anglican church in Jamaica alone jumped from 19,576 to 40,298. Between 1874 and 1880, William Piercy Austin, the bishop of Guiana, was averaging a thousand confirmations a year. Elsewhere in the Caribbean, the growth of the Church of England was steady. In comparison to the Anglican church, the growth of Methodism was solid, but not spectacular.

The phenomenal growth of the Established Church cannot be explained only in terms of the hard and dedicated work done by such competent bishops as Enos Nuttal (of Jamaica) and Piercy Austin or in terms of the determined efforts made

202

by the Society for the Propagation of the Gospel – although these factors were undoubtedly important. The leadership of the Anglican church was good, but it was not superior to that of the Methodists. Its evangelistic efforts were no more determined than the efforts of the Moravians, Methodists and Congregationalists. And these churches had started to evangelise among the negroes long before the Anglicans began to take an interest in the blacks. Undoubtedly, the fact that the Church of England was the established church and the church of the governing classes in the British colonies made membership in that church desirable. In this regard, it must be pointed out that not a few people who were once Congregationalists, Moravians or Baptists, finally became Anglicans. This was particularly so in Barbados, Jamaica and the Bahamas. As people acquired a good enough education to aspire to positions in the teaching profession and in the lower echelons of the civil service, they thought it advisable to join the 'state' church.

The Christians who least approximated to the metropolitan model of what Christian men should be like were those Baptists in Jamaica who were described as Native Baptists. In 1859, they numbered three thousand three hundred in Kingston alone. The white Presbyterian missionaries, William Jameson and Hope Waddell, had thought that their knowledge of Christianity was defective and that they indulged in superstitious absurdities. The British Baptist, James Phillippo, thought that their beliefs combined important truths with extravagant puerilities. By 1859, however, another British Baptist E.B. Underhill, was prepared to admit that the Native Baptists – "whatever their defects"[5] – were exercising a considerable influence for good on the population of Kingston. Underhill was prepared to make this admission now that the Africanisms of the Native Baptists had been eroded. The Congregational minister, W.J. Gardner, however, still felt that the influence of the Native Baptists was inimical to "the advancement of the people" and that behind the pernicious practices of these Baptists were their leaders who were "men of no education."[6]

The fact that social mobility for coloured and black Christians was believed to be related to membership in the Church of England and that some black Christians were either grudgingly admitted to be Christian or dismissed as unchristian, indicates that a consensus had developed by which 'Christian' status could be assessed. This consensus had more to do with such factors as the education of people and their socialisation along

Anglicized lines than with the orthodoxy or otherwise of their beliefs. Even so, there was a limit to social mobility on the part of blacks or coloureds: whatever their church affiliation they could not attain elite status. That status demanded the additional qualification of white skin colour.

British nineteenth century expansionism has been described as 'anti-colonial colonialism'. That is to say that British territorial expansion overseas was criticised and discouraged in Britain. Nevertheless, the establishment of naval and trade bases and of missionary or philanthropical stations overseas led to that expansionism that the British people as a whole deplored. Similarly, it may be said that the missionaries might not have set out to be cultural imperialists. But faced with the prospect of creating a society out of the shambles of slavery they did so, consciously or unwittingly, around cultural values with which they were familiar. These values were as European and as metropolitan as the missionaries were. Their belief that the cultural values of their converts were either, at best, of no account or, at worst, incompatible with the new religion of their converts, would have bred in missionaries the consciousness of their own cultural superiority. Once that happened, it was not long before missionaries would see themselves burdened with the twin responsibility of being evangelists of the gospel and the transmitters of civilisation to their fields of endeavour. It was in this two-fold role that they were to help create the social consensus in the British Caribbean.

3. The Churches and Education

The evangelical churches pioneered in education among the negro slaves and ex-slaves in the Caribbean. The first schools were set up to instruct the blacks in the rudiments of the Christian faith. In the British colonies, the attempt to instruct the slaves in reading and writing met with resistance. In Guyana, for example, while the Governor gave his approval to John Wray to instruct the slaves in the Christian faith orally, he strongly opposed their being taught to read. The Governor felt that literate slaves were a threat to the peace and stability of Demerara. Governor Murray's views were echoed throughout the British Caribbean.

After Emancipation, the education of ex-slaves was greatly encouraged. Education that had been regarded in pre-Emancipation times as inimical to the stability of society was now regarded as vital for the preservation of society. The Rev. John Sterling, an Anglican clergyman who once served in St. Kitts, provided the British Government with the *rationale* for negro education in the Caribbean. In a report to that government dated May 11, 1836, Sterling pointed out:

> About 770,000 persons have been released from slavery by the Emancipation Act, and are now in a state of rapid transition to entire freedom. The peace and prosperity of the Empire at large may be not remotely influenced by their moral condition; the care of this is in itself also a matter of grave responsibility; and lastly the opinion of the public in Britain earnestly requires a systematic provision for their mental improvement. It is plain therefore that something must be done, and it must be done immediately. For although the negroes are now under a system of limited control, which secures to a certain extent their orderly and industrious conduct, in the short space of five years from the first of next August, their performance of the functions of a labouring class in a civilized community will depend entirely on the power over their minds of the same prudential and moral motives which govern more or less the mass of the people here. If they are not so disposed to fulfil these functions, property will perish in the colonies for lack of human impulsion; the whites will no longer reside there; and the negroes themselves will probably cease to be progressive. The law having already determined and enforced their civil rights, the task of bettering their condition can be further advanced only by education.[7]

To finance the educational programme in the colonies, the British Parliament decided in 1835 to make the amount of £20,000 available for the education of the ex-slaves. This grant – the Negro Education Grant – was to continue at that level for five years and then to be reduced annually until it was phased out in 1845. The English policy relating to the education of the blacks was an extension of the domestic educational policy. In Britain, money was expended on popular education because education was considered to be necessary for the social control of the lower classes. It was felt by those who advocated popular education in Britain (e.g. the Philosophical Radicals) that people who had access to useful knowledge could be trusted to behave rationally. Meanwhile, the practical piety inculcated in Sunday schools would make the poor industrious and morally upright. This was believed to be the best guarantee against pauperism.

In the Caribbean, the accent was on instruction that would enhance the moral status of the blacks. The primary objective of education was the inculcation of that kind of morality that would make the ex-slaves respect order and behave in a civilised manner. An inner restraint, as it were, would thus be provided in place of the external constraints that slavery was felt to have provided in the pre-1834 period. The reading material used in schools at first was based almost wholly on the Scriptures; formal religious instruction was also an important part of the curriculum. In fact, the Caribbean educational programme focussed on the four R's — Reading, 'Riting, 'Rithmetic and Religion.

The governments of the several colonies saw in the churches ready agencies to implement their educational policy, therefore it was natural that the churches should be made to operate the Negro Education Grant. After all, for whatever reasons, they had pioneered in the field in the Caribbean. Missionaries, who had always been anxious that their converts should be made literate in order that they might be able to read the Bible, were eager participants in the colonial educational programme. In the changed circumstances brought about by Emancipation, more planters were ready to recognise the potential of education to provide a stabilising force in society.

The other objective of colonial education — the inculcation of habits of industry — would have appealed to planters, particularly since that objective was mooted in official circles. What was even more, the habits of industry were meant to find expression in the cane-piece. Charles Latrobe who came to the Caribbean in 1838 on behalf of Her Majesty's Government to conduct what was in effect an appraisal of the operation of the Negro Education Grant, reported that the finger of Providence pointed to the estate or the plantation as the natural field of industry for the majority of the rising generation of the poor classes in the West Indian islands. Latrobe saw plantation labour on the part of the blacks as necessary not only for providing them with a livelihood, but also for providing society with order, morality and happiness.

Church leaders were at one with Latrobe, not necessarily because they read his report but because they came from a society where "except for 'God' the most popular word in the . . . vocabulary must have been 'work'."[8] In England at that time, children were brought up on the biblical injunction "Work while it is called Today, for the night cometh when no man can work." Idleness was regarded as sinful in that it amounted to an abrogation of God's will. As the 'prophet' of those times, Thomas Carlyle, wrote:

> For there is a perennial nobleness, and even sacredness, in Work. Were he never so benighted, forgetful of his high calling, there is always hope in man that actually and earnestly works: in Idleness alone is there perpetual despair."[9]

We may note in passing that while Victorians such as Carlyle were elevating Work to the status of a religion, at the same time Karl Marx was developing his 'heresy' to the new Victorian religion. According to Marx, labour was indeed the true answer to man's environment. Man was so bound to nature by his labour that it was impossible to conceive of his life without the background of a material universe — the world of objects with which he must work. It was in man's work that he and the world of nature achieved a common purpose. Further, labour made God superfluous since it solved the mystery of world history; 'redeemed' man and nature; and became the instrument of salvation in the universe of man. However, far from work being free, creative, meaningful activity, it became compulsion and poverty, weariness and deprivation and a threat to humanity. Work became alienation. This happened with the development of the class society in which one group gained possession and control of the means of production. Then the labourer worked, but the product of his labour did not belong to him; it belonged to the possessor of the means of production and, in the final analysis, to the real controller of the work process — capital, the power of money. And, under the lordship of capital, the worker would be soon reduced to a product.

Had the blacks in the Caribbean known what Karl Marx had to say about work they might have agreed with him against the Victorians. In the Caribbean, people in positions of power and influence in church and governments saw work in terms of plantation labour. Only the Baptists in Jamaica understood work differently. They encouraged the development of peasant cultivation. Other church bodies were not unlike the Moravians in Barbados who were decidedly of the opinion that negro young people should be trained in the habits of industry, be taught in early life how to use agricultural implements and be initiated into the improved modes of cultivating the soil. All this was bound to redound to the benefit of the plantation which, in post-Emancipation times, badly needed improved modes of cultivation in order to survive the vicissitudes of the sugar industry consequent upon the removal of the heavy duties

207

imposed upon foreign sugars in Britain and upon the influx of beet sugar into the European market.

The staffing of schools posed a problem from the beginning. At first, schools (like churches) were staffed by expatriates, but by the 1840s Normal Schools had been established by the Mico Charity for the training of teachers. In Jamaica, the Presbyterians began teacher-training at Montego Bay, the Moravians at Fairfield and the Baptists at Calabar. These training institutions offered the first real opportunity for blacks to get an education that was higher than that offered by the church schools. In time, the graduates of the Normal Schools came to comprise the lower echelons of the colonial middle class. The members of this class in imitation of expatriate civil servants, ministers of religion and government officials displayed a disdain for manual labour. This disdain helped to strengthen the notion that social mobility was a movement away from the soil — a movement that was, in any case, understandably encouraged by the ex-slaves' abhorrence of plantation labour.

4. *Christianity and Indian Immigration*

As we have already seen, in response to the labour crisis created by Emancipation, planters in the larger colonies of Guiana, Trinidad, Jamaica and Surinam imported immigrant labourers from China, Madeira and India.

Many Chinese became Christians. Their christianisation however, was not achieved without difficulty. When they became Christians, the Chinese belonged mainly to the Roman Catholic and Anglican churches. The first adult Chinese baptism in Guyana was carried out by Bishop Austin on August 16, 1876. In Surinam, the converted Lazarus Fu Ahing, proved of great help to the Moravian mission to his countrymen in the Dutch colony. At the end of their indentureship, most Chinese moved into the urban centres of the several colonies and established themselves in business and commercial enterprises. The wealth that they accumulated in commerce, the non-agricultural nature of their occupation generally, and the fact that so many became Christians, brought this group as a whole respect from, if not absorption into, the burgeoning 'greater tradition' of the colonies. The religious assimilation of the Portuguese who were already Christians was not too difficult. This assimilation, however, was not accomplished in the predominantly Protestant 'greater tradition' of Georgetown, Guyana, without some violent conflict in the late nineteenth century, between the urban blacks and the urbanising Portuguese.

The assimilation of the Indian immigrants posed a serious problem. They were much greater in numbers than the Portuguese and Chinese. The majority of them were Hindus, while the rest were Muslims. From the standpoint of the coloured and the educated Negro classes – people who subscribed to the social consensus – as well as from that of the lower class Negroes, the East Indian appeared uncivilized and contemptible. A Methodist missionary declared that the Indian immigrants in Guyana were a low and filthy lot with dissolute and immoral habits. This same missionary remarked that "of several of them it may be said that they are more fitted to be the associates of wild animals than of humanised – if not even civilised – beings."[10] The biographer of the Rev. 'Martyr' John Smith of Guyana blamed the influx of the hordes of heathens from Madras and Calcutta for the lack of spiritual growth among his Negro charges. A popular ditty of the late 1890s advised: "Mash up de coolie man an' ride he for true," since the "coolie ent nobody."

In Guyana, Congregationalists of the lower Negro classes refused to contribute funds for missionary activity among the 'coolies.' Methodists of those classes were no more charitable. By and large, the lower class Christians shared the views expressed in a letter signed 'Fleta' and addressed to a Guyanese paper.

> Sir, – We have been, and still are enduring the ugly, the immoral, and the uncivilized sight amongst the coolies. The general dress of the Eastern labourer is a swaddling cloth tied around his waist called a *baba*.
>
> It is time that these planter's babies now called unruly heathens, should be legally compelled, without infringement, to adopt the civilized mode of dressing . . . and not continue any longer, to shock by their crude and indecent Indian habits, the feelings of every virtuous family residing throughout the country districts."[12]

The attitude of the creole blacks to the East Indians in Trinidad was not different. The Indians there were regarded as semi-barbarians, the "scum of the effete civilisation of India,"[13] and their religious practices were described as degrading.

209

Things had come a full circle. Sepulveda and his kind regarded the indigenous people of the Indies as little better than monkeys to whom the civilisation of Christianity was to be brought by force if necessary. Edward Long, the Anglo-Saxon Jamaican historian, described the African slave as a finer species of the ape or baboon – the orang-outang. His kind saw the African as incapable of appreciating the message of the gospel. The Negro in the post-Emancipation period, having been inculcated with the blessings of the Anglo-Saxon civilisation, now came to regard the Indian from the standpoint of that much vaunted civilisation as barbarous. He deemed him not even worth the trouble of evangelisation. It was perhaps only in Jamaica that the attitude of Negroes to the immigrants was different.

It was missionaries from the Presbyterian Church in Canada who conducted successful missions to the Indian immigrants of Trinidad and Guyana.[14] In Surinam, the Moravian church conducted such a mission. It is true that the Scots Presbyterians in Trinidad contemplated a mission to the East Indians, but while they were awaiting word from their 'home' base, the Foreign Mission Board of the Church of Scotland, the Rev. John Morton of the Presbyterian Church in Canada fortuitously arrived in Trinidad in 1864. Four years later, he and his wife were to return to Trinidad to evangelise the East Indians in whom Morton developed a strong interest when he first visited the island. From a small beginning at Iɛre Village in South Trinidad, the Presbyterian Mission was to spread to Couva, Tunapuna, Princes Town and other parts of Trinidad. A landmark in the history of that Mission was the dedication of Susamachar on July 7, 1872, as the first church specially erected in Trinidad for East Indian Christians.

The 'Canadian' Presbyterian Church in Trinidad gave valuable assistance to the founding of a mission of East Indians in Jamaica. In about 1892, the Scots Presbyterians in Jamaica undertook a mission to the twelve thousand 'coolie' immigrants in the island. Two years later, assistance was sought from Trinidad for this mission. In response to this request, J. Rajkumar Lal and S. Siboo, two East Indians Presbyterians, were sent; others were to follow. By 1895, various East Indian mission stations were established from Savanna-la-mar in the southwest of the island to Port Antonio in the north-east. Catechists for these stations, J. Ghudar, J.J. Suban, Lal Behari Singh and Pahar Singh, were trained at the Presbyterian College in Trinidad.

210

The evangelisation of the Indian immigrants in Surinam was undertaken by the Moravians from about 1895 at the suggestion of Nicolas Faden, an Indian Christian, who might have come to the colony as an indentured immigrant. The Moravians sought help for this project from the Rev. K.J. Grant, the Canadian Presbyterian missionary, who was then in Trinidad. The resources of the Presbyterians in Trinidad were at that time considerably strained since the mission in Trinidad was supplying the Presbyterians in Jamaica with men for their 'coolie' mission. All that Trinidad could spare was the catechist, Abraham Lincoln. In spite of his name, Lincoln was an Indian. He was baptised in the year of President Abraham Lincoln's assassination. Such was his admiration for the American president that he decided to adopt his name as his Christian name. Lincoln had previously worked as interpreter to the Rev. Thomas Slater at Better Hope on the East Coast, Demerara. In 1895, Lincoln began his labours among his fellow Indians in Surinam under the aegis of the Unitas Fratum

In 1880, the Scots Presbyterians in Guyana invited the Rev. John Morton to the colony for the purpose of investigating the possibility of beginning a mission to the Indian immigrants. Nothing came out of that visit. In 1885, when the Scots Presbyterian Missionary Society decided to seek for someone to spearhead its work at Better Hope on the East Coast, Demerara, Morton advised the Society to apply to the Presbyterian Church in Canada. As a result, in 1855, John Gibson arrived in Guyana. He was followed by men such as J.B. Cropper, James Scrimgeour and Gibson Fisher. These missionaries, together with the East Indian catechists Solomon Sherkhan, Isaas Aliyar Khan, James Bandhu and Timothy Chandan,[15] managed to lay the foundation of the Canadian Mission Presbyterian Church.

The Canadian Presbyterians were responsible for the establishment of primary schools in Trinidad and Guyana. In 1892, a secondary school, Naparima College, was opened in San Fernando, Trinidad, by the Presbyterians; in 1917, the Berbice High School was established in New Amsterdam, Guyana. The success of the Presbyterians among the East Indians in Guyana and Trinidad was due to the fact that, unlike the other religious bodies, they concentrated almost exclusively on the immigrants. This gave the Mission the appearance of an Indian church – a factor that no doubt added to the attraction of this particular denomination as far as the immigrants were concerned.

A number of reasons lay behind the conversion of Indians to Christianity. Not the least among these reasons was the persuasiveness and power of the appeal of the Christian message. But an important factor was the operation of the principle of accommodation among the immigrants. Many Hindus who became Christians (and particularly Presbyterians) did so because they could, wittingly or otherwise, accommodate the Christ of the preaching of catechist and missionary within the framework of their own Hindu beliefs.

Many Hindus found it easy to regard *Yisu Masih* (Jesus Christ) about whom the catechists and missionaries preached, as an *avatar* (incarnation) of Brahma, the principal deity of Hinduism. The burden of the preachers' message was that Yisu Masih was the *Nishkalanki Avatar* (Spotless Incarnation) of popular Hindu belief which represented this avatar as the one who would appear in the last *yug* (era) – the *kala yug* – to reveal the right way to Brahma. Representing Brahma in his more personal aspect as *Ishvara* (Lord), catechists made out that Jesus Christ was the incarnation of Ishvara in such a way that Yisu Masih, Ishvara and Brahma came to be regarded as one and the same deity. It did not enter the consideration of the preachers that the Nishkalanki Avatar was but the last in a series of Brahmanic incarnations which included Krishna and Rama; that, in fact, he was but the re-appearance of these avatars in another guise! But if this theological point eluded the catechists, the presentation of Yisu Masih as the avatar of popular Hindu expectation put Jesus Christ within the tradition of Hinduism and made him acceptable to those Hindus who could be convinced that they lived in the kala yug. It is important to note, in this connection, that the Hindu-Christian debate in Guyana, Trinidad and Surinam in the period before 1920, tended to focus on whether or not mankind was actually living in the kala yug and whether or not Yisu Masih was the Spotless or Sinless Avatar.

The myth of the Nishkalanki Avatar, the use of *bhajans* (Hindu songs of praise) in which Yisu Masih was lauded as *Ishvari-ji* (Lord) and *Sri Bhagwan* (God) – titles long ascribed to Vishnu or Brahma –, the practice of Indian Christian preachers of using sections of the *Bhagavad-Gita*, the Hindu holy book, as the authority for their claims for Jesus Christ, helped to create the belief that Yisu Masih was the Spotless or Sinless Avatar. But, perhaps, no single factor helped to create the belief more, than the use made of the *katha* to propagate the Christian faith among Hindus.

The katha was a Hindu form used for chanting a story or message from Hindu sacred writings or from the stories of the lives of the gods and goddesses. Thus Hindu priests or other persons versed in Hindu religous lore would gather in the temple or at some other place and perform a katha on the life of Krishna or Rama. Following the Hindu priests, catechists used to tell the katha of Yisu Masih. The 'Hindu form of chanting was used and the story was told in Hindustani. Christian bhajans were sung at various intervals during the Yisu Katha.

The following translated excerpt from the story of Jesus' conversation with the Samaritan woman at the well of Sychar (St. John 4) gives an idea of the form and content of the Yisu Katha.

DOHA: (A couplet used for the words of Jesus and for linking the narrative)
This water, whosoever drinks, thirsty he will be again,
Living Water I'll give, who drinks shall never thirst again.

CHAUPA'I (sung narrative)

1   The woman heard this, said (I prefer)
     This water; do, please give to me Sir;
     The Lord Jesus then said to her
     Call and bring your husband hither.

2   The woman said to the Lord in deceit
     "I have no husband" in her conceit;
     The Omniscient, Who all things knows
     Said: You've had five and still you pose.

3   The woman heard, her mind was troubled
     The Omniscient's born and came, I'm humbled;
     When Lord Jesus comes into this world
     He'll deliver us from sin — (foretold).

4   The Lord Jesus listened to her, flowery
     To her He revealed the entire mystery;
     The One to come — I am come in the world
     Sinless (Messiah) to you I speak bold.

DOHA: The One to come, yes He am I, this truth you must believe;
The Sinless Incarnation — I am come; the Lord receive.

CHAUPA'I

5 Listened carefully, then ran the woman
  With joy she shouted and told everyone;
  At the well there is a Gentleman
  Who told me all things I have ever done.

6 He's certainly Lord Jesus the Saviour
  Go and hear Him, His words are nectar.
  Having heard her they came to the Lord,
  Many believed, they heard His sweet word.

7 They all now, of the Lord testified
  The Sinless Christ, this is now verified.
  From beginning He is Lord Everlasting
  In human form, Almighty! Unfolding!

The danger that this kind of presentation of the Christian message led to, was the possibility that message might be interpreted in terms of Hindu theology. The "One to come" of the *Chaupa'I* (verse 4) and the second *Doha,* like the Sinless Incarnation of the second Doha, as well as the "Lord Everlasting in human form" (verse 7), is ominously like the Nishkalanki Avatar of the *Srimad Bhagavatam.*

It was among the East Indian Maldevidan cultists of Martinique that Hindu ideas and Christian beliefs achieved a great degree of syncretism. By 1900, Martinique had an Indian immigrant population of about 10,000; these people had been brought to the French island from southern India. They were evangelised by the Roman Catholic church. In time, l'abbe and *le pretre* became greatly respected among the immigrants, many of whom with their genius for accommodation in religious matters, embraced both Hinduism and Catholicism without any apparent difficulty.

Among the less Catholicised of the Indians, the principal deity worshipped was Maldevidan. The deity was identified with Vishnu, Jesus Christ and Madeyan. He was obviously regarded as an avatar of Brahma. The fact that he was represented by the figure of a man on horse-back would indicate that Maldevidan was the Nishkalanki Avatar whom Hindu mythology spoke of as coming on horse-back, sword in hand, to purge the world of its sins.

In addition to Maldevidan, the immigrants worshipped Mari-Eman whom they identified with the Virgin Mary. Mari-Eman, sometimes called Mari-amma[16] (Mother Mary), was regarded as the queen or the maid servant of Maldevidan; she was also regarded as the goddess who controlled certain diseases. In the

214

French island of Guadeloupe, Mari-Eman was worshipped among Indian immigrants as Mali-Eman. In attributes, Mali-Eman was exactly like Kali Mai (Black Mother) whom we have already encountered.[17] It is very likely that Mari-Eman of Martinique, Mali-Eman of Guadeloupe and Siparia Mai of Trinidad are Catholicised versions of the Madrasi Kali Mai. In the islands where Catholicism was very influential, the tendency was for the immigrants to identify the Virgin Mother with Kali.

Other gods of the Maldevidan pantheon included Katarai who was identified with St. Michael, and Buminaman. The latter god was regarded as evil. He could very well have been Bhauma, the son of Bhumi of the *Srimad Bhagavatam*. Bhauma was known for his hostility to Krishna as well as for his cruelty.

Maldevidan cultists went to the Roman Catholic church to be married. Their babies were baptised and their dead buried by Catholic rites. In their temples they crossed themselves piously in the name of the Trinity. But their temple worship service was not unlike a Kali Mai puja in which the sacrifice of a sheep or a goat was made to propitiate the deities, and, the advice of the gods was given through *l'abbé coolie* who became possessed.

5. 'American' Protestantism in the Greater Antilles

In March 1898, the United States government intervened in the Cuban war of independence. By the Treaty of Paris (December 10, 1898) which brought that conflict to an end, Spain ceded Puerto Rico to the United States. Cuba, for all practical purposes, became an American protectorate. The United States had become a colonising power which from 1898 onwards was to be the dominant political and economic power in the Caribbean. The American influence was also felt in the field of religion.

Americans justified their expansionism in the Atlantic and the Pacific by claiming that it was in fulfilment of their manifest destiny. In the words of Senator Albert J. Beveridge:

> We will not renounce our part in the mission of our race. trustees under God, of the civilization of the world. God has not been preparing the English-speaking and Teutonic peoples for a thousand years for nothing but vain and idle self-contemplation and self-admiration. No! He has made us the master organizers of the world to establish system where chaos reigns. He has made us adept in government that we may administer government among savages and senile people [18]

215

No sooner had Puerto Rico become an American colony that American Protestant missionaries began to converge on the island. Hitherto, it was only at Ponce and on the small island of Vieques that Protestants had established bases. This was made possible because Queen Victoria had, in 1868, petitioned the Spanish crown requesting that the English immigrants in those places be allowed the freedom of Protestant worship. In 1899, the American Baptists established a centre at Rio Piedras, the United Brethren led by Nathan H. Huffman visited Ponce, and Presbyterian missionaries established themselves at Mayaguez and San Juan. The Methodists arrived in 1900, the Disciples of Christ in 1901 and the Congregationalists a year or two later. In 1902, missionaries of the Episcopal Church in the United States arrived and greatly helped the nascent Anglican Church that had been organised since 1873. That church was put under the jurisdiction of the Episcopal Church in the United States and the Rev. James H. Van Buren was elected its first missionary bishop.

The charge has been made that from the time America assumed hegemony over Puerto Rico the aim of the Americans was to "culturally assimilate the Puerto Rican people and make (them) good and loyal North Americans."[19] If this was the case, then the Protestant churches wittingly or unwittingly aided the process. Their religious and educational programmes were conducted largely in English. Their congregations were modelled along the lines of those found in urban North America. The Protestant churches were middle class in outlook, the morality they upheld seemed to have been imported from the States without any alteration, and the churches were financed primarily from American funding. All these factors, gave them the appearance of propagating religious colonialism. With the establishment of the Evangelical Seminary of Puerto Rico in 1919, scope was provided for the training of local pastors. But modelled on the North American theological programme, the training offered at the seminary could scarcely prepare men for an effective ministry in Puerto Rico.

The first Protestants to come to the Dominican Republic were Negro immigrants from the United States who arrived in 1824. At that time, St. Domingo was under Haitian occupation and the Haitian president, Jean Pierre Boyer, in an effort to populate the country decided to stimulate immigration. The immigrants settled at Samana and Puerto Plata. In 1834, two pastors came to serve those immigrants who were Methodists.

216

One was British, the other was from the African Methodist Episcopal Church. In 1898, the Episcopal Church (of America) began work among immigrants in St. Domingo. The Rev. Benjamin I. Wilson was ordained pastor of the Episcopal congregation.

So far, Protestantism was confined to immigrant groups. When the country came under American rule, however, Protestant missionaries began to evangelise the Dominicans. The first missionaries were the Bible colporteurs from Puerto Rico distributing Bibles and tracts. Later, missionaries were sent by the Board for Christian Work in Santo Domingo. The Board comprised the Congregational, Disciples of Christ, Methodist, Episcopalian, Presbyterian and United Bretheren churches. The first three pastors to serve the Board were actually Puerto Ricans — Alberto Martinez, Jose Espada Marreo and Rafael Rodriguez. In 1920, the Evangelical Dominican Church was formed.

Both the Episcopal Church and the Presbyterian Church of the United States started congregations among the Americans and British who settled in Cuba from the mid-nineteenth century. Services were conducted in English since they were intended primarily for the British and American settlers in Cuba. The actual evangelisation of Cuba by Protestants was done by Cubans who had come under the influence of Protestantism while they were in exile in the United States. From 1868 onwards, many Cubans had fled the country because of the crises created by the Cuban struggle for political independence from Spain. They settled among Protestants in the United States. Some became converted to Protestantism and a few decided to become ministers and return to Cuba to work among their fellow Cubans.

One exile who returned was the Episcopalian, Pedro Duarte. He arrived in the island in 1884 and in a short time organised the congregation *Fideles a Jesus* (Faithful to Jesus) at Matanzas. Evaristo Collazo and his wife organised three congregations and a school for girls. Their work came under the aegis of the Southern Presbyterian Church in the United States. In 1883, Alberto J. Diaz returned to the island as a Baptist Bible colporteur to begin a mission for his denomination. That same year, Enrique B. Someillan and Aurelio Silvera were sent by the Florida Conference of Methodist Churches to their homeland to establish a Methodist base there.

During the time that Cuba was under the effective control of the United States government, the Protestant missions experienced significant growth and development with the Methodists outstripping the others in membership. The Presbyterians and Methodists were responsible for establishing schools in Cuba; one of these was the Agricultural School at Playa Manteca in Mayari. While the Baptists organised themselves into the Cuban Reformed Church, the other denominations were administered from abroad. At first, the Episcopal Church came under the jurisdiction of the bishop of Puerto Rico. A bishop was elected in 1940 in the person of the Very Rev. A.W. Knight, but the church itself was greatly under the influence of the General Convention of the Protestant Episcopal Church of America.

In post-revolutionary Haiti, the official religion was Catholicism although other faiths were tolerated. In about 1807, John Brown and James Catts were sent to the island by the British Methodists to minister to black immigrants who had gone to Haiti from the United States and from some of the British Caribbean islands in search of a life of freedom. Brown and Catts were expelled in 1818, but the work begun by them was continued by two local leaders. Meanwhile, in 1816, the American Quakers, Etienne de Grellet and John Hancock, had tried unsuccessfully to begin missionary work in the Republic. The attempt of Thomas Paul of the Massachusetts Baptist Missionary Society.to establish a base in Haiti in 1823 was also abortive. It was not until about 1923 that the Baptists gained a foothold in the island.

In 1861, some one hundred and ten American blacks came to Haiti. Many of them were Episcopalians. They were organised into a congregation by James Theodore Holly. In October, 1863, Holly's church came under the provisional jurisdiction of the Bishop of Delaware. Eleven years later, the Episcopal church in Haiti became autonomous and was named the Apostolic Orthodox Haitian Church. Holly was consecrated the first bishop. On his death however, the church became a missionary district of the Protestant Episcopal Church of America at the request of the Haitian clergy, and so it was to remain for a long time.

6. *The Lutheran, African Methodist Episcopal and Disciples of Christ missions in the Caribbean*

The Lutheran churches in Surinam and Guyana began very much as chaplaincies to the Dutch Lutherans in these two

218

colonies. While the church in Surinam grew both in numbers and influence towards the end of the nineteenth century and into the twentieth century, that in Guyana dwindled to the point where by 1875 it faced extinction. In 1878, however, Jan Vincent Mittelholzer, a former Congregationalist minister, after receiving due recognition from the Evangelical Lutheran Church in Surinam, assumed the leadership of the Lutheran congregations in Guyana. Under the leadership of Mittelholzer, the Lutheran church expanded its work to blacks as well as to Indian immigrants. Opposition to Mittelholzer came from the older Dutch families who, among other things, questioned the validity of his ordination. Mittelholzer appealed to the East Pennsylvania Synod of the Lutheran Church in the United States of America. The Synod upheld Mittelholzer's appeal; and, for all practical purposes, from that time onwards, the Lutheran Church in Guyana became a part of the East Pennsylvania Synod. When Mittelholzer died in 1913, the American synod sent Milton H. Stine to serve as pastor in Guyana. Under the influence of the American Lutherans, the church in Guyana became an American mission.

The African Methodist Episcopal Church came into being around 1816. It sprang out of the Methodist Episcopal Church of Philadelphia, U.S.A. Relationships between the white and coloured members of the Methodist Church of Philadelphia had become so strained that, as early as 1787, the coloured members met to consider their status in relationship to the white leadership of the church. In 1789, Bishop William White of the Protestant Episcopal Church ordained a coloured preacher to serve them in the person of the ex-slave, Richard Allen. Matters came to a head when John Emroy, representing the Methodist Episcopal Church, indicated to the coloureds by letter that white preachers could no longer bear pastoral responsibility for them. The coloureds, in response to Emory's letter, organised themselves into an independent body — the African Methodist Episcopal Church. The doctrines of this new church were the same as those of the Methodist Episcopal Church. Their form of church administration was, but for a few modifications, identical with that of the Methodist Church. The Rev. Richard Allen was elected the first bishop of the African Methodist Episcopal Church.

Between 1816 and 1916, the membership of the African Methodist Episcopal Church grew from four hundred to approximately six hundred and fifty thousand. After the Civil

War, the church became greatly involved in education. In 1856, the Wilberforce University in Ohio was opened under its aegis. One of the most important persons to lecture there was W.E.B. DuBois. Meanwhile, in about 1844, the African Methodist Episcopal Church established a Home and Foreign Missionary Society. The aim of the Society was to promote missions to Africa, South America, the West Indies and Hawaii. Even before the founding of the Society, the African Methodist Episcopal Church had sent Scipio Beanes to Haiti in 1827 to serve the African Methodist Episcopal Church members who had migrated there from the States.

Between 1870 and 1873, African Methodist Episcopal bases were established in the Bermudas and in Guyana; in 1874, work was begun in Santo Domingo, in 1893 in Barbados, in 1898 in Cuba and in 1915 in Jamaica. In the U.S.A., African Methodist Episcopal groups were to lead in the fight for social justice and equal privileges for blacks; but as far as missions were concerned, particularly during the period of American expansionism, the African Methodist Episcopal Church shared in the pro-imperial mood of the day. In the estimation of Bishop Turner, it was the "manifest destiny" of coloured Americans to redeem their unhappy African Brethren. The Rev. G.G. Daniels wrote in the AME journal, *Voice of Missions,* in January 1901:

> . . . The mandate of an imperial policy has gone forth from this great American nation. This is now according to the laws of the Medes and Persians, which cannot be altered. As a Church we have an imperial policy. We must stand by it . . . We have sent out three bishops, with the authority to capture every son of Africa in the vast dominions of Africa, Cuba, Hayti and San Domingo, Porto Rico, the Windward and Leeward West Indies and British Guiana, Canada, Nova Scotia, Bermuda and the far-off Phillipines. [20]

In similar vein, the Rev. A. Henry Attaway of the American Methodist Episcopal Church eulogised American military and naval forces for "breaking the shackles of the oppressed and carrying the munificent blessings of our civilisation to the lowly and oppressed" and for rescuing humanity from barbarism. Attaway continued:

> "The natives must be civilised and christianised. We must do this. The Negro will do his part. Then ten millions of Afro-Americans must form the nucleus of this mighty force." [21]

Attaway felt that the Afro-Americans were best suited to to christianise the natives since they were of the kith and kin

220

of the natives and, at the same time, they were "a favoured integral part of the most powerful nation on earth."

The Disciples of Christ Church was established in Jamaica by James Oliver Beardslee in 1858. Beardslee was for a brief while the minister of the Freeman Chapel, which later came to be called the North Street Congregational Church. Later, the church conducted missions in Puerto Rico and Santo Domingo. The Disciples of Christ or Christian Church was founded in America by two Irish Presbyterians, Thomas Campbell (1763-1854) and his son, Alexander (1788-1866). Thomas Campbell, who served for a while as a Presbyterian minister, was distressed by the divisions which existed among Christians. He therefore urged in his book *Declaration and Address,* that Christians should unite. Campbell felt that unity could be based on the practice of Adult Baptism and in the acceptance of the Bible as the sole authority of faith. When Campbell's position in the Presbyterian Church became untenable, he set up the first independent Christian Church in 1811. The Church was at first associated with the Baptist Churches in America. But in 1833, the Christian Church dissociated itself from the Baptists and established itself as an independent Church that embraced Baptist principles and a Congregational Church Order. The Disciples practised Adult Baptism and weekly Communion.

7. *Protestant Missions to the Amerindians*

We began this work with an examination of the beliefs and practices of the indigenous peoples of the Caribbean. It is perhaps appropriate that we should end with a rapid survey of the later attempts made to evangelise the Amerindians who lived on the fringes of the Caribbean Sea.

The first Protestant churches to undertake missions to the region's indigenous peoples were the Moravians and the Anglicans. As early as 1738, Moravian missionaries were active among the Amerindians on the Wieronie river in Berbice. That mission was destroyed during the Berbice Slave Rebellion in 1763. Meanwhile, F.C. Post was sent by the Society for the Propagation of the Gospel (SPG) to work among the Indians who had taken refuge from the Spaniards by occupying the marshy Mosquito Coast of Nicaragua. The Indians (who came to be known as Mosquitoes) had sought and obtained the protection of the British from 1740. It was an Anglican clergyman in Jamaica who had urged the Society to send a missionary to the Mosquito Coast. It is not known when Post actually went to Nicaragua, but he was formally appointed catechist of the Mosquito Coast in 1767.

The initial attempt to evangelise the Mosquitoes ended in the 1780s when the Spaniards destroyed the mission. The next attempt to work among the Mosquitoes was made in the 1840s by Moravians from Jamaica. By 1875, the second missionary venture could boast some seven stations on the Mosquito Coast. The most important of these were at Pearl Lagoon, Ephrata and Ramah Key. A man who did outstanding work at the Ramah Key station was the Dane, J.I. Jurgensen, who, in addition to evangelising the Indians, reorganised the trading patterns of the island and practically functioned as ruler of the islanders.

Before the Moravians began their missionary work among the Mosquitoes, the Church Missionary Society of the Anglicans had commenced its labours among the Amerinidians in British Guiana. Important pioneer work was done by a Mr. Armstrong at Bartica on the Essequibo River. The work begun by the Church Missionary Society was turned over to the Society for the Propagation of the Gospel. Outstanding missionaries to the colony's hinterland Indians were W.H. Brett, Thomas Youd and James Williams. Brett was a catechist while the others were priests.

Brett began his labours among the Warraus on the Pomeroon and Aripiaco rivers. There was initial opposition to Christianity on the part of the Indians who asserted that, "Christianity (was) good for white men, but not for red men."[21] Not least among the problems which conversion to Christianity entailed for the Amerindians was the conflict generated between the Christian ethnic of monogamy and the Indian practice of polygamy. As an Indian put it: "I really cannot put away my young wife and as for the old one, I certainly will not dismiss her; for she grew up with me, and is the mother of most of my children."[22] Opposition notwithstanding, Brett's missionary enterprise met with great success. This came after Sacibana, a local thief and *piai* man, was converted to Christianity.

Just about the time Brett began his work on the Pomeroon, Thomas Youd was beginning a mission among the Macusis at Pirara in the Rupununi savannahs. Pirara overlooked Lake Amaku, the alleged site of the fabled city of El Dorado, of which Sir Walter Raleigh wrote: "It is founded upon a lake of salt water two hundred leagues long like unto Mare Caspium." Pirara formed part of the area that had been the cause of disputes between the British and the Brazilian governments. In 1840, the Brazilian priest, Father Jose dos Santos Innocentes, a

222

Roman Catholic, stirred up the Brazilian government into sending troops from St. Joaquim to oust Youd from Pirara. The English missionary, in turn, retreated down the Essequibo river only to return with British troops. In the end, both forces withdrew leaving the ownership of the area to be settled by diplomacy.

With the departure of Youd from Pirara, the Rupununi was served from Shenabouie on the Potaro River until May 1908, when James Williams, the vicar of Bartica, was instructed by Bishop Parry to assume responsibility for the savannahs. By 1912, the Rev. Williams was able to report considerable progress in the Rupununi Missions: the establishment of a boarding school at Yupukari, a school at Waipa and some nine chapels in the northern savannahs. The work begun by Youd and continued by Williams was to develop to such an extent that the Anglican Church could lay claim to the northern savannahs as an Anglican sphere of interest and influence. The southern Savannahs were to be evangelised by Roman Catholic priests and missionaries.

In the Upper Mazaruni area, near to the border of Guyana and Venezuela, Anglican missionaries encountered the Alleluia Indians as early as the second decade of this century. These indigenous people hold to beliefs that are recognisably Christian. They claim that their beliefs were taught to them by T'Able (the founder of Truth) and Ichewung, a Mucusi solitary who once lived in the Pakaraima mountains.

The Alleluia people worship on both Saturday and Sunday (which would seem to indicate some contact with Seventh Day Adventists), believe in the Trinity, and look forward to the return of Christ when they would be suitably rewarded for their faithfulness. They have little knowledge of the Bible which is not surprising since they are by and large illiterate in English and the Bible has not yet been translated into any dialect known to them. However, they have a somewhat garbled knowledge of Biblical stories which have been transmitted from generation to generation orally.

Worship consists of prayers, exhortations and long hours of laboured dancing to chants in which their hopes are expressed in Patomona and Macusi words that have been so canonised by tradition and usage that they may not be changed. An annual yam festival is celebrated at Amokokopia, their headquarters, where God first revealed his truth to T'Able and Ichewung.

Notes and References

1 Cited by H.O.B. Wooding in "The Constitutional History of Trinidad and Tobago," *Caribbean Quarterly*, Vol. 6, Nos. 2 and 3, p. 147.

2 Ibid.

3 The Redlegs of Barbados did not fit into this pattern. The Redlegs, or the poor whites of the Barbadian society, are the descendants of Dutch, Irish, Scottish and English indentured labourers who were brought to the island from the middle of the seventeenth century. Their numbers were increased by political prisoners who were *barbadoed* to the island, as well as by vagrants, pirates, prisoners, Quakers, prostitutes, idlers and kidnapped persons, who were sent to the island from Britain. These whites were brought or sent to Barbados in order to offset, to some degree, the numerical imbalance between the whites and the blacks in the island. The Redlegs are concentrated in the Churchview — Newcastle area of St. John's. They consider themselves superior to the lower class blacks with whom they will not intermarry. But from the standpoint of the larger society, the Redlegs are regarded as belonging to the same social class as the poorer blacks.

4 Caldecott, op. cit., p. 133.

5 Cited in Osborne and Johnston, op. cit., p. 123.

6 Ibid, p. 123.

7 Cited in Shirley C. Gordon's *A Century of West Indian Education*, pp. 20-21.

8 Walter E. Houghton, *The Victorian Frame of Mind*, p. 242.

9 Ibid, p. 245.

10 H.V.P. Bronkhurst, *British Guiana and its Labouring Population*, p. 202.

11 J. Van Sertima, "Popular Zoology: The Coolie Porter" *Scenes and Sketches of Demerara Life*.

12 Cited in D.W. Comins, *Note on Emigration from India to British Guiana with Diary*, p. 10.

13 *Calcutta to Caroni, The East Indians of Trinidad*, ed. John La Guerre. p. 44.

14 In Guyana, the Anglicans and Methodists began work among the immigrants before the Presbyterians.

15 The catechists were Indian converts to Christianity.

16 To this day, in Samayapuram, a Tamil village in the Tiruchirrappalli district in South India, the goddess Mariamman is widely worshipped. The Southern Indians who came to the French islands might have been devotees of Mariamman, who was confused with the Virgin Mother, by their Catholicised descendants.

17 Vide supra, p. 219.

18 Quoted in Manues Maldonado-Denis, *Puerto Rico: A Socio-Historic Interpretation*, p. 156.

19 Ibid, p. 78.

20 Quoted in Geiss, *op. cit.*, p. 138.

21 Ibid, p. 140.

22 W.H. Brett, *Indian Missions in Guiana*, p. 185.

23 Ibid.